dang dang doko **dang**

T0125150

OSHO

Extemporaneous talks given by Osho in
OSHO International Meditation Resort, Pune, India

dang dang doko **dang**

The Sound of the Empty Drum

EXISTENTIAL ZEN STORIES

OSHO

This book is a series of original talks by Osho, given to a live audience. All of Osho's talks have been published in full as books, and are also available as original audio recordings. Audio recordings and the complete text archive can be found via the online OSHO Library at www.osho.com/library

OSHO MEDIA INTERNATIONAL
New York • Zurich • Mumbai
an imprint of
OSHO INTERNATIONAL
www.osho.com/oshointernational

Distributed by Publishers Group Worldwide
www.pgw.com

Library of Congress Catalog-In-Publication Data is available

Printed in India by Manipal Technologies Limited, Karnataka

ISBN: 978-1-938755-91-0
This title is also available in eBook format ISBN: 978-0-88050-436-2

contents

preface

The absurd is needed to bring you out of your mind because mind is reasoning. Through reasoning you cannot come out of it. Through reasoning you will move and move, but you will move in a circle.

That is what you have been doing for many lives. One thing leads to another, but the "another" is as much a part of the circle as the first. You feel that you are moving because there is change, but you are following a circle. You go on moving about and about, around and around – you cannot get out of it. The more you reason how to get out, the more you create systems, techniques, methods how to get out, the more you become entangled into it. Because the basic problem is: reasoning cannot bring you out because reasoning is the very phenomenon that you are in.

Something irrational is needed. Something beyond reason is needed. Something absurd, something mad – only that can bring you out. All great masters have been devising things – their devices are absurd. If you think about them, you will miss. You have to follow their line without any reasoning. That's why philosophy is not of much use. Only religion can be of help – religion is absolute madness.

Tertullian has said, "I believe in God because God is absurd." There is no reason to believe in it – is there any reason to believe in God? Has anyone ever been capable of proving that God exists? There is no reasoning which can support it – hence faith. Faith means the absurd. Faith means no reason to believe, and you believe. Faith means no arguments, no proofs to prove, and you put your whole life at stake. Nobody can prove that God is, and you take the jump into the abyss. Anyone who is reasonable will feel that you have gone mad, and that's how all rationalists have always been feeling. A Buddha, a Krishna, a Jesus – they have gone mad, they are talking nonsense.

Osho
No Water, No Moon

CHAPTER 1

freedom is to know that which is

The master Fugai was considered very wise and generous, yet he was most severe both with himself and his disciples. He went to the mountains to sit in Zen. He lived in a cave, and when he was hungry, he went to the village for scraps.

One day a monk called Bundo, attracted by Fugai's austerities, called at the cave and asked to stay the night. The master seemed happy to put him up and next morning prepared rice gruel for him. Not having an extra bowl, he went out and returned with a skull he found lying near a tomb. He filled it with gruel and offered it to Bundo. The guest refused to touch it and stared at Fugai as if he had gone mad. At this Fugai became furious and drove him out of the cave with blows. "Fool!" he shouted after him. "How can you, with your worldly notions of filth and purity, think yourself a Buddhist?"

Some months later the master Tetsgyu visited him and told him that he thought it a great pity that he had forsaken the world. Fugai laughed loudly and said, "Oh, it's easy enough to forsake the world and become a bonze. The difficult thing is then to become a true Buddhist."

Truth is one, but can be approached in many ways. Truth is one, but can be expressed in many ways. Two ways are very essential; all the ways can be divided into two categories. It will be good to understand that basic polarity. Either you approach truth through the mind, or you approach truth through the heart. So there are two types of religions in the world – both true, both meaningful, but both appear opposite to each other – the religion of the mind and the religion of the heart.

The religion of the mind believes that if you become thoughtless, if the mind is dropped, you attain to truth. The mind is the barrier; the no-mind will be the gate. Buddhism, Jainism, and Taoism are the religions of the mind. They are religions of deep analysis, religions of deep awareness, religions of enlightenment.

Then there are religions of the heart: Judaism, Christianity, Islam, Hinduism. They believe that the path goes through the heart, that the heart has to be dissolved into the beloved, into the divine.

The first religions are the religions of meditation. The word *meditation* is not exactly right, but there is no other word to translate *dhyana* into English because the language has never known a religion of meditation, so the word does not exist. All Western languages, in fact, have known only the religion of the heart, so they have the perfect word for that path – *prayer*. But for *dhyana* they don't have any word, so *meditation* is the only word that can be used. In fact, *dhyana* means exactly the opposite; *dhyana* means just the contrary because the word *meditation* comes from a Greek root *medonai* which means to think about. The word *meditation* means to think about, and *dhyana*, which we are translating as *meditation*, means how not to think about; how to be in a state of no thought; how to come to a point where you are, but there is no thinking; a state of no-mind, pure awareness. But *meditation* is the only word, so we will use it.

Zen is the culmination of the Buddhist search. Zen is the uttermost flowering of the path of meditation. The word *zen* comes from *dhyana*. *Dhyana* became *ch'an* in China, then *ch'an* became *zen* in Japan. Remember this: Zen originated in India with Gautam Buddha. When Gautam Buddha attained to his ultimate enlightenment, the state of no-mind, the world came to know the path of analysis, the path of right thinking, the path of right remembering, and the path of how to dissolve all thinking by becoming more and more aware of thoughts.

Just by watching thoughts, slowly, slowly, they fade out – you become simply a watcher. You are not identified with your thinking, you stand aside and you go on watching, just as if you are standing by the side of the road and watching the traffic. The mind is like traffic, very circular, goes on moving in a circle, very repetitive, almost a mechanism. You go on doing the same thing again and again and again. Your whole life is nothing but a prolonged repetition, very circular. The mind is a mandala, a circle, and it moves. If you watch, by and by you become aware of the circle, of the vicious circle of the mind. Again and again it brings the same emotions: the same anger, the same hatred, the same greed, the same ego. And you go on. You are just a victim.

Once you become aware of the mind and you start watching it, the bridge is broken, you are no longer identified with the mind. Once you are not identified with the mind, the mind disappears because it needs your cooperation to be there.

These coming ten days we will be talking about Zen. But to understand it rightly, you have to understand the opposite also – the opposite becomes a contrast, a background.

The path of prayer does not analyze; it does not try to be aware or alert. On the contrary, on the path of prayer one dissolves into one's prayer. You should not witness, you should not be a watcher; you should be drunk like a drunkard and lost, completely lost.

On the path of prayer, love is the goal. You should be loving; you should be so full of love that your ego dissolves into your love, melts into your love. On the path of prayer, God is a necessary hypothesis. I call it a hypothesis because it is a need on the path of prayer, but it is not a need on the path of meditation.

On the path of meditation no God is needed, hence the influence and the appeal of Zen in the West because God has become almost incomprehensible. The very word *God* looks dirty. The moment you say "God," you put people off: hence the appeal of Zen in the West. Christianity is dying because that hypothesis has been used too much, has been exploited too much. The other, just the opposite, is needed.

On the path of prayer you are to be drunk; on the path of meditation you have to be alert. In both the ways the ego disappears. If you are fully alert, there is no ego because in full awareness you become so transparent that you don't create any shadow. If you are fully drunk, in deep love with God, again you disappear because in love you cannot be.

The ultimate is the same: the ego disappears. And when the ego is not there you come to know what truth is. Nobody has ever been able to say what it is; nobody will ever be able to say what it is. The experience is so ultimate, so vast, that it is indefinable. It is so unlimited that it cannot be put into words; words are very narrow, and that experience is tremendously vast, but from both the paths people reach to the same goal.

Truth is one. The Vedas say, "Truth is one, but it has been said in different ways by the seers."

So remember that. All religions are basically, intrinsically, leading to the same goal. Even when they appear very opposite, even when they appear almost diametrically opposite, then too they are leading to the same goal.

So it depends on you which path you would like to choose. If you have a feeling for God – not a belief, belief alone won't do, belief is just a dead thing – if you have a feeling for God, if by hearing the word *God*, you start a subtle throbbing in your being, you feel a trembling, you feel inspired, your heart starts beating faster, if the very word *God* gives you a great awe, then you can move on the path of prayer. Then Zen is not for you, then Zen has to be simply forgotten because then Zen will be a disturbance.

But if the word *God* has no meaning for you, if it has really died for you, if God is really dead for you, it provokes no feeling in you, no emotion in you, it does not vibrate you, it does not pulsate you, it does not whirl your being into the unknown, then Zen is for you. More and more people will have to be moving on the path of Zen because Christianity, Hinduism, Islam, Judaism – all, in a way, have been exploited too much. They have lost their appeal.

Buddhism is still unspoiled, still fertile, and particularly for the modern mind it has a very deep appeal – because the modern mind is made by a scientific attitude, and Zen is absolutely scientific, super-scientific. It goes to the very roots of your mind, and it does not ask you to believe in anything. It has no hypothesis whatsoever. It does not ask that you should believe in something, it has no superstition.

The word *superstition* is very beautiful. It comes from the Latin *superstes*, which means: that which survives, remnants of the past, things which have become futile but still persist out of habit. You go to the church, but you don't have any feeling for going there, and every night before going to the bed you may pray also – but it is just an impotent gesture because there is no heart in it. You simply repeat it with the lips; you pay lip-service to it. It is maybe just an old habit, an old conditioning, because you have been taught from your very childhood to pray, so you continue because the mind goes on repeating the familiar.

So this has to be decided by you. Nobody else can decide it for you. You have to search in your own heart. If you still have that innocence which is needed for the path of prayer, if you are still like a child, if you still can trust, can believe, if you still can have faith, then there is no need to bother about Zen because it will be an unnecessarily arduous path. You can simply melt and merge into God.

I was reading one anecdote – I loved it.

One evening a priest who was visiting Ireland was walking along a country road when he came upon an elderly gentleman. As they walked along enjoying the evening together, a storm suddenly arose, and they took shelter. They talked for a while, and then when silence came upon them, the old man took out a small prayer book and began to pray.

The American priest, observing him, was struck very deeply by a certain kind of hallowedness around him as he prayed. Unintentionally he said aloud, "You must be very close to God."

The old man paused, smiled, and said, "Yes, he is very fond of me."

"Yes, he is very fond of me." That is what prayer is all about. It is not only that you love God – that alone won't help. If you can also feel God's love flowing toward you; if you can feel his presence all around you, only then will prayer become possible.

Prayer is possible as a shadow of his felt presence. You cannot pray in an empty room if he is not present. To whom will you pray? To whom will you utter your heart? To whom? Prayer is futile if the presence is not felt. If the presence is felt, then you are in prayer – whether you say something or not. You may not say a single word, you may be simply so full with awe that you remain silent, but you will feel the presence. Yes, to feel the presence of God is what prayer is all about.

But if God is dead, if you don't feel anything, if no song arises in your heart for God, if the presence has disappeared from the world – you look at trees, and you only see trees and no God hidden there, you look at the sky, and you only see the sky and not his infinite presence – then Zen is going to be your path.

Zen is going to be the religion of the coming century because science has killed, or damaged very badly, the capacity to trust. But there is nothing to be worried about – you can move from another direction. But then there is no question of love, of presence, of God, of prayer – nothing of the sort.

When the Western world for the first time became aware of Buddhism, Jainism, Tao, they could not believe it. What type of religions are these? There is no God in them. They could not believe that a religion could exist without the concept of God; God has always been the center of religion. So they thought that these must be just moral codes. They are not. They are a totally different kind of religion. And India, in the days of Buddha and Mahavira, twenty-five centuries before, reached to the same scientific attitude as the Western world has reached now. Twenty-five centuries before, India realized – at least, those who were very, very intelligent, brilliant, alert realized – that the old God was dead. They realized that the God of prayer was dead.

To say this was simply to say that the heart of man was dead; it was no longer functioning. So a new path had to be found in which the heart was not a basic necessity. Buddha and Mahavira worked out a new sort of religion – the religion of meditation, without any God, without any prayer, without any belief. Nothing is required of you except a seeking, except a searching mind, except a deep inquiry – that's all.

The world is going to be more and more "Zenist." Zen is the ultimate flowering of the Buddha-mind.

Before we enter into the world of Zen, a few things are needed to be understood about the mind. One thing: mind functions because of your cooperation. You can stop it if you withdraw your cooperation. Without withdrawing your cooperation, you cannot stop it. So the whole method of Zen is how to withdraw the cooperation. Many people try to stop the mind without withdrawing the cooperation – then you will go crazy, then you will be doing something absurd, impossible. On one hand you go on pouring energy into the mind, and on the other hand you go on trying to stop it.

It is as if you are driving a car and you go on pushing the brake and at the same time you also go on pushing the accelerator. You will destroy the whole mechanism; you are doing two contradictory things together.

Zen is not in favor of stopping the mind directly, it is in favor of withdrawing your cooperation from the mind in a subtle way. As more energy is withdrawn from the mind, it starts falling on its own accord, and a moment comes when the mind simply disappears – because it is you who are supporting it; it is you who are maintaining it; it is you who unknowingly, continuously, go on pouring energy into it. Through your desires, through your discriminations, through your choices, through your likes and dislikes, you go on pouring energy into it.

So Zen says, if you really want the mind to stop... There is no other way for Zen to come to know the truth unless the mind stops, because if the mind goes on functioning, it is a projector. Then reality functions as a screen, and you go on projecting your mind onto it, you go on seeing that which you want to see, you go on hearing what you want to hear. You never see reality as it is, you never see that which is, you corrupt reality. Mind is a great corrupter.

So mind, the projector, has to be stopped. Then suddenly reality appears as it is because nothing is projected onto it. You are sitting in a movie house, you just see a white screen, and then the projector starts. Then the screen disappears, and you see the film, a great story unfolding. You forget completely the screen, the whiteness, the purity of it, the virginity of it – everything is forgotten. You are lost in a dreamworld. Then the projector stops, and suddenly you realize there has been nothing. The screen has been empty. It was just a game of shadows – you were befooled, you were deceived.

That's why in India we call the world maya, illusion. It is not that there is no truth in it, but the truth is hidden. The truth is hidden like a white screen in a movie house, and you have projected your desires and your dreams on top of it, and you have forgotten completely what reality is.

Zen says stop the projector, put it off, and you will be able to know what is. And to know that which is, is freedom; to know that which is, is to be liberated; to know that which is, is to be enlightened.

So mind is the barrier. And mind is a continuous repetition. Because you have never watched it, you are not aware of it. Nothing new ever happens in the mind; it is always the rotten, old. Nothing new can ever happen in the mind because it is a mechanism. The mechanism can only go on playing the same thing again and again – it is like a gramophone record.

Look at it, and by and by you will be able to see the mechanicalness of it. Gurdjieff used to say that if a man realizes that he is a mechanism, then there is a possibility. If a man realizes that he is only a machine, then there is a possibility to go beyond the machine. Then a man can become conscious.

I was reading a very beautiful anecdote. There is no story in it, just an extract from a petty-cash ledger:

Nov. 1 Advertisement for secretary 50 cents
Nov. 2 Flowers for secretary's desk 80 cents
Nov. 8 Week's salary for secretary $30.00
Nov. 9 Perfume for secretary $6.60
Nov. 11 Sweets for wife 10 cents
Nov. 13 Lunch for secretary and self $9.45
Nov. 15 Week's salary for secretary $35.00
Nov. 17 Bingo for wife and self $1.00
Nov. 18 Theater for secretary and self $6.00
Nov. 19 Sweets for wife 10 cents
Nov. 20 Doreen's salary $40.00
Nov. 21 Theater and dinner for D and self $22.00
Dec. 2 Harley Street Clinic $150.00
Dec. 3 Fur coat for wife $700.00
Dec. 4 Advertisement for male secretary 50 cents

Just take note. Make a small diary of your mind, and you will see circles and circles moving. To make a diary is good, but make it for yourself, not for somebody else to read it. Then look at it, watch it, and you will see – the same pattern again and again bubbles, surfaces. This is a sheer wastage of life because nothing new is happening in it.

Truth is always new, and mind is always old. That's why mind and truth never meet. Mind is always of the past, truth is always of the present. That's why mind and truth never meet. Mind is that which you have already known; truth is that which is yet to be known. Mind is the known, and truth is the unknowable or the unknown. Mind is just a record of all that has happened. Mind is not an adventure; truth is an adventure.

There is an old proverb which says, "There is nothing new under the sun." If you think about the mind, the proverb is true. But if you think about truth, the proverb is absolutely false. Then there is another proverb – which is true – which says, "There is nothing old under the sun." Everything is absolutely fresh and new – like a fresh leaf coming out of the tree. Truth is always young, mind is always old. That's why Jesus says to his disciples, "Unless you become like small children, you will not be able to enter into my Kingdom of God."

Mind is very cunning and clever, but not intelligent. Intelligence is a quality of awareness, and cunningness and cleverness are just substitutes for intelligence. So mind goes on playing tricks of cleverness, and in that cleverness, mind itself is caught. In its own cleverness and cunningness it is lost. Remember this, that you will become intelligent not by being clever, you will become intelligent by being more aware. Cleverness need not be necessarily a sign of intelligence. Even stupid people can be clever. Cleverness comes out of experience: you do things many times, you learn. The mind becomes like a computer – each experience is fed into it, and it goes on learning and accumulating knowledge, and it goes on using that knowledge.

Intelligence has a totally different quality: it has nothing to do with experience, it has something to do with awareness. Cunningness comes out of experience; intelligence comes out of awareness. That's why old people become very cunning. And hippies are right when they say never believe a person who is more than thirty. Because by that time a person becomes cunning, one has learned the tricks and the ways of the world.

But a child is intelligent because a child is more alert, more radiantly alert. See a child watching something. If a child is watching a snail, just watch the child – how alert, how totally in the moment he is as if he has become just the eyes; his whole being is pouring through the eyes. A child is intelligent; an old man becomes cunning and clever. A child has no experience, so he cannot use the past. He has to face the present.

And the whole Zen attitude is that you will have to become a child again; you will have to attain a second childhood in which you drop all your experiences because mind is nothing but a name for the whole accumulated past. Mind is not an entity really, but just piled-up past. If you disperse it, if the dust of the past is cleaned away from the mirror of your being, then you will become intelligent. And only intelligence can know what truth is.

After a lecture a student said to the great philosopher Hegel, "Professor Hegel, I am confused by your teaching because reality looks quite different."

Hegel said, "My dear friend, all the worse for reality."

Zen is not a philosophy because philosophy means some doctrine about reality. Zen is a pure encounter with reality. It has no doctrine, it has no philosophy, it has no scripture. It is just a direct encounter with reality because all scriptures belong to the mind, all philosophies belong to the mind, and all doctrines are the cleverness of the mind. The mind goes on consoling itself through creating philosophies that it knows.

It is very difficult to remain in ignorance because it is very ego-shattering. So the mind creates philosophies and gives you an illusion of knowledge.

Zen is a way of knowing. It has no knowledge. It is just a methodology to know, to face, to encounter – immediate, herenow, direct. It is a direct transmission.

Once the French statesman, Clemenceau, was asked by a diplomat what he thought about diplomats.

Clemenceau said, "Diplomats are people who solve problems that have been created by other diplomats."

That's what philosophers also do, and that's what the whole function of the mind is. Mind creates the problem, and then mind tries to solve it.

Zen completely drops out of this whole game. It is not a mind game. Zen says there are no problems to be solved, and there are no solutions to be sought because there are no problems in the first place. Zen says there has never been a problem in existence. It is the tricky mind which first creates a problem – and of course, when you have a problem, you have to solve it. So it creates a solution. The problem is false, so how can you find a true solution for a false problem? The solution is also false. Then the solution creates ten more problems – and so on and so forth it goes. Philosophies upon philosophies are created, and they are all empty, all gibberish, all crap. Zen is absolutely against philosophizing because Zen is against mind.

Now this Zen story.

The master Fugai was considered very wise and generous, yet he was most severe both with himself and his disciples.

Zen is severe. It is a very arduous path. It is not a game to play with, it is playing with fire. You will never be the same again once you enter into the world of Zen. You will be totally transformed, so much so that you will not be able to recognize yourself. The person who enters into the world of Zen and the person who comes out are two totally different entities. There is no continuity, you become discontinuous with your past. All continuity is of the mind; all identity is of the mind; all name, all form, is of the mind. When the mind is dropped, you suddenly become discontinuous with the past – not only with the past, you become disconnected with time.

And that is the whole secret of Zen: to become disconnected with time. Then you become connected with eternity. And eternity is herenow; eternity knows no past and no future; eternity is pure present. Time knows no present – time is past and future. Ordinarily we think that time is divided into three categories: past, present and future. That is absolutely wrong. Time is divided only into two categories: past and future. The present is not part of time at all. Just watch, just see. When is the present? The moment you recognize that this is the present, it is already past. The moment you say, "Yes, this is the present," it is already gone, it is past. Or if you say, "This is going to be the present," it is still future. You cannot recognize the present, you cannot point at the present, you cannot indicate the present. In the world of time, there is no present.

When you look at the clock, it is already moving, not for a single moment has it stopped. When you were watching it, then too it was moving. That's what Heraclitus means when he says, "You cannot step twice in the same river." The river is flowing. The past is there, the future is there, and the future is continuously being converted into the past. Not for a single moment is there present, not for a single moment does the clock stop, not for a single moment does the river stop. Heraclitus is right. "You cannot step twice in the same river." One of his disciples said to him, "Master, I tried, you are right. But one thing more I would like to add – you cannot step even once in a river." That's exactly how it is. When you touch the river, when your foot touches the river, the river is flowing. When you penetrate one inch into the river, the river is flowing. When you penetrate two inches into the river, the river is flowing. By the time you reach the bottom, the river has flowed so much that you cannot say you stepped even once in the same river.

In time there is no present; the present is not part of time. The present is part of eternity. Present means now, and now knows no past and no future. Once you are discontinuous with mind, you are discontinuous with time. And time and space are together.

In this century Einstein discovered that time and space are not two separate things; rather they are one thing, or two aspects of the one thing. So he called the whole thing "spatio-time" to emphasize the fact that time is nothing but the fourth dimension of space. If time disappears, space also disappears.

So a man who has gone beyond his mind is beyond time and space. He is, but you cannot say where he is; he is, but you cannot say when he is. When and where all dissolve. He simply is, without any definition of where and when. This is what Buddha called enlightenment. This is freedom, absolute freedom because nothing confines you.

But the path is very severe. It has to be so because it is a sort of ultimate suicide. You commit suicide. You commit a mind suicide. You drop out of the mind, you drop out of time, you drop out of space. The world that you have known up to now disappears, and something totally new, something indefinable, arises in your consciousness.

The master Fugai was considered very wise and generous, yet he was most severe... A Zen master has to be severe because he is trying to kill you.

Just a few days before, a sannyasin came and I asked her how long she was going to stay here. She said three months. So I said, "Okay, that will be enough to kill you."

She said, "What?" But now she has understood the point – getting ready to die.

...both with himself and his disciples. He went to the mountains to sit in Zen.

Zen simply means sitting. In Japanese they have the full word, zazen. It means sitting silently, doing nothing.

All doing is of the mind. Whenever you do, the mind comes into being. Whenever you want to do something, the mind immediately starts planning. With even the idea of doing, you start pouring energy into the mind.

Zen is a simple sitting. Not doing anything, not even meditating because to meditate, from the back door the doing again comes in. Zen simply says, sit and don't do anything. Don't think in terms of doing, think in terms of being. Just be. So for years a seeker of Zen simply sits. It is the hardest thing in the world to do, and I can feel you will understand it. It is the hardest thing in the world to do – just to sit. You would like something to do because that something keeps you preoccupied, and you go on feeling that you are doing something, that you are somebody. And at least it never gives you any opportunity to face yourself. Your doing is an escape from yourself, so that you never come face-to-face, so that you never encounter your own being. You go on avoiding.

So people go on doing a thousand and one things, many of them are absolutely unnecessary. Not only are they unnecessary, many of them simply create trouble for them. Just think about yourself. What have you done? You have created a hell around you, but still you go on doing.

People come to me and they ask, "What should we meditate upon? What mantra should we chant?" And if I say, "Nothing, you simply sit. Just face the wall and sit silently and let time pass and don't do anything. Things will settle on their own accord. You simply sit. If you come in and interfere, you will muddle things more. Please just sit on the bank. Let the river flow. They say, "But how can one sit without doing anything? At least give us a mantra, so we can repeat it inside. If there is no activity outside, then let us have some activity inside."

That's why in America, Maharishi Mahesh Yogi has certain appeal. Transcendental Meditation is nothing but the transfer of activity from the outside to the inside. And the American mind is almost neurotic. Something has to be done. If you are not doing something, you are wasting time. Do something! What it is, is not the point, but do something. Speech and activity and aggressiveness – do something, go on doing something, go on moving, fast, fast.

Now, if you simply say, "Don't do anything, sit silently," it looks almost impossible. How can one sit silently? "Give us some inner activity." So a mantra is given. So you repeat inside, "Om, om, om; Ram, Ram, Ram," – anything will do. Any abracadabra. You can make your own mantra. You are foolish to go and ask somebody else for a mantra, you can create your own: "Blah, blah, blah." That will give you the same silence and tranquillity as any Transcendental Meditation because just an inner activity and you feel good.

Zen has no mantra. Zen is not Transcendental Meditation. It is the most arduous thing man has ever tried, not to do anything, zazen, just sitting.

It is unbelievable that sometimes a Zen seeker has sat for twenty years not doing anything – then came the light. Everything became so silent within him, not even a flicker of energy, no occupation, nothing. He was almost dead because all activities disappeared. Then one comes face-to-face with being, then you come to know who you are.

Mind is activity. And if one has to drop mind, one has to drop activity.

He went to the mountains to sit in Zen. He lived in a cave, and when he was hungry, he went to the village for scraps.

He would come down to the village only for a few scraps, otherwise he was sitting in his cave doing nothing.

That which you are seeking is already within you, but you are too much occupied with other things, so you cannot fall into it. When all activity is lost, all clinging disappears. You cannot cling to anything, you simply go on falling in and in and in. Your troubles arise because you hanker for activity. Have you ever heard about anybody who was troubled by the "in"? The "in" has never troubled anybody. That "in," the inner, that very core of your being, is available to you right now, but you are not available to it. You are standing with your back toward it.

Activity is samsara, activity is the world; and when Zen people say leave the world, they don't mean leave the house, leave the market, they mean leave the attachment to activity. Even if you have to do something, do it very passively. If you are walking on the street, walk, but walk very passively. Inside zazen continues; inside you remain sitting, only outside do you move. If you are eating, eat, but inside you remain sitting. By and by that inner posture is attained – when one can do things and yet be without activity. Taoists call it *wu wei*, action without action. Once you know how to sit inside, then you can do things, then it will not be a disturbance. But first one has to come to roots, to a deep grounding, to a centering.

One day a monk called Bundo, attracted by Fugai's austerities, called at the cave and asked to stay the night. The master seemed happy to put him up and next morning prepared rice gruel for him. Not having an extra bowl, he went out and returned with a skull he found lying near a tomb. He filled it with gruel and offered it to Bundo. The guest refused to touch it and stared at Fugai as if he had gone mad.

You can go mad in two ways. One is a wrong way, another is a right way. You can go mad if you are completely lost in your mind. Then you are uprooted from your being. And you may not appear mad to others, but you will be mad. You may not appear mad to others because others are also mad like you. This earth is a great madhouse. Normally everyone is mad; in fact, not to be mad is almost an abnormality. People differ in degrees, but all are mad. And when psychiatrists help you to be normal, they simply bring you back to the level of the social madness, they bring you to the level which is allowed legally. You were going a little beyond the social limit, so they pull you back. That's what they call readjustment.

But a man can become mad in another way, in a right way. One can fall out of the mind into the inner silence, into the inner thoughtlessness, inner emptiness. Then he will immediately appear mad to us. If you look into the eyes of a man who has attained to zazen, you will be frightened. His eyes will be like an abyss, bottomless; you will avoid his eyes. His eyes will be empty. He will look to you, and yet he will not be looking at you. His eyes will be vacant, and you will feel that he has gone mad. In a way he has gone beyond the mind, and to go beyond the mind is to go mad.

So all great people like Jesus or Buddha or Mansoor appeared mad to their contemporaries. When Jesus was crucified, he was crucified as a neurotic who was creating trouble, who had gone out of his mind. He was crucified as one of the most dangerous criminals. When Socrates was poisoned, he was poisoned because he was mad in a certain way. He was leading other people to madness.

Society has always been afraid of people who attain to zazen because their appeal is great, but their behavior is incomprehensible. Their behavior has to be incomprehensible because they function from a totally different center than yours.

For a man of zazen there is no difference between a skull or a bowl. A skull is made of earth as a bowl is made of earth. All skulls by and by will dissolve into earth again, and then you can make a bowl of the earth, and you will not be bothered. But if a skull is brought to you, it will be impossible to touch even; to drink, to eat out of it will be nauseating, vomiting. Impossible.

But for a man of zazen, the inside has happened – all is the same. It is the same reality in different forms. Out of the same gold you can make one sort of ornament or another sort of ornament, it makes no difference. It is the same reality which becomes the skull, it is the same reality which becomes the bowl. So what is the difference?

A man who has been deep inside himself knows that the whole reality consists of one elemental force; it is one energy, even if it takes different forms.

The man could not touch the skull and could not believe that somebody could offer it as a bowl to eat out of it. What was he thinking? His mind was weaving, spinning, "This is a skull of man." The idea, the very idea, was nauseating. He thought that this man Fugai had gone mad.

At this Fugai became furious and drove him out of the cave with blows. "Fool!" he shouted after him, "How can you, with your worldly notions of filth and purity, think yourself a Buddhist?"

All notions are of the mind. To say that this is beautiful, and this is ugly, is of the mind. In fact, nothing is beautiful, and nothing is ugly. If the mind disappears, then what will be beautiful and what will be ugly? Likes and dislikes all belong to the mind.

Just think of the world. Man has disappeared – the Third World War has happened, and man has disappeared from the earth. The earth will remain the same. The flowers will flower, but will they be beautiful? They will be simply themselves, not beautiful, not ugly. Everything will be itself, but there will be no evaluation about it because the valuer has disappeared.

The mind of a man who attains to zazen has disappeared. He is no longer a man because all his conceptions, values, attitudes, prejudices, have disappeared. Now he looks without any prejudices, without for and against. He simply looks. His eyes are empty because he has nothing to project. Then things appear in a totally different way. But to ordinary human beings he will look almost mad because madness simply means one who is out of his mind. In fact, he is out of his mind – but he has moved into his being.

So there are two types of madnesses: you can be out of your mind and not in your being, then you are unhealthy; you can be out of your mind and in your being, then you attain to real health. You become whole, you become holy.

"Fool!" he shouted after him, "How can you, with your worldly notions of filth and purity, think yourself a Buddhist?" Discrimination is of the mind; non-discrimination is of the no-mind.

Fugai was trying to create a situation for this poor man. The man missed. Fugai was creating a device so that this man could be awakened. He was shaking him hard to pull him out of his dreams of likes and dislikes, purity and filth, beauty and ugliness, good and bad. The whole effort was to shatter his mind because the whole of Buddhism consists only of that – how to shatter the mind.

It is said of a Zen master, who in his younger days was a disciple of another master, that he had been working hard at his meditation for months together. Then one day the master came, sat in front of him with a brick and started rubbing the brick on the stone. The sound was there, and it was distracting and disturbing to the young disciple.

Finally, irritated, the young man asked, "What are you doing?"

The master said, "I am trying to make a mirror."

The disciple said, "Have you gone mad? Just by polishing a brick a mirror cannot be made, you may polish it for your whole life. Mirrors are not made that way."

And the master said, "Then I have nothing to say to you. You are trying to polish your mind. Mirrors are not made that way either. I throw away this brick – see – you do the same."

Drop the mind. It is not a question of polishing the mind, modifying the mind, making it more and more clear. It is not a question of changing the mind, it is a question of dropping it utterly.

Buddhism is an effort to drop the mind totally. But how to drop the mind? If you continue in thinking – likes and dislikes, prejudices, this is good, that is bad – then you cannot drop the mind because it is the mind which distinguishes, discriminates, it is the mind which divides, categorizes. All categories are of the mind. That's why Buddhists don't say that God is good and the Devil is bad, because for a Buddhist God and the Devil are both of the mind – good and bad. That's why Buddhists don't say choose heaven and avoid hell – because they say hell and heaven are both are of the mind. Drop the whole mind. And by the dropping of the mind, all distinctions are dropped, and you are in a deep, undiscriminated reality.

That is what truth is. It is not God, it is not the Devil; it is not light, it is not darkness – it is beyond both.

Some months later the master Tetsgyu visited him and told him that he thought it a great pity that he had forsaken the world. Fugai laughed and said: "Oh, it's easy enough to forsake the world and become a bonze. The difficult thing is then to become a true Buddhist."

It is very easy to forsake the world, it is very easy to renounce. Any coward can do that. It is easy to escape from the world, but escape is not a transformation. It is very easy to sit outwardly like a bonze – you can become a statue, still, not moving at all – but the real problem is to drop the movement of the mind, the inner working of the mind. You can sit silently from the outside, but if the inside turmoil continues, then you are not a Buddhist.

A Buddhist means one who has become a buddha, one who has attained to enlightenment. And that happens only when inner movements have ceased, when thinking has stopped, when the mind is no longer the master. When the mind no longer manipulates you, when the mind no longer controls you, when the mind is just a mechanism – if you need, you use it, otherwise you put it aside – you are free of the mind, you have attained your own masterhood.

It is easy to change from the outside, the real change has to happen inside. Remember that. Use the outside to help the inside to change, but never believe that the outside change is all. Sit silently because the sitting posture will help. When the body sits completely immobile, it helps the mind to relax because body and mind are not two separate things – they are one. You are not body and mind, you are bodymind. You are psychosomatic, so everything that happens in the body has subtle vibrations in the mind; and anything that happens in the mind reaches to the body.

That's how if you take alcohol, the mind becomes drunk. The alcohol goes into the body, but it affects the mind. If you take LSD or marijuana or some other drug, it affects the mind. You take it into the body, you inject it into the body, and it reaches the mind. Or if you train your mind, discipline your mind, it reaches your body also. If your mind is happy, if you have trained it...

For example, there are positive philosophies to train the mind, like Émile Coué's philosophy: go on auto-hypnotizing yourself, suggesting to yourself, "I am getting better and better, and every day I am becoming more and more compassionate, kind, loving." If you go on repeating this again and again, the subtle idea will settle in the mind, it will affect your body. That's how many diseases can be cured by hypnosis because in the first place they may be just your suggestions and not real diseases. Out of a hundred diseases almost seventy-five are just pure mental things, but they affect the body. If the mind takes them in, if the mind is affected, then sooner or later the body follows. Mind and body are one, so whatsoever affects one affects the other also. They are parallel, running together. A deep subtle balance is kept between the two.

So I am not saying don't use the outside – you have to use it, but don't think that that is all. Use the outside to change the inside. Then you will not just become a bonze, then you will not be just a statue, you will become a real Buddha.

It happened that a Zen seeker came to a master and asked him, "I have come from a very long distance, I have traveled thousands of miles to come to your feet."

The master asked, "For what? What do you want?"

The man said, "I would like to become a buddha."

The master said, "Get out from here! Already we have too many buddhas here."

The master used to live in a temple which is called "The Temple of One Thousand and One Buddhas." There were one thousand and one statues of Buddha.

So he said, "Get out of it! Immediately out of it. We are tired. We already have one thousand and one buddhas here, we don't need anyone else. But if you want to become yourself, then you can come in."

Remember Zen is not an imitation. No Zen master can ever think of writing a book like Thomas à Kempis' book *Imitation of Christ*. Impossible. The very title will be laughed at.

The real religion is not imitation of anybody else, it is a search to find out your own authentic self, who you are. So just outer discipline will not help; outer discipline can be used as a means, but it is not the goal.

So remember that the basic thing has to happen inside you.

"Oh, it's easy enough to forsake the world and become a bonze. The difficult thing is then to become a true Buddhist." The difficult thing is always to become a true Christian, a true Mohammedan, a true Hindu, a true Buddhist, a true Sikh because the difficult thing is to become true.

Man is a deceiver. He goes on deceiving himself. And it is much easier to become someone, to pretend to be someone; it is much easier to act like someone, than to be. To be is arduous. You will have to pass through many fires; you will have to pass through many deaths and rebirths; you will have to move through a great revolution, a total mutation. It is difficult. It is very easy to pretend, it is very easy to be pseudo. The whole world is full of pseudo-religious people. They go to the church, they go to the mosque, they pray, they pretend to meditate, but one is simply surprised. Whom are they deceiving? They are deceiving themselves and nobody else.

This should be remembered because you are on the path, you are here as seekers. The greatest pitfall for a seeker is to become a victim of self-deception; it is cheap, and it looks like a short-cut. Never pretend. Once pretension settles in, you have taken a wrong move, and it will be very difficult for you to attain to any reality. And you will have to go back one day or other because unless you drop that pretension you will never grow.

For example, if you are at the age of twenty-five and you pretend and you go on pretending up to the age of fifty, and then you realize that a certain pretension happened at the age of twenty-five, you will have to go back and undo it. You will have to relive those twenty-five years again. You will create an unnecessary complexity, and life is already too complex. Unless you go and drop that layer of pretension at the age of twenty-five, all your house will be on a wrong base.

That's what the meaning of Primal Therapy is: you have to go back, regress. Wherever something has gone wrong, you have to re-traverse the path, move to that point, undo that knot and move again.

So don't create any unnecessary complexity. You are here with me – remember one thing: not to pretend. Because you will not be deceiving anybody, you will only be deceiving yourself.

Don't become a bonze. Truth has to be earned. It is not cheap, and there is no short-cut to it.

I was reading a story about a famous Hasid rabbi. He used to tell this story to his disciples:

There was once a man who was very stupid. When he got up in the morning, it was so hard for him to find his clothes that at night he almost hesitated to go to bed for thinking of the trouble he would have on waking.

One evening he finally made a great effort, took paper and pencil, and as he undressed, noted down exactly where he put everything he had on. The next morning, very well pleased with himself, he took the slip of paper and read: "Cap" – there it was. He set it on his head. "Pants" – there they lay.

He got into them. And so it went until he was fully dressed.

"That's all very well, but now where am I myself?" he asked with consternation. "Where in the world am I?"

He looked and looked, but it was a vain search. He could not find himself.

"And that is how it is with us," said the rabbi to his disciples.

Remember, you may dress like a sannyasin, you may be in the ochre robe, but that doesn't make much difference unless you know where you are, unless you know who you are. You may be well-dressed like a sannyasin, but that is not going to help much. So don't believe in cheap things. It is a great help in a way, it is a gesture that you have become sannyasins, it is a gesture that you are ready to commit to yourself, it is a great gesture that you are ready to go into the unknown, into the unfamiliar, it is going to make a great difference, but don't take it as the whole. It is just the beginning of the journey, not the end.

One great poet, Robert Frost, used to say:

Two roads diverged in a wood, and I –
I took the one less traveled by,
And that has made all the difference.

You have chosen with me a path not ordinarily traveled by people, not traveled by the majority, by the crowd, by the mass. It is going to make a great difference, but it is just a beginning. Never for a single moment forget it that this is just a beginning. And the end is very far and much effort, much discipline, much inner transformation will be needed. And nobody else can do it for you. You have to be born for yourself, nobody else can be born for you. You have to live for yourself, nobody else can live in your place. And you have to love, and you have to die, nobody else can do it for you. Life is intrinsically individual. All that is meaningful, all that is significant, has to be done by you. That which can be done by servants is irrelevant; that which can be done by the priest is irrelevant. This transformation you have to bring to yourself. It is going to be arduous, but take it as a challenge. It is good that the path is arduous, otherwise where are we going to prove our mettle? Where are we going to prove our crystallized soul?

This challenge is a blessing. But never try to pretend.

Enough for today.

CHAPTER 2

existence flows in and out of you

The first question:

Osho,
Yesterday while sitting in zazen, I felt myself get hit with a stick on my head. But Pradeepa that time had not hit me. Also today during the lecture, I got hit twice on the head, but no stick-hitter was around. Is this magicless magic?

It is sheer imagination, and on the path of meditation imagination is the greatest pitfall. Be aware of it. You can imagine so deeply, and you can believe in your imagination so intensely that it can appear more real than the real.

Imagination is a great force. On the path of meditation, imagination is a barrier; on the path of love, imagination is a help. On the path of love, imagination is used as a device: you are told to imagine as intensely and passionately as possible. But on the path of meditation, the same thing becomes a barrier.

Imagination simply means that you visualize a certain thing, but you put so much energy into it that it almost becomes real. Every night we all dream. While dreaming, every dream looks to be real.

To come to know in a dream that it is a dream will be the end of it; then you will find yourself awake. The dream can continue only if you believe that it is real. And even people who are very skeptical, doubting, of the scientific attitude, even they go on believing in the night, they go on believing in their dreams.

Every morning you find that it was just imagination, but again every night you become a victim to it. And again when the dream unfolds you start believing it. On the path of meditation, that hold of the dream faculty has to be loosened. Gurdjieff used to say to his disciples. "Unless you can remember in a dream that it is a dream, you will never awake." This whole world is a dream – a dream is a private world, the world is a common dream. If you cannot awake while dreaming, it will be impossible to awake while you are awake, because now the dream is very big, and it is not only your energy that is creating the dream, it is the energy of all. It will be difficult. If you cannot come to see that something in your dream is false, when you alone are to decide and nobody else can interfere... It is nobody else's business. You cannot invite anybody else into your dream because it is so private.

It happened that two patients of a psychoanalyst tried to play a trick on the analyst. It was the first of April and perfectly appropriate.

They decided that the next day they would come, separately, and they would relate the same dream – they decided on the details of the dream – to the psychiatrist and watch how he feels. It is impossible to dream the same dream together, two persons have never dreamed one dream together, so they wanted to shock him.

The first related his dream. When he left the second came, and he related his dream. And he waited for some hint that the psychiatrist was shocked or surprised, but he was not surprised at all. He simply listened as if there was nothing out of the ordinary, as if it was just usual, as if it were an everyday affair.

The man asked, "Are you not surprised?"

The psychiatrist said, "This is the third time I have heard this dream."

The man said, "Third time? Who is the third person?"

He was shocked because only two persons knew about the dream. Who was this third person?

The psychiatrist laughed. He said, "You cannot play a trick like that on me because no two persons can dream the same dream. It is impossible."

It does not happen that way because a dream is an absolutely private world. You cannot invite anybody else into your dream, you cannot ask anybody else's opinion about your dream – whether it is true or untrue. It depends absolutely on you. And if you cannot even awake in this, how will it be possible for you to awake in the great maya, the great illusion that the world is?

So Gurdjieff used to say that the first effort is to awake in a dream and see the dream as a dream. He had a few techniques for how to awake in a dream. He would teach his disciples that every night when they were going to sleep, they should go on repeating as deeply as possible, as passionately as possible, "This time when I start dreaming in the night, I will raise my hand and touch my head. And immediately when I touch my head, the remembrance will happen to me that this is a dream." For months together the disciple would think, autosuggest. Every night falling into sleep, they would repeat it again and again with deep passion, so that it entered into the very unconscious layers of the mind.

When it enters deeper than the dream, then one day it happens; while dreaming, automatically the hand goes to the head, and suddenly he remembers that this is a dream. But the moment he remembers that it is a dream, the dream simply withers away, fades out. He is awake while asleep, and the dream has left him.

Once it happens that you awake in a dream, in the morning the whole world has changed. It is no longer the same world because your eyes are clear, you have attained to a certain clarity of perception. Now dreams cannot deceive you, now you see things as they are. You don't project.

Beware of imagination. You would like me to tell you that yes, it was I. You will feel very much fulfilled that it was I hitting your head. People like to believe in miracles; hence miracles happen because people like to believe. People feel happy believing in their dreams; they go on giving energy to their dreams. That's how you have lived for many, many lives in a dream world.

I am not going to cooperate with you in any way. It was sheer imagination, you imagined it. Now you want my help also.

I have heard...

The rabbi of Chelm was distracted by children as he was preparing a sermon. He hollered out the window to chase them away, "Hurry down to the river where a terrible monster is in the water. He is breathing fire, and is an ugly dragon."

The children ran to see what was going on. People followed them, the crowd grew.

As the rabbi saw the mob running, he asked, "Where is everyone going?"

"Down to the river where there is a monster breathing fire. It is an ugly green dragon."

The rabbi joined the race. "True, I did make it up," he thought as he panted. "Still, you never can tell."

You may be creating something, but if others start believing it, you will start believing it. This is your imagination. If I say, "Yes, it was true," then you will suddenly believe in it, and you will think that you have believed in me. You simply have taken my support for your own dream.

Mind is a great liar, it goes on lying to you. Beware of the tricks of the mind.

A little girl was always lying. She was given a St. Bernard dog, and this little girl went out and told all the neighbors that she had been given a lion.

The mother called her and said, "I told you not to lie. You go upstairs and tell God you are sorry. Promise God you will never lie again."

She went upstairs and said her prayers and then came down.

Her mother said, "Did you tell God you are sorry?"

The little girl said, "Yes, I did and God said that sometimes he finds it hard to tell my dog from a lion too."

That's how it goes on and on. But I am not going to help you in any way, because any hint of help will be destructive for you. On the path of meditation, on the path of Zen, all imagination has to be avoided. You have to be indifferent about it.

And the more you enter into meditation, the more and more imagination will try to distract you. It is not a new phenomenon, it has always happened. All the great meditators have come across it.

Buddha is distracted by Mara, the god of devils. Jesus is distracted by the Devil. Sufi mystics are distracted by Satan. There is no Satan, no Mara, no Devil – the real devil is in your mind, the imagination.

There are stories of Hindu seers that when they reach to the final step of their meditation, they are distracted by Indra. He sends beautiful maidens, *apsaras*, to distract them. But why should anybody distract these poor saints? Why? They are not doing anybody any harm. They have left the world, they are sitting under their trees or in their caves in the Himalayas, why send beautiful maidens to them?

Nobody is sending anybody. There is no agency like that. Imagination is playing the last tricks, and when your meditation goes deep, deeper layers of imagination are provoked. Ordinarily your meditation is not there, you live on the surface of the mind. Of course your imagination is also superficial. The deeper you move in meditation, the deeper the layers of imagination will be revealed to you, they will be more real. They will be so real that you cannot even think that they can be imagination.

Now you can even bring proofs that they are not imagination. For example, this sannyasin who has been hit twice yesterday can even show his head, and you can find the marks. Now, he will say, "How can it be imagination? Nobody has hit me – and these marks are here?" Then ask people who know about hypnosis. In deep hypnosis the hypnotist suggests that he is putting fire in your hand, and he puts nothing – but the hand gets burnt. Now what has happened? It was just that the imagination worked so tremendously. The body is also under control of imagination. So if you think yourself beautiful, you will become beautiful. If you think yourself ugly, you will become ugly. Your imagination will give a mold to your body.

That's how fire-walkers walk on coals. If your imagination takes it deeply that you are not going to be burnt and God is protecting you, you will not be burnt. You can pass through a pit full of burning coals without being burnt. But if even a slight suspicion arises in your mind, then immediately you will be burnt. Because that slight suspicion is a loophole in your imagination. Then you are no longer protected by the seal of your own imagination.

So the deeper you go in meditation, the deeper will be the games of imagination. Sometimes it will come as *apsaras*, beautiful maidens, dancing, provoking, seducing you. Sometimes it will come as tremendous fear, monsters throwing fire from their mouths. Or anything that you can imagine will surround you. And if you get caught into it, if for a single moment you forget that this is imagination, then the imagination has destroyed your penetration into meditation. You are thrown back to the surface again. Then you will have to seek the path again. So if you are sitting in zazen, as the sannyasin has said, then remember it.

And this is a good indication. That you could imagine so deeply shows that meditation is going deep. The deeper the meditation, the deeper will be the imagination. Only at the last point does meditation take over. Until the last, the struggle continues between imagination and meditation. And sometimes the imagination is so beautiful... This is not such a beautiful imagination, you have been hit twice! Still you want to believe in it, just to think that miracles have started to happen to you, just to think that your master is working so hard on you, just to think that he goes on making you aware and hits on your head when you were falling asleep, is very ego fulfilling.

There are many beautiful imaginations – they will come. Flowers will shower on you, and you can almost smell them. It is possible that you can imagine very deeply that roses are falling on you, and you can smell them. That's okay – but somebody else passing by your side may be able to smell your roses. Then it becomes tremendously powerful.

It means your imagination is not only passive, it has become active. You are creating a certain smell inside your body by your imagination. Your body has all that the earth has. The earth creates the rose. If the rosebush is not there, you cannot smell roses in the earth, there is no smell. But if you put a rosebush there, one day suddenly it flowers, and the smell is there. The earth was containing the smell, and the rosebush helped the smell to come to an expression. Your body is earth, it contains all that is contained by earth. If your imagination is tremendous, not only will you smell, others also can smell the rose. But still it is imagination. Your imagination functioned just like a rosebush; it helped to express something that was hidden within you.

Man is earth. The word *human* comes from *humus. Humus* means the earth. The Hebrew word *adam* comes from a Hebrew root which means the earth. We are made of earth, we are miniature earths. We carry all that is hidden in the earth, that is our potentiality also. Once you help through imagination, your potentiality starts becoming actual.

But on the path of meditation, even beautiful experiences like these are to be avoided because once you get into them, you are getting into the mind, and the whole effort is how to drop the mind, how to get rid of the mind. Once the mind is not there, then you are completely separate from the body – mind is the bridge, mind connects you with the body. Mind dropped, there is the body, the earth, and there are you, the sky – totally separate realities. Then you have become a witness.

So if next time this magicless magic happens to you, and you feel a hit on the head, don't be concerned by the hit, simply remain aware. Just watch. Whether it is true or untrue is irrelevant, remain a witness. Simply remain a watcher, don't get involved in it in any way and soon it will disappear. And once you have learned the technique of how to drop the games of imagination, it is going to be tremendously beneficial to you. Because the more you go into meditation, the more and more imagination will be coming. Stronger and stronger waves of imagination will pass through your being, and you will have to be aware and alert.

If it is difficult for you, impossible for you, then the path of meditation is not for you. Then the path of love, then the path of *bhakti* and devotion, where imagination is not avoided but used, is for you. Then you forget all about zazen, that path is not for you. Then you forget all about Buddha, Mahavira, that path is not for you. Then you move into the world of Meera, Chaitanya, Mohammed. Then you move into the world of devotion.

Remember, one thing can be a help on one path, and the same thing can be a hindrance on another path. For example, there are rails, the train runs on them, they are a help, without rails the train will not run. But if you start moving a car on those rails, you will be in difficulty. They are a help for trains, but they cannot be a help for cars. Cars need a more free way, more freedom. So remember always, a thing which is a hindrance on one path need not be a hindrance on another path.

But if you choose zazen… I think the sannyasin who has asked this question will be tremendously benefited on the path of zazen – because to have such imagination that he could believe it to be true simply shows that his sitting is helping. He is relaxing into deeper layers of consciousness.

The second question:

Osho,
While practicing zazen, just sitting, I discovered that I had become the greatest fool on earth. But suddenly I remembered one proverb: when ignorance is bliss, it is folly to be wise. Though this stupidity has made me a fool, I have never been so full as I am now. I have now fallen in love with this zazen stupidity. I invoke your blessings, so that I may remain a fool till eternity.

Yes, there is a foolishness which is wisdom, and there is a foolishness which is enlightened. There is a foolishness of the wise. Why call it foolishness? It is foolish in the eyes of the world, in the eyes of the worldly because it belongs to a different realm. It is not of the world of calculation, cleverness. It is innocent.

Jesus looked like a fool. Lao Tzu also looked like a fool. In India for the fool we have a term, *buddhu* – it comes from *buddha*. Buddha must have looked like a fool, tremendously like a fool, hence the term *buddhu*. We call a man *buddhu* if we want to call him an idiot. *Buddhu* means buddhalike.

Buddha must have looked like a fool when he renounced his empire. He was going to be the king, and he became a beggar. Can you find more foolish a person? He had the most beautiful women around him, and he escaped from the palace. What foolishness. When Buddha escaped, renounced, he didn't stay in his father's kingdom because the spies of his father would have followed him, and they would have caught hold of him again. He immediately left the kingdom, went outside, and entered into another kingdom.

But the king was a friend of his father. So when the king came to know, he came to see Buddha and he said, "What foolishness you are doing. If you are angry with your father, don't be worried; come to my palace, get married to my daughter and be a king here. If there is some trouble with your father, forget all about it. I am just as loving toward you as your father. He is my old friend, and my kingdom is not lesser than your father's kingdom. So come. But what nonsense are you doing, begging on the street? You are not a beggar. Your family has been royal for centuries."

Buddha laughed and he said, "As far as I know, I have been a beggar for many lives. I don't know about my family, but I know about me. And I come through my father, but I don't belong to him. He has just been a passage."

Yes, if you move deeper than the mind, you will start looking foolish to others – even to yourself you will start looking foolish, because you will fall out of line. That is the meaning of the word *idiot* – one who has his own idiom of life, his own private style of life. That is the meaning of *idiot*. If you have a language of your own, nobody will be able to understand it. Then people will say, "Why are you talking like an idiot? It is gibberish." You may be using a perfect language of your own coinage, but unless it is social, it cannot be accepted as language. Unless your life belongs to the society, you cannot be thought intelligent. People who are thought to be intelligent are those who are in the rat race in this competitive world, hankering to cut each other's throat, trying to reach to the topmost, trying to become the first in the world.

Jesus says blessed are the meek, the non-competitive; blessed are the poor, those who have nothing. Of course he's talking nonsense. If Jesus is right, then all the politicians are foolish. If Jesus is right, then all the rich men are foolish. Then what about Alexander the Great? If Alexander the Great is right, then of course Jesus is a fool. And Alexander the Great seems to be right because the crowd believes in him. Jesus is lonely, Lao Tzu is lonely, Zen masters are lonely – solitary beings, idiots, they have their own idiom. They live their life according to their own being, they don't bother a bit, they don't fulfill the formalities of the society. They live as individuals, that is their foolishness. They don't live just like mechanical parts of society, they are not robots. They are alive beings.

If you are alive, if you are really alive and vibrating with life, you will look foolish; that's why children look like fools. Old people look wise because they are dead, stiff – all life has oozed out of them. They are alive only for name's sake. They may have died a long time before.

I have heard about one man who made a will before he died. And in the will he said, "Write on my tomb: Born such-and-such year, died when thirty, buried when seventy."

Almost always it happens that people die near about thirty, then they are buried at seventy. That's another thing: burial is one thing, dying is another thing. When society comes to know that you are dead, that's another thing.

I have heard about a priest – a Catholic priest, of course – who died, and for three days he could not understand what had happened. Then he came to his church and tried to communicate with his successor, and said, "Be aware. I died, but for three days I did not think that I was dead because I was more dead while I was alive. I was feeling more alive, so I did not think that I was dead. It took three days for me to realize the fact that I had died."

Children look foolish, and Jesus says, "Unless you are like small children, you will not be able to enter into my Kingdom of God." In fact he is saying, "Blessed are the fools."

Children are fools, that's why everybody tries to make the children wise. The very effort to make them wise simply kills them. By and by they become afraid to live; their streaming life is crippled from everywhere, only a very narrow passage which is socially acceptable is allowed for them to live in. Then only through that tunnel, they somehow cling to life. That tunnel is just a very small thread – they don't die, that's all, but they don't live either. They don't live at all. They somehow drag.

So if you sit in zazen and you move deeply into it, your mind will start falling away, and your mind has up to now been your cleverness, your so-called intelligence. Your mind has accumulated all your experiences, your past. And when the past starts withering away and you become fresh and alive in the moment, you are again like a child, again a fool.

Lao Tzu said, "Everybody is clever except me. Everybody seems to be very calculating, I am just muddle-headed."

It is related that Rabbi Hanuk told this story...

For a whole year I felt a longing to go to my master, Rabbi Bonon, and talk with him. But every time I entered the house, I felt I was not man enough. Once though, when I was walking across a field and weeping, I knew that I must run to the rabbi without delay.

He asked, "Why are you weeping?"

I answered, "I am, after all, alive in this world, a being created with all the senses and all the limbs, but I do not know what it is I was created for and what I am good for in this world."

"Little fool," he replied, "That's the same question I have carried around with me all my life. You will come and eat the evening meal with me today."

Ordinarily we think people who know answers are wise. They may be learned, but they are not wise. They may be very well-informed, but information has nothing to do with wisdom. People who are really wise, in fact, have no answers. They have a quest, an inquiry, a tremendous inquiry in them, but no answers. By and by they come to understand that all questions are meaningless, so they drop questions also. A man becomes perfectly wise when he has no answers and no questions.

Ordinarily if you have many answers, you will be thought wise. But religiously, in the Zen way, if you don't have any answers and no questions... Questions exist in the mind, and then mind tries to find out answers. Then through answers mind creates more questions, and so on and so forth it goes. It is an endless chain, it goes on ad nauseam. Once you understand this – that this whole game is a mind game – you simply drop it. You don't hesitate in dropping it, you don't postpone it for tomorrow – "I will drop it tomorrow" – you drop it right now. You say, "This is just foolish."

Then, of course, when you drop your foolishness, you will look a fool to the world. If somebody asks you, "Who are you?" and you say, "I don't know," will you look wise? He will think either you are a fool or a madman. "You don't know? You don't know your name? You don't know who you are? You don't know your identity?" The man will become suspicious of you; he will report to the police immediately that here is a man who seems to be suspect, who could be dangerous. But if you say, "Yes, my name is this. My address is this," then everything is settled.

Socrates said in his last days, "When I was young, I knew many things, and I used to think of myself as the wisest man in the world. The more I grew, the more I became aware that I didn't know much. And then the last thing happened – one day I suddenly realized that I knew nothing."

It is said that the oracle at Delphi declared that Socrates was the wisest man in the world. People who had heard the oracle came to Socrates and told him that the oracle has declared that he was the wisest man in the world. Socrates looked shocked, and he said, "There must have been some mistake because just today I have realized that I don't know anything at all. I am the most ignorant man in the world. Please go and correct the oracle." And they went, and they told the oracle that Socrates himself says that he is the most ignorant man in the world. The oracle said, "That's why I have declared him the wisest."

The more open you become, the more innocent, the more child-like you become, the more the winds of existence start flowing in and out of you. The more you are knowing and have the gesture of knowledge, the more you are closed. Then you don't allow the winds of existence to enter you, then you are always distrustful, you don't trust life. A fool is one who goes on trusting; a fool is one who goes on trusting against all his experience. You deceive him, and he trusts you; and you deceive him again, and he trusts you; and you deceive him again, and he trusts you. Then you will say that he is a fool, he does not learn. His trust is tremendous; his trust is so pure that nobody can corrupt it.

Be a fool in the Taoist sense, in the Zen sense. Don't try to create a wall of knowledge around you. Whatsoever experience comes to you let it happen, and then go on dropping it. Go on cleaning your mind continuously; go on dying to the past so you remain in the present, herenow, as if just born, just a babe. In the beginning it is going to be very difficult. The world will start taking advantage of you; let them. They are poor fellows. Even if you are cheated and deceived and robbed, let it happen because that which is really yours cannot be robbed from you, that which is really yours nobody can steal from you. And each time you don't allow situations to corrupt you, that opportunity will become an integration inside. Your soul will become more crystallized.

I have heard...

A thief visited the house of a Sufi mystic at night and spread his shawl to wrap up the loot. After a long search he had not found anything. In the meantime the dervish sleeping on the floor had rolled over onto the shawl. When the thief came to pick up his shawl, he saw the dervish sleeping on it.

Just as he was leaving empty-handed, the dervish woke up and called after him, "Please shut the front door."

"Why should I?" the thief answered, "I came and supplied your mattress, someone else might come and bring your blanket too."

So remain open, don't be worried – even a thief cannot steal anything from you. He may supply a mattress or a blanket, that is another matter. He may give something to you, but he cannot take anything from you because that which can be taken is not yours. That which cannot be taken, only that is yours.

Be a fool. Zen is the effort of dropping the mind, destructuring it, so that your innocence that has become hidden behind the structure reveals itself again. You were born without knowing anything. You were born with clear eyes with no thoughts in them, with no clouds. Your inner sky was pure. Then you were taught, conditioned, a thousand and one things – and you became cluttered with knowledge from the school, the college, the university, and life's experiences. And you were taught how to doubt, because doubt is the intelligence of the worldly man.

Trust is the intelligence of the religious man. You were taught to doubt, trained to doubt, but because of doubt you became closed. A man who doubts cannot remain open; a man who doubts always feels insecure. A man who doubts always thinks about the world as if it is the enemy; the man who doubts is constantly fighting. That fight is going to end in your defeat because the part cannot win over the whole. That's not possible.

So you are fighting a doomed fight. You are going to be defeated finally. You may have small victories here and there, but they don't count. Finally death comes, and all is taken away. And in this fight you could not enjoy, you could not delight in life. To delight in life one needs to be a fool, trusting.

Read Dostoyevsky's *The Idiot*. The main character in *The Idiot* is a Zen character, a Tao character, a prince who is foolish, totally foolish. But his doors are open, he is not in any way fighting the world. He is relaxed. All tensions gather in you because of doubt, all tensions make their abode in your being because of fear, insecurity. And you are just a small wave in the ocean, but you are afraid of the ocean, and you are trying to fight with the ocean. You will simply waste an opportunity which could have become a celebration, which could have become festive.

The same energy which could have laughed is turned sour and bitter and becomes poisonous. To be alive... When I say "to be alive" I mean to be alive in the whole spectrum of life. Alive to cry and alive to laugh; alive to weep and alive to love – the whole spectrum. I see thousands of people living half-heartedly. They have chosen a certain color of the spectrum, and they have narrowed down their being.

Now they are missing, they are missing much because you can enjoy life only when you are a rainbow.

A man was deeply in love with a woman, but he was a very shy man. Finally he succeeded in persuading her to be at least friendly toward him.

This man was a friend of Henry Miller, and Henry Miller was asking again and again, "What is happening in your love affair?"

One day he came and he said, "I was almost on the verge of succeeding. I had succeeded so much that I persuaded her to undress completely, but more than that she would not do. What do you suggest I should have done?"

Miller said, "Why, you should have wept."

"Wept?" The man could not believe what he was saying.

He said, "What else can you do? Laughter I cannot see in you, it is impossible. It is very, very far away because you have not even wept yet."

Laughter is possible only if one is able to cry and weep deeply. The child cries – that is the first relationship with the world. Every child born cries first. That is the first rung of the ladder. Miller says rightly, "You should have wept because I don't know that you can do anything else. But this much you can do because this much you must have done when you were born. You should have wept."

A fool is one who lives the whole rainbow – he cries, tears are flowing from his eyes, he is not blocked in any way. He can cry in the marketplace, he is not ashamed of life. Unashamedly he lives, and lives totally. That's why he is a fool, or thought to be a fool. He laughs, and he delights. He is a rainbow. And godliness comes only to those who are like a rainbow.

Blessed are the fools.

The third question:

Osho,
I feel the word *God* has no heartfelt potential, yet the sky and plants can bring me to my knees, and there is a heartache for something unknown. Zen attracts me with its freshness, coolness, but its demands make me feel impotent. You seem the most

attractive, you warm my heart and have the coolness of a stream. Are you possibly a third way? – because I can't decide.

I am not a way at all, I am just a presence. You have to understand it because you are going to be with me. You have to understand it as deeply as possible.

I am not a way. A way leads you somewhere, it connects you with the there, and my whole effort is to bring you here. A way is there-oriented, and I am here-oriented. A way is needed if the goal is far away from you. If the goal is away, distant, then the way is needed. As I see it, the goal is within you; you are the goal, you are the target. So there is nowhere to go, a way is not needed. In fact, dropping all the ways, dropping the very search and just being yourself is enough. Because you cannot do that, you have to be shown a few ways to walk and get tired. That is just to exhaust you.

The whole effort is to exhaust you. When the effort is exhausted and you are really tired and you fall down, and you say, "Now I don't want to go anywhere," and you relax, you reach. Seeking is not the way to reach, but seeking is needed because you are very active.

Even to reach God, ways are needed – and God is herenow. He is your surround, he is within you and without. It is as foolish as a fish seeking the ocean and living already in the ocean. You are in truth because there is no other way; only in truth can you be. You may have forgotten it, or you may not be able to recognize it because it is so obvious. It is so close that there is no distance to see it – distance is needed to have a perspective, you cannot see things from very close. And God is not only close, he is not only the closest – he is you. God is not a "seen," he is in the seer; and God is not a goal, he is in the seeker. The seeker is the sought.

So I am not a way. I talk about ways because you are mad. I talk about medicines because you are ill, and you cannot understand the vision of no-way. You will have to walk, seek, get frustrated. When I say there are two ways, I mean there are two ways to get frustrated. One is of love, and another is of meditation.

But I am not a way. I am just a presence. And those who will understand me will not need anything more than just being with me. That's what in the East we call *satsang* – just being with me, just being in my presence, just relaxing in my presence, just allowing me to enter you, not resisting, not fighting with me.

And suddenly one day you will start dancing, singing, celebrating. One day suddenly you will start laughing. What were you seeking? You were seeking yourself. How can you seek yourself? You are already that.

The questioner says: "I feel that the word *God* has no heartfelt potential…" I know it. Theologians have killed it. They have killed a very beautiful word, *God*.

Jews were right because they were very reluctant to call the name of God in any way. They were very reluctant. They were right because if you use the name of God too much, use will destroy its beauty. Before Jesus, Jews were not allowed to utter the name of God. Even now, if you look in Jewish books, and if they write *God*, they don't write G-o-d. They simply write G-d; they leave out the *o*. Because how can you pronounce his name in totality? He is so big. Whatsoever you call him is going to be incomplete, so they write G-d, not G-o-d – the *o* is left out. And it is good that they leave out *o*. *O* is the symbol of emptiness, *shunya*. *O* is void, zero. That is the very soul of God, *o*, zero, that is his very being – so they leave it out.

For many centuries only the high priest in the temple of Jerusalem was allowed to utter the name of God, and that too only once in a year, and that too in total aloneness. People would wait, millions of people would wait together outside the temple. Then the high priest would go into the innermost shrine, all the doors would be closed, nobody will be able to hear, and there, in the innermost shrine, he would whisper the name. That's all.

It was good because words like *God*, *love*, should not be used too much otherwise their beauty is lost. Theologians killed the beautiful word *God*. Now it is almost ugly, it is almost vulgar.

How theologians have killed it has to be understood. Each of you has a theologian inside. You have been conditioned for so many centuries that the theologian has almost become a part of you. God is wild, has to be, but the theologian is always afraid of the wild God, the theologian is always afraid of anything alive. So by and by he cuts out all wildness from God. He polishes, trains, and conditions the very word *God*.

If you go to the old scriptures of the world, God was wild, as wild as you can imagine. He used to be angry also; he used to fall in love also; he used to run after women also. He was very human, down-to-earth, and very alive, throbbing and kicking.

But then it was not acceptable to the theologians because it was difficult to categorize him, and it was difficult to use him. So by and by, limb by limb, they destroyed God. Now only a mummy, a dead body, exists preserved by chemicals in churches. Churches are the tombs of God where God has died. They made God more and more far away from man because it was impossible for their egos to understand that God could be in any way related to man. The creator and the created, the creator and the creature, how can they be related? No! The creator is far away in the seventh heaven, and we are just like worms crawling on the earth, sinners asking to be forgiven. They condemned man, and they went on raising God higher and higher. A moment came when the bridge broke.

It is so simple to see that the creator has to be related with the creation. A poet is deeply related with his poetry, has to be so, he loves his poetry. A painter is deeply related with his painting – it is his life, his flowering, his expression. A sculptor loves the statue he has made. Watch a sculptor when he has finished a statue, how he touches and feels it – almost as if it is the girl of his dreams, his beloved. Watch a sculptor when in difficult circumstances, he has to sell his artwork. Tears come to his eyes.

If God is the creator, he has to be close to creation, he has to be deeply in love with his creation. But then you cannot condemn man, and then you cannot make man feel guilty. And if you cannot force man to feel guilty, then churches cannot exist, then their whole business disappears. The whole business of the church exists only if you are guilty. Because of your guilt, you need their help; because of your guilt, you need salvation.

If God is already close to you, and if God is already breathing in you, singing in your heart, then what is the need of any salvation? If God has created you, then how can you be sinners? Then you cannot be condemned, the signature of God is on you.

But then the whole business of religion disappears. So they went on making God more and more clinical. Now he smells almost like a hospital – no life but everything clean. They became so afraid of the germs of life that they killed all the germs. But God also is killed.

The word *God* has lost the heartfelt potential.

One of my sannyasins has sent a beautiful anecdote to me. Listen to it, meditate over it.

The anecdote...

Yesterday somebody knocked on my door, and I opened it, and it was God. And he asked me if he could use my bathroom. I said, "Sure, come on in."

When he finally came out of the bathroom, he explained that he had been having some trouble finding somebody who would let him use their bathroom, because most people like to think God never has to go to the bathroom. Then he thanked me and told me he was looking for somebody to be the messiah, and he thought I showed promise.

I asked him if he really thought so. And he said he liked my bathroom.

God is eccentric, otherwise why should he create such an eccentric world? But theologians have killed him completely. They cannot think that he needs a bathroom, there is no provision in heaven for that. He simply sits on his throne, he never goes to the bathroom. An inhuman God is a dead God. God has to be made alive again, he has to be brought home. Then your heart will start throbbing for him. If you drop theology, then religion is beautiful, but if theology is always there between you and religion, then the theology is ugly, and it makes religion look ugly also.

"I feel that the word *God* has no heartfelt potential, yet the sky and the plants can bring me to my knees. And there is a heartache for something unknown." That's good. That's how one should approach God, without theology. Don't use even the word *God*, there is no need because the word *God* is not God. The word *love* is not love – drop the word, just carry the innermost core of it, the significance of it, the song of it. That's the only real way to enter into his temple – nature, the trees, the birds, the sun and the stars. He is all around you, calling you in many, many ways. Don't go to the church. That is the last place you can hope for him to visit. Last! Maybe in some crisis, but otherwise not.

He's alive in the flowers, he's alive in the rainbows, he's alive in the birds. Listen to him. In fact if you learn how to listen, you cannot avoid him for long. Love – if you know how to love, you cannot escape from him for long. Love is his shrine, and listening is the way to help him come into you.

There is an anecdote in the annals of Hasidism...

"Where is the dwelling of God?" This was the question with which the Rabbi of Coates surprised a number of learned men who happened to be visiting him.

They laughed at him. "What a thing to ask, Rabbi. Is not the whole world full of his glory?"

Then the Rabbi answered his own question. "God dwells wherever man lets him in."

Let him in. He is knocking at your doors, allow him in. You need not go anywhere. Just relax, trust. His hand is already searching you. Just allow him to find you, and immediately a great transformation happens.

So that is the right way.

"The sky and the plants can bring me to my knees, and there is a heartache for something unknown." Yes, God is the eternally unknown. Even by knowing him, one never knows him; even by knowing him, he remains unknown. His unknowability is his mystery. And it is good that man cannot know him, otherwise he will become part of science, otherwise he will be just caught in a test-tube somewhere in a lab. And you know what scientists can do. They will torture him if they can find him. They will poke him from here and there to find out secrets, just as they are torturing monkeys and other animals. They will torture God if they can find him.

No, God can never become knowledge. The word *science* means knowledge. God can never become knowledge and can never become science. He is not a riddle to be solved, he is a mystery to be lived, a dance to be danced, a song to be sung, a love to be dissolved in. Yes, you can come to feel him, but you can never come to know him. The unknown God is the only God there is.

There is a story about St. Paul...

When he came to Athens to the Greek world to preach Christianity, he was very much surprised. In the center of Athens there was a temple dedicated to the Unknown God. There was no image; the temple was absolutely empty and silent. There was no one inside it. Just on the door of the temple there was an inscription: Dedicated to the Unknown God. And people used to come to pray there, to feel God there. There was no priest, and there was no theology and no philosophy around it.

St. Paul destroyed it because he started teaching people, and he laughed at the stupidity of this temple. He is reported to have said that it was absolute foolishness. How can you love an unknown God? Here he was, and he would show them the known God. God had become known in Jesus Christ.

He was thinking that he was doing a great service to humanity, but he is one of the greatest criminals. He destroyed the concept, or no-concept, of an unknown God. That is the only God there is. He may have been reflected in the eyes of Jesus but he still remains unknown. In fact, by knowing him, he is not known, you also become part of his mystery and become unknown. Jesus has become a mystery by knowing him – not that he has become known through Jesus. There is no way. He is so vast it is impossible to put him down as a formula, as a theory, as a dogma, as a creed.

Forget the word *God*. Don't make that your obsession. It has nothing to do with God. You can drop the word. Dropping the word will be helpful because with that word all that theologians have done up to now will be dropped. You just look around, look into the eyes of a child, or into the eyes of your beloved, your mother, your friend – or just feel a tree. Have you ever hugged a tree? Hug a tree. And one day you will come to know that it is not only that you have hugged the tree but that the tree also responds, the tree also hugs you. Then for the first time you will be able to know that the tree is not just the form, it is not just a certain species the botanists talk about, it is an unknown God – so green in your courtyard, so full of flowers in your courtyard, so close to you, beckoning you, calling you again and again.

Forget the word. Forget all words. If you can dedicate your being to the unknown, that is the best dedication possible. Theologians, priests, and people who do the business of religion have different things in their minds. They are not concerned with you or with God. Religion has become a great investment. In fact, it is the biggest trade in the world. No millionaire is so rich – and he cannot be – as churches are. No company – Burma Shell or Standard Oil – is so rich, they cannot be. When religion becomes an investment, then there are other reasons than religious, other considerations.

I have heard an anecdote...

It happened in a Jewish temple. Jewish temples and synagogues do not pass the plate as do the Christian churches, consequently they have to raise money in other ways. One of them is the sale of tickets for reserved seats for the high holy days when business is best.

On one holiday a young man went to the synagogue in Philadelphia to look for his uncle. The guard refused him admittance because he had no ticket.

"Look," the youngster said, "I must see my uncle. It is very important."

"Not a chance," said the guard. "Everybody says that. Nobody gets in here without a ticket."

But the boy pleaded, "It is a matter of life and death. Please, I will only be two minutes."

"Well okay, if it is so important," the guard said. "But don't let me catch you praying."

This can happen in this ashram also. This happens always. Because whenever something of the unknown descends on the earth, immediately man's cunning mind starts changing it into a commodity that can be sold in the market. Immediately the profit motive comes in. The word *God*, the churches, the temples, the synagogues, they have become marketplaces. You cannot find your heart there. The only way to find your heart is to seek the unknown again. You will have to move alone, you will have to go alone. You cannot follow a crowd. If you follow a crowd, you will reach some temple, or some synagogue, or some church. If you want to find the wild God, the godliness of this universe, the unity, the cosmos, then you will have to seek on your own, alone.

Pray to a tree, pray to a river, pray to a rock. Feel, there is no need for words. Let your heart communicate. Melt yourself into the world, and let the world melt into you. This communion is prayer.

The person who has asked the question will be helped if he moves on the path of love. Zen will not be helpful for him. He has a very feeling heart. Listen to the heart.

Many other questions are there, questions about making a synthesis of love and meditation, of heart and mind, of thought and feeling because many people would like to move on both the ways together.

Synthesis comes, but you cannot make it. If you follow the path of meditation, one day you will attain to love as a consequence. If you follow the path of love, one day you will attain to meditation as a consequence. Synthesis comes, but you will have to follow one path.

If you try to follow two, you will be in confusion. Synthesis comes at the end on its own accord, so don't be worried.

It is always so: if meditation happens, love is bound to happen. If love does not happen, then that simply shows meditation has not happened yet. If love happens, meditation also happens as a shadow. If meditation has not happened through love, then your love is not yet real. If it has not happened yet, you may be thinking about it, but you have not moved into the world of love. So don't be worried about synthesis. You cannot make a synthesis. It is not for you to worry about it. Follow one, whichever feels more close to you.

There are a few questions which ask, "Both seem to be almost fifty-fifty, so what to do?" If both seem fifty-fifty, then Zen is your way. Because a person who cannot decide is not the man of the heart; a person who cannot decide is the man of the mind. If it is heart, it is always decisive. Have you ever fallen in love with two women together, fifty-fifty? If you fall that way, then one thing is certain, it is not love. There may be other considerations. One is rich, another is a daughter of a prime minister or something like that. Love is not a consideration. If love is the consideration, then immediately you choose one, then there is no problem.

So if you have a problem to decide, then it is decided: you are the mind type, you will have to follow Zen. If you can decide, then good; if you cannot decide, then take it for granted that the very doubt, the indecisiveness, shows that you are a mind type, thinking, doubting, analyzing, thinking about pros and cons. And then your greed says, "Is there not a way to make a compromise of both?"

Remember, compromise is not a synthesis. Compromise is a dead thing; synthesis is organic unity. You can make a compromise, but through compromise nobody has ever grown; you cannot make a synthesis, it comes.

You start growing on one path because both the paths use different devices, not only different, diametrically opposite. If you try to make a compromise, it will be impossible because one goes to the south, another goes to the north. So one leg will be going to the south, another will be going to the north. You will not be able to reach, you will be divided, you will become split. In making the compromise, you will become a schizophrenic. That's how the human mind has become schizophrenic, split.

Don't bother about compromise. It always comes. Those who

have attained through zazen have attained to the same love as those who have reached through devotion, *bhakti*.

A man, a Christian, came with the Bible to a Zen master and started reading the Sermon on the Mount. After a few lines the master said, "Stop, there is no need. Whosoever has said these words is a buddha."

He had never known anything about the Bible, he had never heard anything about Jesus, he used to live in a faraway cave, completely out of the society. But he said, "No need to read it anymore. Even one sentence is enough. It has the taste of the sea. Whosoever has said this is a buddha – is enlightened." If you ask Buddha, Meera is enlightened, Chaitanya is enlightened. If you ask Meera and Chaitanya, Buddha is enlightened, Bodhidharma is enlightened.

Let me put it in this way. If you follow love, devotion, surrender, one day you will suddenly find you are full of meditation. If you follow meditation, one day you will find the beloved has come, he has knocked at the door.

Enough for today.

CHAPTER 3

only the center can win

After Bankei had passed away, a blind man who lived near the master's temple said to a friend: "Since I am blind, I cannot watch a person's face, so I must judge his character by the sound of his voice. Ordinarily when I hear someone congratulate another upon his happiness or success, I also hear a secret tone of envy. When condolence is expressed for the misfortune of another, I hear pleasure and satisfaction, as if the one condoling was really glad there was something left to gain in his own world.

"In all my experience, however, Bankei's voice was always sincere. Whenever he expressed happiness, I heard nothing but happiness, and whenever he expressed sorrow, sorrow was all I heard."

Man is split. Schizophrenia is a normal condition of man – at least now. It may not have been so in the primitive world, but centuries of conditioning, civilization, culture and religion have made man a crowd – divided, split, contradictory. One part goes one way, another part goes in just the diametrically opposite way, and it is almost impossible to keep oneself together. It is a miracle that man is existing at all. He should by now have disappeared long before. But because this split is against his nature, deep down, somewhere hidden, the unity still survives. Because the soul of man is one, all the conditionings at the most destroy the periphery of the man. But the center remains untouched; that's how man continues to live, but his life has become a hell.

The whole effort of Zen is how to drop this schizophrenia, how to drop this split personality, how to drop the divided mind of man, and how to become undivided, one, integrated, centered, and crystallized.

The way you are, you cannot say that you are. You don't have a being. You are a marketplace – many voices. If you want to say yes, immediately the no is there. You cannot even utter a simple word yes with totality. Watch; say yes, and deep inside the no also arises with it. You cannot say a simple word like no without contradicting it at the same time. In this way happiness is not possible; unhappiness, because you are constantly in conflict with yourself. It is not that you are fighting with the world, you are every moment fighting with yourself. How can there be peace? How can there be silence? How can you be for even a single moment at rest? Not for a single moment are you at rest. Even while you are sleeping, you are dreaming a thousand and one things. Even while sleeping you are tossing this way and that – a continuous conflict. You are a battlefield.

You say to somebody, "I love you," and the more you say it, the more you have to repeat it. It appears there is suspicion behind it. If you really love, there is no need even to say it because words do not matter. Your whole being will show your love; your eyes will show your love. Your presence will show your love. There will be no need to say it, there will be no need to repeat it continuously. You repeat to convince the other and at the same time to convince yourself, because deep down, jealousy, possessiveness, hatred, the urge to dominate, a deep power politics, are hidden.

In his epistles St. Paul uses "in Christ" one hundred and sixty-four times. He must have been a little doubtful about it. "In Christ. In Christ. In Christ..." one hundred and sixty-four times. It is too much. Once would have been enough. Even once is more than enough. It should be your being that shows that you live in Christ, and then there is no need to say it.

Watch. Whenever you repeat a thing too many times, go deep within yourself. You must be carrying it, but you cannot falsify it. That is the problem. Your eyes will show that it is hidden behind.

Have you watched? You go to somebody's house, and he

welcomes you, but there is no welcome in his presence. He says, "I am very happy to see you, glad to see you." But you don't see any gladness anywhere; in fact, he looks a little anxious, worried, apprehensive. He looks at you as if trouble has come to his home. Have you watched people saying to you "Take any seat," and simultaneously showing you a certain seat to take? They say "Take any seat," but they show you, in a subtle gesture, "Take this seat." They go on contradicting themselves.

Parents go on telling their children, "Be yourself," and at the same time they go on teaching how one should be. "Be independent," and at the same time they go on forcing the child to be obedient. They have their own idea about how the child should be, and when they say, "Be yourself," they mean, "Be the way we want you to be." They don't mean, "Be yourself."

There is continuously something else present, and you cannot really falsify it. But man has become cunning about that also. We don't look into each other's eyes because eyes can show the truth, so it is thought to be part of etiquette to avoid eyes. Don't look into somebody's eyes too much, or you will be thought a little uncultured, transgressing, trespassing. It is very difficult to falsify the eyes. You can falsify the tongue very easily because the tongue, the language, is a social byproduct. But eyes belong to your being. You say something, but your eyes continually show something else. Hence in all the societies of the world, people avoid each other's eyes. They don't encounter because that will be looking into the truth.

But you can watch these contradictions in yourself, and it will be a great help. Because unless your inside is just like your outside, and your outside is just like your inside, you can never be at rest.

In Tibet, in Egypt, they say, "As above, so below." Zen says, "As within, so without."

Unless your within becomes like your without, you can never be at rest because your periphery will continuously be in conflict with your center. The problem is that the periphery cannot win. Ultimately only the center can win. But the periphery can delay, postpone; the periphery can waste time and life and energy. If you go on living on the periphery and just go on pretending, not really living, you will have many faces, but you will not have your original face.

I have heard...

Abrahamson had reached the grand old age of eighty and

decided to celebrate. All his life he had been orthodox, had worn a long beard, black hat, black suit and black overcoat. Now to celebrate his birthday, the old man shaved off the beard, replaced his somber black clothes with the latest style green checked suit, a burgundy tie and blue striped shirt and headed for the massage parlor.

As Abrahamson crossed the street, he was struck by a truck and killed. In heaven he spoke to his maker, God, "Why me? I was a good husband, I gave to all the charities, I have always been a religious man. Why me?"

"To tell the truth," said the Lord, "I did not recognize you."

And I would like to tell you even God will not be able to recognize you either. He changed his dress only once and became unrecognizable, and you change your periphery every moment, you change your dress every moment, you change your face, your mask, every moment. Forget about God; you cannot recognize yourself. You cannot say who you are.

In Zen they have a koan, a deep object for meditation, to find out one's original face. The master says to the disciple: "Go and sit silently and try to find out your original face." And what do they mean by "the original face?" They mean the face that you had before you were born or the face that you will have after you have died; because the moment the child is born, the society starts giving him false faces; the moment the child takes his first breath, corruption starts. The child has entered into the world of politics, falsification, untruth. Now, layer upon layer, there will be many faces.

And the clever man has many more faces than the simple man. So whatsoever the need he immediately changes his face. He adjusts his face.

Have you watched? You are sitting in your room, and your servant passes by. You have one face for the servant, a very indifferent face. In fact, you don't look at your servant, he is not worth looking at. You don't recognize that a man, a human being just like you, has entered the room. It is as if a mechanism has passed. You don't recognize the humanity of the servant. But if your boss comes into the room, immediately you are standing, wagging your tail, smiling – all smiles. You have a different face for your boss. If your wife comes, you have a different face. If your mistress comes, you have a different face. Continuously you go on adjusting, manipulating. One has to understand, otherwise one cannot find one's original face.

A man who has an original face has a unity. He remains the same. Buddha is reported to have said that the taste of an enlightened person is just like the taste of seawater – wherever you taste it, whenever you taste it, it always tastes of the salt.

The enlightened person always shows one face. Not that he is monotonous. Remember, don't misunderstand me, he is not monotonous at all. In fact, you are monotonous because your faces are all dead. He is alive, growing, but his face is his. The face goes on growing, it goes on becoming richer and richer, it goes on taking on more and more awareness, it goes on becoming more and more radiant, alive, beautiful. A grace goes on increasing around it, it is surrounded by a light, but it remains the same face. You can recognize it. There is a discontinuous continuity, or a continuous discontinuity. He changes and yet he remains the same. He remains the same, and yet he goes on changing. You can recognize the continuity, and you can also recognize a constant growth.

Growth always happens to the original face; remember. False faces cannot grow, they are dead. They have no life in them, how can they grow? You can bring plastic flowers; they cannot grow. You can keep them, you can deceive people, but they cannot grow. Real flowers grow. Only life grows.

If you are not growing, you are dead. Remember that each moment should be a growth moment. One should continuously go on moving and yet remain centered, rooted in one's being.

You can deceive others, you cannot deceive yourself. But there are also very, very clever people who can deceive themselves also. They are the worst enemies of themselves.

I have heard...

Mulla Nasruddin had been pulled from the river in what the police decided was a suicide attempt. When they were questioning him at headquarters, he admitted that he had tried to kill himself. This is the story he told:

"Yes, I tried to kill myself. The world is against me, and I wanted to end it all. I was determined not to do a halfway job of it, so I bought a piece of rope, some matches, some kerosene, and a pistol. Just in case none of those worked, I went down by the river. I threw the rope over a limb hanging out over the river, I tied the rope around my neck, poured kerosene all over myself and lit the match. I jumped off the bank, put the pistol to my head and pulled the trigger.

"Guess what happened. I missed! The bullet hit the rope before I could hang myself, so I fell into the river, and the water put out the fire before I could burn myself. And you know, if I had not been a good swimmer, I would have ended up drowning my fool self."

That's how things go. You want to do a thing, and yet you don't want to do it. You go on, and yet you don't want to go. You live and yet you don't want to live. You even try to commit suicide, and yet you don't want to commit suicide. That's why out of ten suicide attempts, only one succeeds. And that too seems to be by some error. Nine attempts fail.

People are contradictory. They just don't know how to do something totally. And it is natural. It can be understood that when they try to commit suicide, they cannot be total because they have never been total in their lives. They don't know what totality is. They have never done a single act with their total being. Whenever an act is total, it liberates; whenever it is half-hearted, it simply creates a conflict in you. It dissipates energy, it is destructive, it creates bondage.

You have heard the Indian word *karma*, the very cause of all bondage. A karma is a karma only if it is half-hearted; then it binds you. If it is total, then it never binds you, then there is no bondage for you. Any act lived totally is finished. You transcend it, you never look back. Any moment lived totally leaves no trace on you – you remain unscratched, untouched by it. Your memory remains clean, you don't carry a psychological memory about it. There is no wound.

If you have loved a woman totally and she dies, she dies; there is no wound left. But if you have not loved her totally and she dies, then she continues to live in the memory. Then you weep for her, you cry for her because now you repent. There was time, there was opportunity when you could have loved her, but you could not love her. And now there is no opportunity; now she is no longer there. Now there is no way to fulfill your love.

Nobody weeps and cries for somebody's death; you cry and weep for the lost opportunity to love. Your mother dies. If you have loved her really, totally, then death is beautiful, there is nothing wrong in it. You go and say good-bye to her, and you don't carry any wound. You may be a little sad, naturally, she has occupied your heart for so long, and now she will not be there, but that is just a passing mood. You don't carry a wound, you don't go on crying continuously, you don't hang with the past. You did whatsoever you could – you loved her, you respected her – now it is finished. One understands the helplessness of life. You are also going to be finished one day. Death is natural; one accepts it.

If you cannot accept death, that simply shows there has been a contradiction in your life. You loved and yet you were withholding yourself. Now that withholding creates the problem.

If you have enjoyed food, you forget all about it. Once you are finished, you are finished. You don't go on thinking about it. But if you were eating and you were not eating totally – if you were thinking about a thousand and one other things and you were not at the dining table at all, you were just physically there, but psychologically you were somewhere else – then you will think about food. Then food will become an obsession.

That's how sex has become an obsession in the West. While you are making love to a woman or to a man, you are somewhere else. It is not a total act, it is not orgasmic, you are not lost in it, so a greed arises. You try to satisfy that greed, that unfulfilled desire, in a thousand ways: pornography, blue movies, and fantasy, your private movie. You go on fantasizing about women. When a real woman is there and she is ready to love you, you are not there. And when the woman is not there, you have a woman in your fantasy.

This is a very sad state of affairs. When you are eating, you are not there and then you are thinking about food, fantasizing about it. This is happening because you are not total in your act, you are always divided. While making love you are thinking of *brahmacharya*, celibacy. Then while being a celibate you're thinking of making love. You are never in tune, never in harmony.

And one goes on pretending that everything is okay, so one never faces the problem.

I have heard about one couple who was known all over Poland as the most ideal couple ever. Sixty years of married life and never had there been a conflict. The wife was never known to nag the husband, the husband was never known to be rude to the wife. They had lived very peacefully, blissfully – at least it appeared so.

They were celebrating their sixtieth wedding anniversary. A journalist came to interview them.

"How old is your wife?" inquired the journalist.

"She is eighty-seven," said the husband, "and God willing, she will live to be a hundred."

"And how old are you?" inquired the journalist.

"Eight-seven too," answered the husband, "and God willing, I will live to be a hundred and one."

"But why," asked the journalist, "would you like to live a year longer than your wife?"

"To tell the truth," said the old octogenarian, "I would like to have at least one year of peace."

Appearances are very deceptive. Appearances may give you respectability, but they cannot give you contentment. And some day or other, in some way or other, the truth has a way of surfacing.

Truth cannot be repressed forever. If it can be repressed forever, eternally, then it is not truth. In the very definition of truth one should include the fact that truth has a way of bubbling up. You cannot go on avoiding it forever and ever. One day or other, knowingly or unknowingly, it surfaces, it reveals itself.

Truth is that which reveals itself. And just the opposite are lies. You cannot make a lie to appear as truth forever and ever. One day or other the truth will surface, and the lie will be there condemned.

"And are mine the only lips, Nasruddin, you have ever kissed?" asked a woman Mulla Nasruddin was in love with.

"Yes," said Nasruddin emphatically, "and they are the sweetest of all."

You cannot avoid truth. It is better to face it, it is better to accept it, it is better to live it. Once you start living the life of truth, authenticity, of your original face, all troubles by and by disappear because the conflict drops, and you are no longer divided. Your voice has a unity then, your whole being becomes an orchestra. Right now when you say something, your body says something else; your words say something, and your tone says something else; your tongue says something, your eyes go on saying something else simultaneously.

Many times people come to me, and I ask them, "How are you?"

And they say, "We are very, very happy." And I cannot believe it because their faces are so dull – no joy, no delight. Their eyes have no shining in them, no light. And when they say, "We are happy," even the word *happy* does not sound very happy. It sounds as if they are dragging it. Their tone, their voice, their face, the way they are sitting or standing – everything belies, says something else. Start watching people. When they say that they are happy, watch. Watch for a clue. Are they really happy? And immediately you will be aware that something else is saying something else. And then by and by watch yourself.

When you are saying that you are happy and you are not, there will be a disturbance in your breathing. Your breathing cannot be natural. It is impossible because the truth was that you were not happy. If you had said, "I am unhappy," your breathing would have remained natural. There was no conflict. But you said, "I am happy." Immediately you are repressing something, something that was coming up, you have forced down. In this very effort your breathing changes its rhythm; it is no longer rhythmic. Your face is no longer graceful, your eyes become cunning.

First watch others because it will be easier to watch others. You can be more objective about them. And when you have found clues about them, use the same clues about yourself. And see when you speak truth, your voice has a musical tone to it; when you speak untruth, something is there like a jarring note. When you speak truth, you are one, together; when you speak untruth, you are not together, a conflict has arisen.

Watch these subtle phenomena because this is the way you can become happy one day. Happiness is a consequence of togetherness. So whenever you are together, not falling apart; whenever you are one, in unison, then suddenly you will see you are happy. That is the meaning of the word *yoga*. That's what we mean by a yogi: one who is together, in unison, whose parts are all interrelated and not contradictory, interdependent, not in conflict, at rest with each other. A great friendship exists within his being. He is whole.

Sometimes it happens that you become one, in some rare moments. Watch the ocean, the tremendous wildness of it – and suddenly you forget your split, your schizophrenia; you relax. Or, moving in the Himalayas, seeing the virgin snow on the Himalayan peaks, suddenly a coolness surrounds you, and you need not be false because there is no other human being to be false to. You fall together. Or listening to beautiful music, you fall together. Whenever, in whatsoever situation, you become one, a peace, a happiness, a bliss, surrounds you, arises in you. You feel fulfilled.

There is no need to wait for these moments. These moments can become your natural life. These extraordinary moments can become ordinary moments. That is the whole effort of Zen. You can live an extraordinary life in a very ordinary life: cutting wood, chopping wood, carrying water from the well, you can be tremendously at ease with yourself. Cleaning the floor, cooking food, washing the clothes, you can be perfectly at ease because the whole question is if you are doing your action totally, enjoying, delighting in it.

The society is not in favor of an integrated man, so remember society cannot help you. It will create all sorts of hindrances for your growth because only a disintegrated man can be manipulated; the politicians can dominate him, the teachers can dominate him, the religious priests can dominate him, the parents can dominate him. Only a disintegrated soul can be forced into slavery.

Integrated, you are free; integrated, you become rebellious; integrated, you start doing your own thing; integrated, you listen to your own heart, and follow it wherever it leads. Such types of individuals can be dangerous for the dead so-called society. They can create trouble; they have always created trouble. A Jesus, a Socrates, a Buddha have always been troublesome because they are so integrated that they can be independent. And they are living so blissfully that they don't bother about other nonsense.

Try to understand it. If you are unhappy, you will become ambitious; if you are happy, ambition will disappear. Who bothers to become a prime minister unless he is a little insane? Who bothers to become the richest man in the world unless he is mad? Who bothers about fame? – you cannot eat it, you cannot love it, you cannot sleep with it. In fact, the more famous one becomes, the more difficult it becomes to be happy.

The richer you are, the more worries you have – problems of security, future. Whatsoever you have hoarded, you have hoarded against others. They are constantly watching for a right opportunity to take it back. Whatsoever you hold, you hold out of violence. Of course, if you have been violent, then others can be violent to you. They are just waiting for the right moment. The richer you get, the more worries, more problems, more fears you have. Who bothers, if one is happy?

It is said that a Taoist mystic was sought by the emperor of China because he had heard that the mystic was very wise, and he wanted him to become his prime minister. Two ambassadors with many presents from the court were sent to him. A golden chariot followed them.

The two ambassadors were puzzled because they found this wise man sitting on the bank of a small river fishing, very poor, just ordinary. But the king had ordered, so they told him, “The king wants you to become his prime minister. You are welcome. We have come to take you.”

The mystic looked at the ambassadors, and then he looked around. A turtle was wagging his tail in the mud, enjoying, just by the side of the river, in a small pool.

The mystic said, “Look at that turtle.”

The ambassadors said, “We don’t understand. What do you mean?”

He said, “I have heard that there is a turtle in the emperor’s palace three thousand years old – dead of course – encased in gold, with valuable diamonds, very precious. The dead turtle is worshipped. If you ask this alive turtle, ‘Would you like to become the dead turtle in the king’s palace? You will be encased in gold, surrounded with precious stones, and you will be worshipped by the king himself,’ what do you think this turtle will choose? Would he like to go to the palace, or would he like to wag his tail in the mud?”

They said, “Of course, he would like to wag his tail in the mud.”

The mystic said, “Do you think I am more foolish than the turtle? Go back. I would like to wag my tail here in this mud, and I would like to be alive.”

Who has ever heard of anybody living in a palace and being alive? Difficult, almost impossible. If you are unhappy, then you become ambitious because an unhappy person thinks, “If I attain much wealth, I will become happy.” The unhappy person thinks, “If I become the prime minister, the president, then I will become happy.” An unhappy person starts projecting into the future; a happy person lives here and now. And he is so happy, so infinitely happy, that he has no future. He has no concern for the future.

That's just what Jesus means when he says, "Think not of the morrow. Look at the lilies in the fields. Even the great King Solomon was not so beautiful, arrayed in his precious dresses, as these poor lily flowers. Look at the grandeur. And they toil not, and they think not of the morrow."

The whole society depends on creating ambition in you. Ambition means a conflict, ambition means that whatsoever you are, you are wrong; you have to be somewhere else. Wherever you are, you are wrong; you have to be somewhere else. A constant madness to be somewhere else, to be somebody else, is what ambition is.

So every child is corrupted, destroyed. The parents were destroyed by their parents, and they go on destroying their children, and so on and so forth. Of course, they don't know what else to do. They simply repeat the old pattern: whatsoever was done to them by their parents, they do to their children. The parents say, "Go to school and come first. Go to university and attain the gold medal." Then for their whole life they are always chasing and chasing the gold medals. They live in a dream, and because of this, they have to follow many things which are against their nature, they have to do many things which are against their nature. If they are to attain some goals in society, they have to follow the society.

And society is constantly trying to force something on you: a certain morality, a certain religion. Whether it suits you or not is not the problem; whether it is going to help your being flower is not the problem. The society goes on enforcing things on you.

One day I met Mulla Nasruddin on the road. He was walking with his two children. So I said, "How are your children?"

He said, "Both are good."

I said, "How old are they?"

He said, "The doctor is five, and the lawyer is seven."

Already the future is fixed in the mind of the father. One has to become a doctor, the other has to become something else. The children have not been asked. Now the father will enforce. He can enforce, he has power. The children are helpless. And if the child was going to become a singer and he cannot become a singer but has to become a doctor, he will never feel at ease. He will be false. He will be carrying something false – continuously dragging himself. His whole life will be destroyed. It will be a sheer wastage. There are doctors who would have been beautiful singers or dancers or poets, and there are poets who would have been better as doctors or surgeons. There are poets who should have been engineers, scientists, and there are scientists who should have been somewhere else. It seems that everybody is in some wrong place because nobody has been allowed to be spontaneous and to be himself.

The society forces you to be something that you are not meant to be. Nobody else can know who you are meant to be, your destiny has to unfold within you. It is only you, left to yourself. A society can help. If a real, right society exists some day in the world, it will simply help you. It will not give you directions, it will give you all support to be yourself. But this society first tries to make you somebody else – imitators, carbon copies – and when you have become a carbon copy, then people start saying that you are not yourself.

A Jewish momma found herself sitting next to a young man on a bus. She looked at him quizzically for a few moments, then nudged him in the ribs and said confidentially, "You are a Jewish boy, aren't you?"

He said, "Er, no, as a matter of fact, I'm not."

She laughed and said, "Oh, go on, I'm Jewish myself. I can always tell. You're Jewish, aren't you?"

He said, "No, Missus, I'm not."

She said, "What's the matter? You ashamed of it or something? You *are* Jewish."

So just to keep her quiet, the young chap said, "All right, if it'll make you happy, yes, I'm Jewish."

She said, "That's funny, you don't look Jewish."

That's how it goes on. First everybody is trying to convince you that you are this, and once you are this, suddenly you find – and everybody else starts saying – that you don't look yourself. "What is wrong with you? You look unhappy, you look sad, you look frustrated, you look depressed; what is the matter with you?" First they try to force you to be somebody that you are not, and then they want you to be happy also. This is impossible.

You can be happy only if you become yourself. There is no other way to be happy. Nothing can be done about it, that is how it is. You can be happy only if you are yourself, but it is very difficult to find out now who you are because you have been so confused, you have been so crippled. And society has entered so deep down in you that it has become your conscience. Now your parents may be dead, your teachers may be dead – or even if they are alive, they are no longer sitting on your head – but still whatsoever they have taught you goes on speaking in subtle whisperings within you.

It has become your conscience. The parental voice has become your ego. If you do something against it, it immediately condemns you. If you do something accordingly, it applauds you, appreciates you. Still you go on being dominated by the dead.

I have heard...

Rothstein owed a hundred dollars to Wiener. The debt was past due, and Rothstein was broke, so he borrowed the hundred dollars from Spevak and paid Wiener. A week later Rothstein borrowed back the hundred dollars from Wiener and paid Spevak. Another week went by and Rothstein borrowed back the hundred dollars from Spevak to pay back Wiener. He repeated this transaction several times until finally he called them up and said.

"Fellers, this is a lot of bother. Why don't you two exchange the hundred dollars every week and keep me out of it!"

This is how it has happened. First your father, your mother, your teachers, your priests have put things in your mind. Then one day they come and they say, "Now be on your own. Leave us out." Now the conscience goes on functioning as a subtle agent.

Remember, the conscience is your bondage. A real man is conscious, but he has no conscience. An unreal man is unconscious and has a very strong conscience. Conscience is given by others to you; consciousness has to be attained by you. Consciousness is your earned being, your earned quality of awareness. Conscience is given by others who wanted to manipulate you in their own ways. They had their own ideas, and they manipulated you, they coerced you, tortured you into certain directions. They may not have been aware of it themselves because they were tortured by their parents. This is how the future is dominated by the past, and the present is dominated by the dead.

A real man has to drop his conscience. The parental voice has to be dropped.

There are a few sayings of Jesus which are very rude but true to the very core. He says, "Unless you hate your father and mother, you will not be able to follow me." Now this looks very rude. The language is rude, but what he means is what I am saying to you – drop the conscience. He is not saying you should hate your father and mother, he is saying you should hate the mother's and father's voice inside you. Unless you drop that, you will never be free. You will remain split, you will have many voices in you, you will never become one.

You have lost your original face. People have painted your face too much according to their own ideas. They have made you. Now you have to take the whole process in your hands; you have to become aware that you are not here to fulfill anybody's expectations. You are here to attain your destiny. So don't choose the safer way which you have been choosing up to now. It is safer to follow society because then society does not create trouble for you. It is very, very dangerous to follow your own voice, very dangerous to follow yourself because then you are alone, and society is not there to support you.

They used to tell a story of the Russian dictator, Stalin. The dictator walked into a movie incognito and sat in the last row. Suddenly his picture flashed on the screen, and everybody rose in salute. He remained seated, enjoying the spectacle of his power when suddenly an usher poked him in the back and whispered harshly: "You'd better get up too if you know what's good for you. I don't like him any more than you do, but you'd better get up. It's safer."

We have been choosing the safer, the secure, the socially approved. You will have to get out of it. There are two ways to get out of the socially approved: one is the way of the sinner, the criminal; another is the way of the saint, the holy man. These are the two ways to get out of the structured being that the society has given to you, out of the role that the society has given you to play.

One is the criminal way. That is a reactionary way, foolish. It is not going to help you. You may get out of the social structure, but you will find yourself in prison. That is not going to help much; you cannot go very far on that way. That too is a way of getting out of the bondage of society; the criminal is also trying to be free. Of course, he does not know how to be free, so he gets more into bondage. But his desire is the same as that of the saints. He is moving in the wrong direction, but his desire is the same. Society has forced many people to be criminals because the structure is too strong, and people don't know how to get out of it. So they do something wrong, just to get out of it.

The saint is also doing the same, but he is trying to create devices. Meditation is a device, zazen is a device to get out of society without becoming a criminal.

So remember, that danger is there. If you understand me and you think, "Right, I will get out of society," and you don't understand what I mean by meditation, you will become a criminal.

That's what hippies are doing in the West. They are hankering for freedom, and their desire is right, absolutely right, they have absolute birthright to be free, but they don't yet know the way of the saint. So knowingly, unknowingly, they are moving onto the path of the sinners. Sooner or later they will be crushed by society.

Just to be free of society is not enough. To be free and responsible, to be free and responsibly free – only then are you free, otherwise you will be caught in another pattern. The hippie is reacting, the people of Zen are rebelling. In reaction you just go to the opposite: if the society says no drugs, you say drugs are the only panacea. If the society says do this, you immediately do just the opposite. But remember, in doing the opposite, you are still in the trap of society because society has decided what you should do. Even the opposite is decided by society. The society said no drugs, so you say, "I am going to take drugs." By saying no, the society has decided your direction.

So the one who is conventional is within the society, and the one who has reacted against it again gets caught in the same society. One says yes to the society, another says no to the society, but both react to the society. The man who really wants to be free says neither yes nor no.

The language is created by the society, so the language is simply contradictory. Either you have to say yes, or you have to say no. Sometimes you don't want to say either yes or no, but there is no word. Just lately Edward de Bono has done a great service to humanity. He has invented a new word, *po* – just in the middle of no and yes. Because there are situations when you would like to say *po*. You mean, "I don't want to say yes, I don't want to say no, I don't want to take any alternative between these two. I want to be free. If I say yes, I am caught, you decided my yes; if I say no, you decided my no in the opposite direction. I say *po*."

A Zen person says *po*, the hippie says no, and much is the difference, great is the difference.

The language is decided by the contradictory mind, so everything is divided into two: heaven and hell, God and the Devil, yes and no, good and bad, the sinner and the saint. Everything is divided into two, and in life, in fact, it is totally different – it is a rainbow. All the seven colors are there. There are many stages between the saint and the sinner; there are many possibilities between yes and no. And dark and light are not only two possibilities – they are two poles. Between these two poles are all the rays, all the colors of the rainbow.

But the Aristotelian logic, which is the logic of the society, divides only into two. That two creates a falsity in man. If you don't want to say yes and you don't want to say no, what you will do? The language does not give you any other alternative. Somebody says, "Do you love me?" What are you going to say? If you say yes, it may not be true, if you say no, that also may not be true. You may like to remain uncommitted, you may like simply to shrug your shoulders, but in language there is no way to shrug your shoulders.

I have heard about a man who went to visit a church with his wife. The church had the inscription over the portal: This is the house of God. This is the Gate of Heaven.

The man must have been a logician, a follower of Aristotle.

He glanced at these words, tried the door and found it locked.

Then he turned to his wife and said, "In other words, go to hell!"

Because the door to heaven is closed, so where to go? "In other words, go to hell!"

Life is divided into two; that is too miserly a division. Life is much richer. Life is neither white nor black, it is gray. White is one end of it, black is another end of it, but life is gray.

If you don't know that language is also a social trap, morality is also a social trap, formality is also a social trap, etiquette is also a social trap, you will not be able to get out of it. And this is possible only if you become very, very aware, very keenly aware, sincerely aware. Then you will see traps all around. Don't react to them. Sinners have always been there, criminals have always been there – they tried to break out of the bounds of the society, but they never could get very far; they were always caught.

The only way to get out of it is a very subtle one, and that is to get within yourself so deeply that the society cannot reach there. That's the only way – to become true, to get to your center. That's what Zen is all about.

Once, at a scientific gathering, a young physicist approached the British astronomer Sir Arthur Eddington and asked, "Is it true, Sir Arthur, that you are one of the only three men in the world who really understands Einstein's theory of relativity?"

Then noticing the look of discomfort that came into the astronomer's face, he apologized. "I'm sorry," he said. "I didn't mean to embarrass you. I know how modest you are."

"Not at all," said Eddington. "I was just wondering who the third man could be."

All your social formality, modesty, politeness, is just a layer, a very thin layer – as if you pour oil on water, and a thin film of the oil covers it. It is not even skin deep. Don't be deceived by it. The only way to get beyond is to go within. You can become rude – that is happening. Just to become sincere, some people are becoming rude. That is not the way. Just to be honest, people are becoming violent. Just to be true, they are becoming angry and insane. That is not the way. If you want to be true, move to the center because if you remain on periphery, you will remain untrue.

Let your center dominate the periphery. Move to the center, and be in a hurry. I don't mean be impatient. I mean don't be lazy. Because the problem is that if you have lived too long in the society and you have followed its rules and regulations for too long, one becomes accustomed to it. One forgets that it is a bondage, one forgets that these are chains. The chains start appearing like ornaments. You in fact start protecting them.

It happened...

To celebrate their thirtieth wedding anniversary, Mulla Nasruddin came home and presented his wife with a little monkey. "Are you crazy or something?" shouted Mistress Nasruddin. "Where the hell are we gonna keep a monkey?"

"Don't worry," said Nasruddin. "He will sleep right in the bed with us."

"And what about the smell?"

"If I could stand it for thirty years, he will get used to it soon. Don't be worried."

Be in a hurry because once you get settled, it will be difficult; difficult because you will not realize that you are in bondage. If you can escape younger, it will be easier. The older you grow, the more difficult it becomes.

Now, the story.

After Bankei had passed away, a blind man who lived near the master's temple said to a friend: "Since I am blind, I cannot watch a person's face, so I must judge his character by the sound of his voice. Ordinarily when I hear someone congratulate another upon his happiness or success, I also hear a secret tone of envy. When condolence is expressed for the misfortune of another, I hear pleasure and satisfaction, as if the one condoling was really glad there was something left to gain in his own world.

"In all my experience, however, Bankei's voice was always sincere. Whenever he expressed happiness, I heard nothing but happiness, and whenever he expressed sorrow, sorrow was all I heard."

This is the greatest homage that can be done to a man, to the memory of a man.

Bankei was one of the great Zen Masters. This blind man who used to live near the temple could not see people's faces. Blind people become very, very perceptive. Because they are blind, they become very perceptive. Because their eyes are not functioning, the whole energy and the capacity to see moves to their ears. Their ears become substitutes for eyes.

And there is a difference between eyes and ears. Eyes are linear, they look only in one direction. Ears are not linear. The ears hear from all directions, the sound is caught from all directions. Ears are more total than eyes. Eyes just focus; eyes are more concentrated. Ears are more meditative; hence all the meditators close their eyes. Because with the eyes your mind becomes linear, it is easier to concentrate with the eyes; difficult to meditate. Remember the difference: when you concentrate, you focus your mind exclusively on something, and everything else is excluded out of it. You include only the certain thing on which you are concentrating, and everything is excluded. You focus. But ears are more meditative. They include all, everything that happens around. If you are listening to me, you are also listening to the birds. It is happening simultaneously. To the ears, existence is simultaneous; to the eyes it is linear, gradual. If I start looking from this side to that side, first I will see Amida, then somebody else, then Teertha, then somebody else. You are all here together, but eyes will create a linear procession which is a falsification of reality. You are not here in a queue, you are all here together. But if I listen with my ears, with closed eyes, to your breathing, your being, then you are all here together.

Ears are closer to existence than eyes, and it is a misfortune that ears have been neglected, and eyes have become very predominant. Psychologists say that eighty percent of human knowledge is gained through the eyes. Eighty percent! It is too much. It has become almost dictatorial. The eyes have become the dictators. Ears are closer to existence, to the diffused existence, to the togetherness of existence.

There are methods, particularly in Zen, where one simply sits and listens; listens to existence, not concentrating anywhere. It is easier for eyes to be closed; you can open them, you can close them. Your mind can manipulate your eyes, but you cannot close your ears. They are always open.

So if your emphasis moves from eyes to ears, you will become more open. The eyes can be manipulated more easily, the mind can play tricks with the eyes. With ears it is more difficult to play tricks.

If you have come across a blind man, you will see, it happens. He starts seeing by his ears. And he can see many subtle nuances which eyes cannot see. He becomes more perceptive. By the sound, by the tone, by small waverings in the tone, fluctuations in the tone, he starts seeing deeply into you. And because he is not part of the society – society belongs to those who have eyes – a blind man is almost an outcast, out of the society. So you don't know how to deceive a blind man. You know how to deceive people who have eyes, but you don't know how to deceive a blind man. You have never practiced it, it has never happened. Rarely do you come across a blind man.

He starts seeing many things. Even by your footsteps, by the sound of your footsteps, he starts recognizing many things in you. Are you a man rooted in the earth? Grounded in the earth? A blind man can see just by your footsteps. He can hear whether you are grounded or not.

Every person moves in a different way, walks in a different way. If a buddha walks, he is tremendously grounded. His legs are almost like the roots of a tree. He is in deep contact with the earth. He is nourished by the earth, the earth is nourished by him. There is a continuous transfer of energy.

Ordinarily people are uprooted trees. They walk as if they are uprooted; they don't have roots in the earth, they are not grounded. You try sometimes. Just stand with naked feet on the earth or on the sand on a beach, and just feel that your legs are like roots and that they are reaching deep into the earth. And start swaying with the wind like a tree. Forget that you are a man, think of yourself as a tree, and soon you will see something transpiring between your feet and the earth. It may take a little time because you have forgotten the language, but one day you will see something is transpiring. Something is given by the earth to the feet, and you are also returning, responding. And the day it happens, you will start walking in a totally new way – rooted, solid, not fragile, not sad, more alive, full of energy. You will be less tired, and your footsteps will have a different quality.

A blind man can immediately say whether this man is rooted in the earth or not.

A man who is a thief walks in one way – continuously afraid. The fear enters into the footsteps, into the sound of the footsteps. A man who is walking in his own home – at home, at ease – walks in a different way.

The blind man who lived near Bankei's temple must have known thousands of people. He was a beggar. He said, when Bankei died: *"Ordinarily when I hear someone congratulate another upon his happiness or success, I also hear a secret tone of envy."*

When people congratulate others, deep down they are jealous. The envy is there. It is just a social formality that they are fulfilling. Their voice will show it. You watch, you start watching life. It is a beautiful thing to watch. Many things are happening around you continuously. You are missing tremendous experiences. Watch people's voices – somebody congratulating someone. Just try to see what his voice says – not what he is saying, but what his voice says. And immediately you will understand what this blind man means. There is a subtle jealousy, envy, pain, misery, frustration that somebody else has succeeded and he has not succeeded. It is just a lip service.

"When condolence is expressed for the misfortune of another, I hear pleasure and satisfaction..." The second thing is still deeper. The first thing you can understand. You can say, "Right, true. There is jealousy when you congratulate somebody." But the blind man says that when you condole, when you see somebody has died or somebody has gone bankrupt or somebody's house has burned, and you go and you sympathize and you say, "It was very bad," deep down there is a subtle satisfaction and pleasure. Because deep down you are feeling good that your house has not been burned, somebody else's has; that your wife has not died, somebody else's has; at least your child is still alive, somebody else's has died. God has not been so cruel to you. You feel a subtle joy.

Whenever you sympathize or express condolence, watch. Or when you watch others doing that, just look deep down into their voice. Something else is also present; that is bound to be so. In your love, hatred is present. Even when you laugh, something deep down goes on crying within you. Your laughter is not pure; your laughter can be changed into crying very easily, your crying can be changed into laughter very easily. You know it. You love a person, and you can hate him any moment. You were ready to die for him, and now you are ready to kill him. A friend can become foe any moment. Man is contradictory, split, schizophrenic.

And the blind man said: *"In all my experience, however, Bankei's voice was always sincere. Whenever he expressed happiness, I heard nothing but happiness..."*

It was pure, uncontaminated by the opposite, uncorrupted, uncontradicted. It was simple. It was not complex. It was sincere.

"...and whenever he expressed sorrow, sorrow was all I heard." This simplicity is the goal of Zen; this sincerity is the goal of Zen.

I was reading a few lines of T. S. Eliot the other day:

A condition of complete simplicity
(Costing not less than everything)
And all shall be well and
All manner of things shall be well
When the tongues of flame are in-folded
Into the crowned knot of fire
And the fire and the rose are one.

They express the very essence of Zen. "...And the fire and the rose are one." There comes a moment of simplicity when the energy that is invested in hatred and the energy that is invested in love are released from their polar opposites. "...And the fire and the rose are one."

The man is simply simple. He has no contradictions in him. You can taste him; his taste is always the same. And whatsoever he does, he does it totally; there is no other way. He cannot do even a small thing without being total in it. Even a small gesture of his hand and he is totally there in that gesture. He looks at you, and he is there in his look – totally there. He touches you, and it is not only his hand that touches you, it is his whole being.

Ordinarily we are manipulating things – chairs, tables, a thousand and one things – and we have forgotten that hands are meant for something more also, not just manipulating things. So when you touch your beloved's hand, you touch as if you were touching a table. You have forgotten that hands are not just to manipulate, they are to give also. The hands have become dead.

When a man like Bankei touches, then you will know what touch is. He will flow from his touch totally into you; he will pour himself into you. His touch will be a gift, his look will be a gift because he has attained. He has given the ultimate gift of his own being to himself: "...And the fire and the rose are one."

Listen to your heart, move according to your heart, whatsoever the stake: "A condition of complete simplicity (Costing not less than everything)..."

To be simple is arduous because to be simple costs everything that you have. You have to lose all to be simple. That's why people have chosen to be complex, and they have forgotten how to be simple.

But only a simple heart throbs with existence, hand in hand. Only a simple heart sings with existence in deep harmony. To reach to that point, you will have to find your heart, your own throb, your own beat.

"This is my way;" Nietzsche used to say, "where is yours? Thus I answered those who asked me 'the way.' For the way – that does not exist."

"This is my way; where is yours? Thus I answered those who asked me 'the way.' For the way – that does not exist." Only ways exist – *the* way does not exist. Your way, my way, yes – but *the* way, no.

Zen is an absolutely individual path. It is not a religion in the sense of Christianity, it is not a religion in the sense of any organization. One has to become individual. The word *individual* is good. It simply means: one who cannot be divided. Indivisible means individual. You are not yet individuals because you are split. Become one and you will become individuals.

Great is the stake, great is the risk, but it is worth it.

Enough for today.

CHAPTER 4

understanding is more than enough

The first question:

Osho,
"Happiness is not being smart enough to know what to worry about." Please comment.

This must have been said by a very unhappy man, and yet a very egoistic one, because he cannot recognize the fact that unhappiness is created by being unintelligent. He is trying to save his ego. He is saying that the grapes are sour.

To be unhappy no intelligence is needed. Everybody is capable of being unhappy, but happiness is very, very rare. Great talent is needed. Not only intellect, intelligence is needed. Only rarely does a Buddha, a Krishna become happy. It is almost impossible to be happy.

So let us try to understand what unhappiness is. Unhappiness is the incapacity to understand life, the incapacity to understand oneself, the incapacity to create a harmony between you and existence. Unhappiness is a discord between you and reality; something is in conflict between you and existence. Happiness is when nothing is in conflict; when you are together, and you are together with existence also. When there is a harmony, when everything is flowing without any conflict, smooth, relaxed, then you are happy. Happiness is possible only with great understanding, an understanding like the peaks of the Himalayas. Less than that won't do.

Anybody is capable of being unhappy any moment, that's how the whole world is so unhappy. To be happy you will have to create such a great understanding about you and about the existence in which you exist, that everything falls in line, in deep accord, in rhythm. And between your energy and the energy that surrounds you a dance happens, and you start moving in step with life.

Happiness is when you disappear. Unhappiness is when you are too much. You are the discord, your absence will be the accord. Sometimes you have glimpses of happiness when by some accident you are not there; looking at nature, or looking at the stars, or holding the hand of your beloved, or making love, in some moments when you are not there. If you are there, even there will be no happiness. If you are making love to your beloved and it is really as you express it, a "making," then there will be no happiness.

Love cannot be made. You can be in it or not in it, but there is no way to make it. The English expression is ugly. To "make love" is absurd. How can you make it? If the maker is there, the doer is there, the technician goes on existing. And if you are following some techniques from Masters and Johnson, or Vatsyayana, or some other source, and you are not lost in it, happiness will not happen. When you are lost, you don't know where you are going, you don't know what you are doing. When you are possessed by the whole, the part does not exist separate from the whole, then there is an orgasmic experience. That is what happiness is.

For happiness you will need tremendous intelligence, and I say intelligence, not intellect, knowingly. Intellect you can get from the market, intellect you can get from the books, intellect you can get from the university. Intellect is transferable, intellect is mechanical, intellect is of the biocomputer you call mind. Intelligence is not of the mind, intelligence is of the no-mind – what Zen people call no-mind. Intelligence has nothing to do with information, knowledge; it has only one element in it, and that element is of awareness.

If you are intelligent, then your life will be of happiness. Why is intelligence needed? Because life in itself is meaningless. Meaning is not something sitting there, and you have just to reach and possess it.

Meaning has to be created. People come to me and they ask, "What is the meaning of life?" As if life has any meaning. Life has no meaning; that is the beauty of life. That's why it is freedom. You are free to create your meaning, and I am free to create my meaning. If life has a meaning, then we will all be just slaves, and that meaning will not be worth anything. Life is freedom. It does not impose any meaning on you; it simply gives you an opportunity to create your own meaning. The meaning has to be created. It is not like a thing that you can uncover, you will have to become your meaning, you will have to give a rebirth to yourself. That's why I say much intelligence is needed. Only when you feel meaning in life, will you be happy, not before it.

Life has no meaning in itself, you have to bring meaning into it. Life is just raw material, you have to create your meaning out of it. You have to create your godliness. Godliness is not there waiting for you. You have to create it within your heart, within your innermost core of being. Only then will you be happy.

To create meaning you will have to be a creator. Painters paint, create paintings; poets write, create poetry; dancers create dance, but these are all just fragments. A religious person creates himself; the religious person is the greatest artist there is. All other artists are just finding substitutes, so one day or other they will become frustrated. You have written many poems, and then one day you realize, "What is the point? Why go on writing?" You have painted, then one day suddenly you realize, "What is the point? For whom? For what?" One day you will die, and all will be left and will disappear. So what is the point?

Unless you feel a point of immortality in whatsoever you are doing, you cannot be happy, and that point of immortality is felt only when you create immortality within yourself.

Gurdjieff used to say, and very rightly, that man is not born with a soul. All other religions say that man is born with a soul, but Gurdjieff's saying is tremendously significant: man is not born with a soul. And unless you create it, you will not have any soul, you will exist empty, and you will die empty. You will have to create it, that's why I say great intelligence is needed.

This statement must have been made by someone who was very unhappy and yet so egoistic that he could not or would not recognize the fact that it is he who is creating his unhappiness. So he says, "Happiness is not being smart enough to know what to worry about." He is saying that to be happy one has to be ignorant, to be happy one has to be stupid. Then a Buddha is stupid, then a Jesus is stupid, then people who are in madhouses are the only intelligent people in the world.

But this man is trying to save his ego. To be intelligent is arduous, it will need tremendous effort on your part. You will have to destroy much that is rubbish within you, you will have to create almost a fire of consciousness so that what is useless is burned, and only that which is pure gold is saved. Very few people are ready to go through that hardship, through that discipline which creates intelligence. People want short-cuts.

A man went to see his psychiatrist and said that every night he was visited by a ten-foot monster with two heads, and he was suffering tremendously. Sleep was not possible, he was becoming more and more miserable, and any day he could collapse. He had even thought about committing suicide.

"Well, I think I might be able to cure you," said the psychiatrist, "but I am afraid it will be a lengthy process, and it will cost you about three hundred dollars."

"Three hundred dollars?" said the man. "Forget it! I will just go home and make friends with it."

That's why is so difficult to be intelligent, and it costs so much. It costs all. You have to put at stake whatsoever you have. It is a cross. In fact, you have to die to be intelligent because only when you are reborn will you be intelligent, not before it. And the cross has to be carried on one's own shoulders, nobody else can carry your cross. You will have to carry your cross to your own Golgotha, there is no other way. Many times you will stumble on the road, many times you will be so tired and exhausted that you would like to rest. Many times you will think that people who have never desired intelligence, awareness, are blessed. "What have I chosen?" Many times doubt and suspicion will arise in your mind. "Is there any goal, or am I simply carrying a cross and wasting my life?" Many times you would like to go back to the world, there will be many temptations. But if you can stick with it, if you can remain on the path against all odds, one day intelligence flowers.

It is almost like a seed: the seed cannot know what is going to happen. The seed has never known the flower, and the seed cannot even believe that he has the potentiality to become a beautiful flower.

Long is the journey, and it is always safer not to go on that journey because unknown is the path, nothing is guaranteed. Nothing can be guaranteed. Thousand and one are the hazards of the journey, many are the pitfalls – and the seed is secure, hidden inside a hard core. But the seed tries, it makes an effort, it drops the hard shell which is its security, it starts moving. Immediately the fight starts: the struggle with the soil, with the stones, with the rocks. And the seed was very hard, and the sprout will be very, very soft and dangers will be many.

There was no danger for the seed, the seed could have survived for millennia, but for the sprout there are many dangers. But the sprout starts: toward the unknown, toward the sun, toward the source of light, not knowing where, not knowing why. Great is the cross to be carried, but the dream possesses the seed, and the seed moves one day, and there is much competition: there are other trees, there are other plants, and he has to pass all of them. Only then will the sun and the sky be available. And then, no one knows. But one day it flowers, it happens.

The same is the path for man. It is arduous. Much courage will be needed.

It is said about Dr. Albert Schweitzer that he was playing host to several European visitors at the hospital in Lambarene in French Equatorial Africa.

"This heat is unbearable," one of the visitors moaned. "What is the temperature?"

"I don't know," said Schweitzer. "We don't have a thermometer here."

"No thermometer?"

"No," replied the doctor. "If I knew how hot it was, I don't think I'd be able to endure it either."

People remain unintelligent because if you know, if you start understanding, it will be almost impossible to endure the life that you are living. You are living in hell.

I have heard about a man, a very intellectual man, a philosopher, who died. He came naked before God, and God opened the book of the man's life. God went on to recount all the sins of the man written therein. The man had been guilty of practically all sins including cruelty, lack of charity, thievery, ingratitude, disloyalty, lust and lack of love. To all these charges the man answered, "Even so did I."

Thereupon God closed the book of the man's life and said, "Surely, I will send you to hell."

The man said he could not do so because hell was where he had always lived.

So then God, feeling a little disturbed that he could not send this man to hell, feeling almost impotent, not knowing what to do – because he was right – how can you send a man to hell who has always lived in hell? So then God said he would send him to heaven just to save his ego.

And the man cried out, "Thou canst not!"

And God said, "Wherefore can I not send thee to heaven?"

And the man answered and said, "Because never, in no place, have I been able to imagine it."

And there was silence in the House of Judgment.

How can you send a man to heaven who cannot even imagine it, who has never tasted it? How can you send a man to heaven who has not created it in his own soul? Impossible. He defeated God. Hell is not possible because he has lived there, and there is no other hell. Heaven is not possible unless you create it. Unless you carry it within yourself, you cannot find it anywhere.

It is said in all the religious books of the world that saints go to heaven, but it is a half-statement. They go to heaven because they live in heaven; they go to heaven because they have created their heaven. In fact, to be in heaven, you will have to have heaven within you; there is no other way.

To be intelligent is to create your own heaven, is to create your own happiness, otherwise there is none. If you create it, you have it. It is just like breathing: if you breathe, you are alive; if you don't breathe, you are not alive. If you create happiness, you are happy; if you don't create, you are unhappy. Unhappiness needs no creativity on your part. Unhappiness is a negative state, it need not be created. Happiness is not negative, it is a positive state, it has to be created. Absence can be there, but the presence has to be created.

Remember it and don't become victims of such quotes. In the West there are many foolish statements in circulation. These statements may appear to be very penetrating; they are not.

The second question:

Osho,
During my dancing meditation I kept having flashes about what you said concerning the society, drugs, etc. And wondering that now that I am intoxicated by the ultimate drug – you, Osho – can anyone take that away from me? Bring me down from that eternal high?

No one except you. You can destroy it, nobody else. It is totally your creation. You can destroy it, or you can nourish it. Remember it because it is so difficult to move on heights. We are not attuned for heights, we are attuned for crawling on the earth. That's why whenever you attain to a high, you cannot remain on that altitude for long. Sooner or later you descend back into the dark valley of your life. Then it becomes just a memory. Not only that, it becomes a frustration because now you know that height is possible. And you have lost your path, and you are back in the valley. In fact, you were better before, in a way. You had not known the height, you had not known the light, so you were thinking that the valley is the only life. Now that you have tasted something, you will never be at rest in the valley.

So if you are feeling high, if you are touching some altitude within your consciousness, if some sky is opening, then be very careful because very fragile is the flower of consciousness – very, very fragile. It can be destroyed in a single moment of unawareness. It needs lives together to create it, and a single moment of unalertness to destroy it. It is very fragile.

Nobody else can take it from you, that is certain: nobody can rob you of it. It is something within you. So you can be killed, but it cannot be killed. It is absolutely yours. Even if I want to take it back from you, I cannot take it because, in fact, I have not given it to you. You have given it to yourself. My presence may have helped as a catalytic agent, but that's all. Even I cannot take it back from you.

But don't be satisfied with this – that nobody can take it. You can destroy it. The danger will come from you, the trouble will come from you. So don't look around for the enemy, look within. It is a great gift that you have given to yourself, now watch for the inner enemy: the anger, the hatred, the jealousy, the envy. They are watching. They are watching you flying so high, they are getting ready to pull you down, to pull you back to the valley where they think you belong. Watch there; the enemy is within, just as the friend is within.

Mahavira has said that you are your enemy if you are not alert, you are your friend if you are alert.

A great treasure is happening to you. You cannot remain unconscious, as you were before, because before you had no treasure; there was nothing to be guarded. Now the more you grow inside, the more you will have to guard, to protect.

The third question:

Osho,
I kept wondering what you meant about our having to go astray; wondering what I would have to do, and then suddenly I realized: we are astray.

True. A great insight has happened to you. Man is astray. The sin is not to be committed, it has already been committed. That is the meaning of the Christian parable that Adam committed the sin – the first man. Man is born astray, that is the meaning of it, we are already in sin.

The word *sin* is very, very beautiful. The original root from which it comes means "missing the target." Sin does not mean sin, it simply means missing the target.

We have gone astray. From the very beginning man is astray, so there's nothing for you to do to go astray. Wherever you are, you are missing your goal, your target. You don't know who you are, you don't know why you are, you don't know where you are headed – and for what. You just go on like driftwood, wherever the winds carry you.

Remember, this "I am astray" is the first realization which will make you come back to the path. The moment Adam realized, "I have committed the sin," he was returning back home. The moment you realize that whatsoever you are and wherever you are, you are wrong… It is very difficult to realize it because the mind tries to protect, to rationalize. The mind belongs to the world. It goes on protecting you – not exactly you but your "astrayness."

You will have to drop all protections, all rationalizations. Once you understand that you are astray, you suddenly realize that you have nothing to save in this world – the wealth, the power, the prestige, nothing is of worth. It is all rubbish. And you are losing something tremendously valuable for rubbish; you are selling yourself and purchasing toys; you are destroying the possibility of creating a soul for nothing.

This is a basic realization, the first breakthrough. Feel happy about it if you have recognized the fact that you are astray, if you have recognized the fact that you are wrong – and not wrong in any particular way, but in a general sense. Not wrong because you are angry, not wrong because you are full of hatred, not wrong because you have done this or that; not in any particular way but in a general sense, one feels one is astray. Then only the door opens for growth; then suddenly you start looking in another dimension. Then you don't look out, you start looking in because whatsoever you do outside will lead you more and more away. The more you chase shadows outside, the more you will be losing yourself in the world.

One starts closing one's eyes, one starts feeling and touching one's being. The first thing to know is "Who am I?" Everything else is secondary. And if this basic thing is solved, if this basic problem is solved, if this basic mystery is penetrated, then all else is solved automatically. And if you don't solve this, and you don't answer the basic quest of man – "Who am I?" – then whatsoever you do is irrelevant.

What are you doing? You are not trying to realize yourself, you are trying to compete with others. Nobody is trying to be oneself, everybody is trying to defeat the other. The whole world lives like a competitive madhouse: somebody purchases a car, now you have to purchase a car, and a bigger one. You may not need it, but now your ego is hurt. Somebody makes a big house, now you have to make one, and a bigger one. This is how life goes on being wasted. Why should you be worried about what others are doing? That is their thing to do; if they feel good, let them do it. You should look at your own need.

But there are two types of people ordinarily: one who is competing with others and another type who goes on condemning others that they are doing wrong. Both are wrong. Who are you to decide? If somebody is making a big house, who are you to decide if he is doing right or wrong? It is none of your concern. It is for him to think about. You should only think about whether what you are doing is right for you to do.

People go to absurd lengths in competition, and people go on dying every day. One day death possesses you, then you remember that your whole life was wasted with fighting others. And it was pointless. You should have put your whole energy into realizing yourself.

I have heard a very beautiful anecdote...

A Catholic church and a synagogue happened to be on opposite sides of the same street. And a rivalry sprang up between the parish priest and the rabbi. When the church was repainted, the synagogue had to have stucco work done. When the priest organized a parish procession of one thousand witnesses through the town, the rabbi organized a procession of two thousand of the faithful.

The priest bought a new car, so the rabbi bought a bigger one. Then the priest had a solemn ceremony outside his church of blessing his new car, and the rabbi came out with a large pair of pliers, went up to his car and cut three inches off the exhaust pipe.

Circumcision! People go on to absurd lengths. One has to defeat the other anyhow. One has to take over the other.

Remember, this foolishness is very ingrained in humanity, and unless you drop this foolishness you will not be able to know yourself, you will not be able to come back home. You will go on moving further and further away, going more and more astray. And one day suddenly you will realize that the whole edifice has collapsed. It was foundationless, you were making a house of cards. A small breeze came, and everything disappeared. Or you were trying to sail in a paper boat.

Man as he is, is simply living in a dream – the dream of the ego, ambition, power, prestige. The religious man is one who has come to understand that this is all going astray.

One day it happened...

I was at Mulla Nasruddin's house. Mulla Nasruddin's teenager son had dented a fender of the family car.

"What did your father say when you told him?" I asked him.

"Should I leave out the cuss words?" he said.

"Yes, of course."

"In that case," said the boy, "he did not say a word."

All cuss words! One day when you look back on your life, you will not see a single act that was intelligent – all were stupidities, foolishnesses. You will feel simply ashamed. The sooner you realize it, the better.

This is what sannyas is all about: a recognition that the way you have lived up to now was absurd; a gesture that you would like to discontinue with your past. By changing the name and by changing the dress nothing is changed, it is a simple gesture that now you feel ashamed with the old identity. It was so foolish that it is better to forget all about it. A new nucleus, a new name, so you can start fresh. That's all.

And it is easier to drop the past than to renovate it. It is easier to be completely cut off from the past rather than to modify it. You can paint a foolish thing, you can modify it, but you cannot make it wise – it will remain foolish. It is better to drop it.

So if this recognition has come to you that we are astray, feel blessed, and don't forget it. Remember it continuously. Unless you have come back to the path, go on remembering it. Just recognizing it once won't do, you will have to live it, remember it for a long time continuously, again and again, so the hammering continues – whatsoever you have done in the past, it is finished.

At least if you remember that it was all wrong – and I say *all* wrong; don't try to decide that a few things were good. I insist: either all things are wrong, or all things are right. There is no other way. It is not possible that a foolish man can do a few things that are right. And the vice versa is also not possible: that a wise man can do a few things that are wrong. A wise man does all right, and a fool goes on doing all wrong. But the fool would like to choose at least a few things right, the fool would say, "Yes, I have done many things wrong, but not all." Then those things that he saves and says were right will become the center for his ego again. So be totally frustrated with your past.

Fritz Perls used to say that all therapy is nothing but skillful frustration. The great therapist is one who goes on frustrating you skillfully; that's what I am doing here. I have to show you that whatsoever you have been doing was wrong because only that understanding can save you. Once you recognize that the whole past was wrong, you simply drop it, you don't bother to choose. There is nothing to choose. It all came out of your unawareness, and it was all wrong. Your hatred was wrong, your love also; your anger was wrong, your compassion also. If you seek deep down, you will always find wrong reasons for your compassion and wrong reasons for your love. A foolish man is foolish, and whatsoever he does is foolish.

So it will have to be remembered continuously, it should become a constant remembrance – what Buddha used to call mindfulness. One should remain mindful so it is not repeated again. Because only mindfulness will protect, and you will not be able to repeat your past again and again; otherwise the mind tends to repeat it.

The fourth question:

Osho,
I have fallen in love with Chuang Tzu, with Joshu, with Mumon, with Bodhidharma. How can I not follow them? I feel already they have transformed me through you. How can I not be thankful?

Let me tell you one anecdote first...

When Rabbi Nor, Rabbi Mordekai's son, assumed the succession after his father's death, his disciples noted that there were a number of ways in which he conducted himself differently to his father, and asked him about this.

"I do just as my father did," he replied. "He did not imitate, and I do not imitate."

Meditate over this anecdote. He said, "I do just as my father did. He did not imitate, and I do not imitate." If you really understand Joshu, Bodhidharma or me, you will not imitate because I have not imitated, because Bodhidharma never imitated anybody.

Joshu used to say to his disciples, "If you utter Buddha's name, go and rinse your mouth immediately." Joshu also used to say, "If you meet the Buddha on the way, kill him immediately," and he used to worship Buddha every day.

Ordinarily Zen looks puzzling, but it is clear-cut. It is following Buddha. When Joshu says, "If you meet the Buddha on the way, kill him," he is a right disciple because that is Buddha's essential message. When Buddha was dying, his last utterance in this world was, "*Appo deepo bhava*" – "Be a light unto yourself." Don't follow anybody.

Anand was crying, weeping because Buddha was leaving the body, and he said to Buddha, "You are leaving, and I have not yet become enlightened. What about me? What will happen to me? The world will be absolutely dark for me; you were the light. And now you are going. Have compassion on us." Buddha opened his eyes and said, "*Appo deepo bhava.*" "Be a light unto yourself, Anand, nobody else can be a light for you."

When Joshu says, "Kill the Buddha if you meet him on the way," he is a true follower of Buddha. In Zen following is very, very delicate. Great intelligence will be needed if you want to be a follower of Zen. It is very easy to be a Christian or a Hindu; it is very mathematical. To follow Zen, it is very, very delicate and poetic because the very following means not following; because that is the message of the Zen masters, don't follow.

It is reported that it happened in China...

A Zen master had organized a great celebration. People asked him about it because that type of celebration was only arranged on one's master's birthday. Nobody had ever known this man to follow anybody. He had been to a certain master, but it was known that the master had refused to accept him as a disciple. So for whom was he celebrating?

He said, "Because that master refused to accept me as his disciple, he is my master."

They said, "We don't follow. What do you mean? When he refused, he refused. He never accepted you as his disciple."

He said, "That's why I am celebrating. If he had accepted me, I would have been lost. He threw me to me, to myself. He said, 'Be a light unto yourself.' When he rejected, he accepted me. He said, 'I will not allow you to imitate me. I will not allow you to become a disciple of mine. I will not allow you to become an imitator, a carbon copy.' His compassion was great, he loved me tremendously, that's why he rejected me."

Zen is a little difficult to understand; its ways are very poetic, zigzag. Christianity is like a superhighway; Zen is more like a zigzag labyrinth in a forest. It turns, moves, sometimes in this direction, sometimes in that, sometimes in almost the opposite direction; you were going to the east, and suddenly you turn and start moving to the west. But that's how it is, and that's how it should be because life is not mathematics and life is not like a superhighway. Life is wild. In fact, no path exists; you walk and you create your own path.

The questioner has said, "I have fallen in love with Chuang Tzu..." Good, but falling in love with Chuang Tzu means falling in love with oneself. If you want to follow Chuang Tzu, you will have to follow yourself; there is no other way. People like Chuang Tzu don't give you ordinary commandments, they don't give you ten commandments; do this, don't do that. They don't give you a morality. In fact, they don't give you any discipline, they simply impart their awareness because they know that any commandment, any fixed commandment, is going to become a slavery to you; it will not liberate you. And life changes so much that something that is right this moment may not be right the next moment, and you will be caught in your discipline. Discipline is rigid, discipline is dead, discipline never changes, discipline is not a process. Once fixed, it is fixed forever. Look at the Judaic Ten Commandments. Moses fixed them, he brought these commandments written on a stone, slabs of stone, dead. Now Jews and Christians have followed them, and you may not improve upon them, you may not change them. Life goes on changing. They have become a dead weight, and nobody follows them, but still people go on paying lip service to them.

Zen masters have not given any rigid discipline to anybody. They simply impart their awareness. They say, "Be aware, and you will find your discipline moment to moment."

I have heard, it happened...

The sales manager believed in super-efficiency. "Jones," he said to the new traveler, "you will take the nine forty-five to Leeds. Your task there will take you two hours and fifty minutes, so you will have time for a sandwich and a cup of tea in the station buffet before catching the three forty-five to Manchester. At Manchester go straight to Mennin and Company and get the details of that order. That will take you thirty-five minutes which will enable you to catch the five-thirty back here. Is that all clear?"

"Yes, sir," said the helpless representative, and off he went.

But at one, the sales manager was enraged to receive a telegram from the new salesman which read: "Leeds buffet out of sandwiches. Stop. What shall I do?"

This is going to happen. If details are so important, this is going to happen.

Zen masters have not given any details. They simply impart their awareness and say, "Be aware. Awareness will show you the way in each moment. What is needed, you will know. Respond knowingly, alert, that's all." How can it be decided beforehand what you should do? Who knows? Each circumstance is so unique that it is difficult to decide. And people who decide always encage humanity, imprison humanity.

Zen is a path of liberation. It liberates you. It is freedom from the first step to the last. You are not required to follow any rules; you are required to find out your own rules and your own life in the light of awareness.

So keep your light of awareness there, keep your lamp burning; that's all. Then you know what to do, where to move, where not to move. Once a rigid discipline is given, it makes you a prisoner.

So if you love Bodhidharma, you are falling in a very dangerous love. If you love me, you have fallen in a very dangerous love. I am not going to give you any rigid discipline. People ordinarily expect everything ready-made. They want somebody else to fix their lives because that's how they have been brought up. Everybody says to them from the very childhood, "Do this, don't do that." They have lived on do's and don'ts. From the mother's milk they have received commandments, and they don't know, if they are left to themselves, what to do. Even sometimes they want to be left to themselves – because there is a deep urge to be free – but then they don't know what to do. Again they will start finding somebody to lead them. People have been forced to become followers. You are not being trusted to become your own leader and your own follower.

Zen is a way which makes you the follower and the master. The master is there just to indicate: subtle indications, very indirect. And if you are looking for rigid rules, you are looking in a wrong direction.

And remember, you say that you have fallen in love with them, how can you not follow them? Love does not force anybody to follow: love wants to make you free, love wants to give you freedom. In fact, the person who is forcing you to follow him may be on an ego trip himself, may be trying to dominate you, may be trying to destroy you, may be trying to cripple you. No, people who have known don't destroy you. They help you to be yourself, they don't force you to follow them. They only want you to understand them. That's enough. Understanding is more than enough. Nothing else is needed.

Imitation is a substitute for understanding, and a very poor substitute. If understanding is there, there is no question of imitating or of following: you will follow understanding. Keep this very clear: if you follow your understanding, you will be following me. By and by you will see that your path and my path are running parallel. By and by you will see that you are following me if you follow your understanding. If you follow me and forget your understanding, sooner or later you will see that I am gone and you are left in darkness. The real way to follow me is not to follow me but to follow your understanding; then even when I am gone, you will be following me. It looks paradoxical, but Zen is paradoxical.

"How can I not follow them? I feel that already they have transformed me through you. How can I not be thankful?" Be thankful, be grateful, but there is no need to follow them or imitate them.

Gratefulness is a totally different thing. Thankfulness is a totally different thing than following a person. Gratitude is needed, it is good to be grateful, it will help you to flower. Gratitude never cripples anybody, but if just because of gratitude you think that you have to follow, then already you have destroyed gratitude, already you have destroyed the freedom, the flowering that gratitude gives to you, already you have started to pay.

If you think by following, you are paying a debt, then you are not grateful, you are bargaining. One day suddenly you will see that you have paid enough. Or you may even get annoyed that you have paid more than enough. And if you are paying your master in any way trying to pay the debt, then you don't love your master because these things cannot be returned, there is no way. You can pay everybody else back, but you can never pay your master back because it is not a bargain, it is not a commodity. He gives you out of his fullness, he gives you because he has too much and he does not know what to do with it, he gives you because he has to give – in fact, he is grateful to you that you accept it, he is grateful to you that you didn't reject his gift. You could have rejected it. It is such a deep exchange that the master is grateful to the disciple that the disciple accepted his gift, and the disciple is grateful to the master that he thought him worthy. But there is no returning, you cannot pay it back. That would be almost profane, a sacrilege.

Be grateful, be thankful forever and ever, but don't try to make it a duty – that because you are grateful, you have to follow – otherwise sooner or later you will get very angry. If you are grateful toward me because you have to be, then sooner or later you will be angry also.

Duty is not a good word, it is a four-letter dirty word. Love is religious; duty is social. Love is spiritual; duty is moral. Love is of the transcendental; duty is legal. You serve your mother because you say, "This is my duty." Better not serve her, leave her and let her die, but don't call it duty, it is ugly. If it is love, from where does this word *duty* come in? Duty is something forced upon you; reluctantly you have to do it, it is a social obligation, a commitment. It is because she is your mother that you have to do it – not because of love. If you love her, then you serve her, but then service has a fragrance. You are not burdened, deep down you are not thinking about when she is going to die, deep down you are not planning that when she dies, you will be finished with this burden. You are flowing, flowering while serving her; you are enjoying it, it is a delight that your mother is still alive. When your wife is just your wife and not your beloved, then it is a duty, but when you love your wife, then it is different.

A friend of Mulla Nasruddin was talking to him. He said, "My wife is an angel."

Mulla said, "But mine is still alive."

We don't love each other, we have forgotten the language of love.

Feel thankful, feel loving, deep in gratitude, but go on your way. Try to create more awareness and understanding and intelligence. Radiate with intelligence to express your gratitude; there is no other way.

The fifth question:

Osho,
I have got a future-ego. It keeps telling me what a super person I am going to turn out to be in a few years' time when I am finished with this trip. It is very smug and in the meantime, like right now, it is pretending to be so humble, so malleable, so adaptable, and so untouchable. Could you help me to get at it? It is bugging me.

Who is this me?

If you think the ego is bugging you, who are you? It is again an ego trip. Now the ego is taking a very subtle form. When the ego is not, you are not. Ego is all that defines you, that makes you say "I" or "me." Ego is your definition, your boundary, ego divides you from others. It is ego, that's why you can say "I" and "you." If the ego disappears, who is "I" and who is "you"?

Now you are taking a very subtle form. You say the ego is bugging you. Who are you then? Just see the point. If you don't see the point, you can go on playing the game ad infinitum. You can become humble, and the ego will be there. You can even become egoless, and the ego will be there. Ego is very subtle, and very cunning are its ways.

A psychiatrist once asked his patient, Mulla Nasruddin, if the latter suffered from fantasies of self-importance.

"No," replied the Mulla. "On the contrary, I think of myself as much less than I really am."

Now you are going on a very pious trip. The ego can become pious. It can become so humble that nobody can feel it. You may even start thinking, "Now it is not bugging me," but if the "me" is there, it is there.

The poison has become very purified, but a purified poison is more poisonous. That's why ordinary people have ordinary egos, but the so-called religious people have pious egos; they are more dangerous.

And you say, "I have got a future-ego." No, the ego is always of the past, it cannot be of the future. Even when you are thinking of the future, it is nothing but projected past. Even if you are thinking, "Tomorrow I am going to become the greatest man in the world," but the idea of the greatest man and the idea of the tomorrow both come from your past. The past accumulated is the substance of the ego. In the past many things were happy, and many things were unhappy. In the future you will like to modify, you would like to drop all that was unpleasant, and you would like to collect all that was pleasant. That is your future ego, but it is not future, it is simply the past reshuffled, chosen again, selected. In the past there were many things you did not like; in the future you will drop them. But the ego belongs to the past, ego is of the past, ego is a ghost following you; it comes from the past, and it is already dead.

Just think: if you have no past, can you have any ego? Meditate over it. If your mind is suddenly completely washed of the past – now there are techniques available, mind-washing techniques – if your mind is completely washed of the past, will you have any ego? How will you have an ego? You will again become like a child, again innocent, you will again have to start from *abc*. Again you will create an ego because mind-washing cannot help, the roots are deeper. The seeds are hidden very, very deep inside you; again they will sprout, again the tree of the ego will start spreading. But it is of the ego, it is of the past.

You don't know the future, so how can you think about it? You can only think about the past redecorated, refined, modified.

"It keeps telling me what a super person I am going to turn out to be in a few years' time when I am finished with this trip." If this is a trip, you will never be finished with it. You may be finished with this, but then you will choose another trip. Trips never end, they never come to any end; one changes one train for another, one town for another, one master for another, one religion for another, but the trip continues. If this is not a trip, only then can it end. If to be with me has nothing to do with the future, if to be with me is of the present, if you are here now with me, then it is not a trip. We are not going anywhere; at least, I'm not going anywhere. You may be going, but I'm not going anywhere. So with me there is going to be no trip. If you want to be with me, you have to drop all trips.

Sannyas is not a trip. It is an understanding in which you drop all the trips, in which you say, "Now I have arrived. Finished. Now I am not going anywhere. Now there is no future and no desire to go anywhere. Now I have come to terms with the present, now I will be living in the herenow."

If sannyas is also a trip for you, then it is not going to help much. It will become like other trips; sooner or later you will be fed up with it, frustrated with it because every trip is going to end in a frustration. No trip can fulfill you because the fulfillment is herenow, and a trip is directed somewhere else. A trip is desire, hope; fulfillment is not a desire, not a hope. Fulfillment is just to be herenow and just to accept the way you are, the being you are.

And start enjoying. I am not preparing you for any subtle enjoyment in the future, my whole method is to enjoy it right now. Who knows? There may be no future. Why waste this moment? Enjoy, delight! There is no need to sacrifice this moment for any other moment because any other moment, if it is ever to come, is going to be just like this moment. So why sacrifice this moment? I am against all sacrifice. I don't tell you to sacrifice the present for the future; that has been told to you by your parents, your teachers, your educational system, your society. They all say sacrifice the present for the future. I say don't sacrifice anything. Live it, delight in it, so that you can learn how to be blissful. Once you know it, even in the future you will be able to delight.

Those moments are going to be the same, can't you see the fact? In the past it is the same time. In fact, the very idea that time is passing is stupid. We are in time, nothing is passing. It is our desire that gives the delusion of passing time. Once you drop the desire, suddenly you start laughing: nothing is passing, everything *is*. It is the same, it has always been the same, it will always be the same. It is the same eternity surrounding you like an ocean. Live in it, enjoy it. Through enjoyment you will become capable of more enjoyment; more brings more. The richer people become richer, poorer people become poorer. Says Jesus – a very Zen saying – that if you have, more will be given to you, and if you don't have, even that will be taken away. Very anti-communist, very Zen. If you have, more will be given to you. And if you don't have, even that will be taken away from you. It looks unjust.

But Jesus is saying a tremendous truth. Yes, that is the truth, one of the most fundamental. If you have, more will be given to you because you will create the capacity by having it. Nobody is going to give unless you have more capacity.

Have you seen? If you don't use a machine, it lasts. If a watch is guaranteed for ten years and you don't use it too much, it may last for twenty years, thirty years. But just the opposite is the case with life. If you don't use it, it will not last more, it will simply disappear from you. If you don't use your legs, your legs will disappear; if you don't use your eyes, your eyes will disappear; if you don't use your awareness, your awareness will disappear. That's why man is not a machine. Don't use the machine, and it lasts longer; don't use man, don't use your potentiality, don't use your body-mind, and you will start disappearing.

It is life's nature – the more you use it, the more you get. Enjoy, otherwise your capacity to enjoy will disappear, will be atrophied, paralyzed. And tomorrow you will be there paralyzed, atrophied – then who is going to enjoy tomorrow?

Omar Khayyam says that he is worried about these religious people. They say that in heaven wine is flowing in streams – Mohammedans say that – but they prohibit wine here on the earth. So Omar Khayyam says, "I am very much worried about these people. If they don't get accustomed here, how are they going to enjoy heaven? And in heaven there are beautiful women, and here these religious people say don't enjoy them here. That is a sin." Omar Khayyam seems to be absolutely logical. He says, "What will you be doing there?"

When I was reading Omar Khayyam, I remembered an anecdote.

Two old women – eighty years old – were talking. One woman said to the other, "Are you aware or not that your husband is chasing girls?"

She said, "I know it, but let him chase them. He is like a dog who chases a car, but when he gets it, he cannot drive it."

So these religious people, if they enter heaven some day, they will be like dogs chasing cars. Once they get it, they don't know what to do, they cannot drive it.

Enjoy. Heaven is not in the future, it is herenow, already present. It is your surroundings. The more you enjoy, the more you become capable of enjoying.

Yes, Jesus is right. If you have, more will be given to you; if you don't have, even that will be taken away from you. And when I say these things, remember, everything is addressed to you personally. The mind is very cunning. If I say something, you can always rationalize that I am saying it to somebody else. This is not your question certainly, so I am addressing it to somebody else; you can laugh and enjoy. The question may be anybody's, but my answer is addressed to you personally. Never think of the neighbor; think only of yourself.

I will tell you an anecdote.

Father Moran was delivering his Sunday sermon. "Someday" he said, "every man in this parish will die."

Suddenly the priest heard MacLean laughing in the third row, but he continued. "As I was saying, every man in this parish will die." Again MacLean began chortling.

Father Moran looked at him and said, "Why, why do you laugh when I say everyone in this parish will die someday?"

"Ha Ha!" exclaimed MacLean. "I am not from this parish."

Remember it!

The sixth question:

Osho,
Yesterday in your discourse you said that one needs to choose the path best suited to one's temperament, either the path of meditation or the path of the heart, but I do not feel both paths to be totally separate. Can one travel a path that is somehow a fusion of the two?

Never heard of it. A fusion is not possible, and in the name of fusion only a dead compromise will happen because the directions are so totally, diametrically, opposite.

If you love, you will have to use imagination, romance, dreams, all the faculties of dreaming, of autohypnosis. If you meditate, you have to drop all the dreaming faculties, autohypnosis, imagination, love; you have to drop everything. But don't be afraid. If meditation happens, in the end you will find that love simply follows. And then that love is totally different from the love that you were trying to fuse with in the beginning. It is totally different. It comes out of your meditation, out of your silence. It has no desire in it, no passion in it. It is cool. It is not a disturbance, it is not an excitement, it has no madness in it.

And if you follow the path of love, one day meditation will come, and the meditation will be totally different than you can think of right now. That meditation will not be dry like a desert, it will be like an oasis. That meditation will not make you renounce the world, it will make you capable of enjoying and delighting in it more. That meditation will not be against love.

But you have to follow one path. A fusion is not possible because both paths move in different directions, use different techniques.

And if you make a fusion, who will be making it? You will be making the fusion. What is your understanding? How can you synthesize? Synthesis is possible only when you have gone beyond. When you have become greater than both love and meditation, then you can synthesize, not before it. A buddha can synthesize, but he never synthesizes because he knows that synthesis has happened in him. And if he synthesizes, it will not be of use to anybody. It will be simply useless, abstract. He insists on the path of meditation – so much so that he has to deny the path of love; he has to say that it is absolutely wrong. If he says, "Not absolutely wrong," then you will start thinking, "Why not move on both? Why not be safe? Who knows which is right? So be clever." But your cleverness will help only your ego-confusion to persist and nothing else.

I have heard...

George M. Pullman decided to build a model community on the outskirts of Chicago many years ago. It was during the early part of 1880, and the Pullman Company had purchased more than four thousand acres of prairie, twelve miles south of the Chicago business district. On this tract there were going to be constructed shops and a town to house almost ten thousand people.

Mr. Pullman engaged the services of Solon Spencer Berman, a well-known New York architect, who was to be the master designer of the master town which was to be completed in 1884.

As the town was nearing completion Berman was so proud of his new city with its public buildings, residences, paved streets, paths, playgrounds, freeway system and water supply that he went to Mr. Pullman one day and suggested that it would be quite appropriate to name the city "Berman" after its architect.

Pullman readily admitted that Berman was a pretty name and that Berman had done a great deal to help bring his dream to fruition, but in response to Berman's request he said, "Berman, I will compromise with you. We will use the first syllable of my name and the second syllable of your name. The city will be called Pullman."

This is how ego goes on trying for its own way. It was going to be called Pullman anyway; now he shows that he has made a compromise; he has taken in half of the name of the architect.

Don't be clever, otherwise you will remain the same, you will not change. Half-techniques on the path of love and half-techniques on the path of meditation will create much confusion in you. They will not help. They may destroy you. You may go berserk.

It is as if you are trying two different "pathies" together: allopathy and ayurveda. It can be dangerous. Or allopathy and naturopathy, it can be dangerous. Their whole understanding is different, their gestalt is different. Both work, but they are complete systems. Once you accept one, it is better to accept that and don't bother to create any synthesis on your own.

Why does this idea of synthesis arise? Because you are so confused you cannot understand which path is your path. Rather than recognizing your confusion, you start creating a compromise. Drop all idea of compromise, just recognize that you are confused. These are the three possibilities: one, the person knows well that he is a man of the path of love or, second, he knows that he is the man of the path of meditation or one knows the third possibility – that he is confused.

If the first two are the case, then there is no need; if the third is the case, then I am here to help you. But to ask for help is against the ego, so you try to compromise. This compromise will be more dangerous, it will confuse you more because, made out of confusion, it will create more confusion.

So try to understand why you hanker for compromise. Sooner or later you will be able to understand that compromise is not going to help. And compromise may be a way of not going in either direction, or it may be just a repression of your confusion. It will assert itself. Never repress anything, be clear-cut about your situation. Even if you are confused, remember that you are confused. This will be the first clear-cut thing about you: that you know that you are confused. You have started on the journey.

I have heard...

A friend of Mulla Nasruddin said to him, "Come and have a drink."

Mulla Nasruddin came up and took a drink of whisky.

"How is this, Mulla?" asked a bystander. "How can you drink whisky? Sure it was only yesterday ye told me ye was a teetotaler."

"Well," said Nasruddin, "you are right. I am a teetotaler, it is true, but I am not a bigoted one."

People go on finding some way or other. But on the path of growth these deceptions are not good.

Another anecdote...

Flagherty sneaked into the room and started making love to his sleeping wife until she awakened and shouted, "Is that you?"

"It better be," snorted Flagherty.

"When are you gonna stop this sinning?" she demanded. "Moody quit smoking, Paine stopped gambling, what are you gonna give up?"

"All right," said Flagherty through bloodshot eyes, "from now on you sleep in the bedroom, and I will sleep in the spare room."

Three weeks went by with Mrs. Flagherty sleeping alone. Finally unable to contain herself for one night more, she tip-toed to the spare room and tapped lightly on the door.

"What is it?" shouted Flagherty.

"I just wanted to tell yer," said his wife, "that Moody has started smoking again."

You cannot repress anything. Howsoever subtle are your ways, you cannot repress anything, you will have to face it. If you are confused, face it.

The last question:

Osho,
Are you the trick or the treat?

Po!

CHAPTER 5

nothing changes a man except awareness

There was an old woman in China who had supported a monk for over twenty years. She had built a hut for him, and she fed him while he was meditating.
One day she decided to find out just what progress he had made in all this time.
She obtained the help of a girl rich in desire, and said to her: "Go and embrace him, and then ask him suddenly, 'What now?'"
The girl called upon the monk and immediately started caressing him, and asking him what he was going to do about it.
"An old tree grows on a cold rock in winter," replied the monk somewhat poetically, "nowhere is there any warmth."
The girl returned and related what he had said.
"To think I fed that fellow for twenty years!" exclaimed the old woman in anger. "He showed no consideration for your need, no disposition to explain your condition. He need not have responded to passion, but at least he should have experienced some compassion."
She at once went to the hut of the monk and burnt it down.

An ancient proverb says:

Sow a thought, reap an act. Sow an act, reap a habit. Sow a habit, reap a character. Sow a character, reap a destiny.

And I say to you: sow nothing, and reap meditation or love. Sowing nothing – that's what meditation is all about, and its natural consequence is love. If at the end of the journey of meditation love has not flowered, then the whole journey has been futile. Something went wrong somewhere. You started, but you never reached.

Love is the test. For the path of meditation, love is the test. For the path of love, meditation is the test. They are two sides of one coin, two aspects of the same energy. When one is there, the other has to be there. If the other is not there, then the first is also not there.

Meditation is not concentration. A man of concentration may not reach to love; in fact, he will not. A man of concentration may become more violent because concentration is a training to remain tense, concentration is an effort to narrow down the mind. It is deep violence with your consciousness, and when you are violent with your consciousness, you cannot be nonviolent with others. Whatsoever you are with yourself, you are going to be with others.

Let this be a fundamental rule of life, one of the most fundamental: whatsoever you are toward yourself, you will be toward others. If you love yourself, you will love others. If you are flowing within your being, you will be flowing in relationships also. If you are frozen inside, you will be frozen outside also. The inner tends to become the outer; the inner goes on manifesting itself in the outer.

Concentration is not meditation; concentration is the method of science. It is scientific methodology. A man of science needs deep discipline into concentration, but a man of science is not expected to be compassionate. There is no need. In fact, a man of science becomes more and more violent with nature. All scientific progress is based on violence toward nature. It is destructive because in the first place the scientific man is destructive to his own expanding consciousness. Rather than expanding his consciousness, he narrows it down, makes it exclusive, one-pointed. It is a coercion, violence.

So remember meditation is not concentration, but neither is meditation contemplation. It is not thinking. Maybe you are thinking about godliness; even then it is thinking. If there is "about," there is thinking. You may be thinking about money, you may be thinking about godliness; it basically makes no difference. Thinking continues, only objects change. So if you are thinking about the world, or about sex, nobody will call it contemplation. If you are thinking about godliness, virtue, if you are thinking about Jesus, Krishna, Buddha, then people will call it contemplation.

But Zen is very strict about it: it is not meditation, it is still thinking. You are still concerned with the other. In contemplation the other is there, although of course not so exclusively as it is in concentration. Contemplation has more fluidity than concentration. In concentration the mind is one-pointed; in contemplation the mind is oriented toward one subject, not toward one point. You can go on thinking about it, you can go on changing and flowing with the subject, but still, on the whole, the subject remains the same.

Then what is meditation? Meditation is just being delighted in your own presence; meditation is a delight in your own being. It is very simple – a totally relaxed state of consciousness where you are not doing anything. The moment doing enters, you become tense; anxiety enters immediately. How to do? What to do? How to succeed? How not to fail? You have already moved into the future.

If you are contemplating, what can you contemplate? How can you contemplate the unknown? How can you contemplate the unknowable? You can contemplate only the known. You can chew it again and again, but it is the known. If you know something about Jesus, you can think again and again; if you know something about Krishna, you can think again and again. You can go on modifying, changing, decorating, but it is not going to lead you toward the unknown. And godliness is the unknown.

Meditation is just to be, not doing anything – no action, no thought, no emotion. You just are. And it is sheer delight. From where does this delight come when you are not doing anything? It comes from nowhere, or it comes from everywhere. It is uncaused because the existence is made of the stuff called joy. It needs no cause, no reason. If you are unhappy, you have a reason to be unhappy; if you are happy, you are simply happy. There is no reason for it. Your mind tries to find a reason because it cannot believe in the uncaused, because the mind cannot control the uncaused; with the uncaused the mind simply becomes impotent. So the mind goes on finding some reason or other. But I would like to tell you that whenever you are happy, you are happy for no reason at all, whenever you are unhappy, you have some reason to be unhappy because happiness is just the stuff you are made of. It is your very being, it is your innermost core. Joy is your innermost core.

Look at the trees, look at the birds, look at the clouds, look at the stars, and if you have eyes, you will be able to see that the whole existence is joyful. Everything is simply happy. Trees are happy for no reason because they are not going to become prime ministers or presidents, and they are not going to become rich, and they will never have any bank balance. Look at the flowers. It is simply unbelievable how happy flowers are for no reason.

The whole existence is made of the stuff called joy. Hindus call it *sat-chit-anand – ananda*, joy. That's why no reason, no cause is needed. If you can just be with yourself, not doing anything, just enjoying yourself, just being with yourself, just being happy that you are, just being happy that you are breathing, just being happy that you are listening to these cuckoos for no reason, then you are in meditation. Meditation is being here, now. And when one is happy for no reason, that happiness cannot be contained within yourself. It goes on spreading to others, it becomes a sharing. You cannot hold it, it is so much, it is so infinite. You cannot hold it in your hands, you have to allow it to spread.

This is what compassion is. Meditation is being with yourself, and compassion is overflowing with that being. It is the same energy that was moving into passion that becomes compassion. It is the same energy that was narrowed down into the body or into the mind. It is the same energy that was leaking from small holes... What is sex? Just a leakage of energy from a small hole in the body. Hindus call these holes. When you are flowing, overflowing, when you are not moving through the holes, all walls disappear. You have become the whole. Now you spread. You cannot do anything about it.

It is not that you have to be compassionate, no. In the state of meditation you are compassion. Compassion is as warm as passion; hence the word *compassion*. It is very passionate, but the passion is unaddressed, and the passion is not in search of any gratification. The whole process has become just the reverse. First you were seeking some happiness somewhere; now you have found it, and you are expressing it. Passion is a search for happiness; compassion is an expression of happiness. But it is passionate, it is warm, and you have to understand it because it has a paradox in it.

The greater a thing, the more paradoxical it is, and this meditation and compassion is one of the highest peaks, the uttermost peak. So there is bound to be a paradox.

The paradox is that a man of meditation is very cool, not cold; cool yet warm, not hot. Passion is hot, it is almost feverish, it has a temperature. Compassion is cool yet warm, welcoming, receptive, happy to share, ready to share, waiting to share. If a person of meditation becomes cold, he has missed. Then he is just a man of repression. If you repress your passion, you will become cold; that's how the whole humanity has become cold because passion has been repressed in everyone.

From the very childhood your passion has been crippled and repressed. Whenever you started becoming passionate, there was somebody – your mother, your father, your teacher, the police – who immediately became suspicious of you. Immediately your passion was curbed, repressed. "Don't do it!" Immediately you shrank within yourself.

And by and by one learns that to survive, it is better to listen to people who are around you. It is safer. So what to do? What is a child supposed to do when he feels passionate, when he feels full of energy and he wants to jump and run and dance, and his father is reading the newspaper? It is rubbish, but he is reading his newspaper, and he is a very important man, he's the master of the house. What to do? The child is doing something really great – in him it is existence who is ready to dance – but the father is reading his newspaper, so there has to be silence. He cannot dance, he cannot run, he cannot scream. He will repress his energy; he will try to be cold, collected, controlled.

Control has become such a supreme value. It is not a value at all. A controlled person is a dead person; a controlled person is not necessarily a disciplined person. Discipline is totally different. Discipline comes out of awareness; control comes out of fear. The people who are around you are more powerful than you, they can punish you, they can destroy you. They have all the power to control, to corrupt, to repress. And the child has to become diplomatic.

When sex energy arises, the child is in difficulty. The society is against it; the society says it has to be channelized, and it is flowing all over the child. It has to be cut out.

In the schools what are we doing? In fact, the schools are not so much instruments for imparting knowledge, as they are instruments of control. For six, seven hours a child is sitting there. This is to curb his dancing, to curb his singing, to curb his joy; this is to control him. Sitting for six, seven hours every day in an almost prisonlike atmosphere, by and by the energy deadens, the child becomes repressed, frozen. Now there is no streaming, the energy does not come, he lives at the minimum; that's what we call control. He never goes to the maximum.

Psychologists have been searching, and they have come to recognize a great fact of human misfortune; that is that ordinarily persons live only ten percent. They live ten percent, they breathe ten percent, they love ten percent, they enjoy ten percent; ninety percent of their life is simply not allowed. This is sheer wastage. One should live at the hundred percent capacity, only then is flowering possible.

So meditation is not control, it is not repression. If somehow you have got the wrong idea – you are repressing yourself – then you will become very controlled, but then you will be cold. Then you will become more and more indifferent, not detached. Indifferent, non-caring, unloving; you will almost commit suicide. You will be alive at the minimum. You can be called "just so-so" alive. You will not be burning from both sides, your flame will be very dim. Much smoke will be there, but almost no light.

It happens to people who are on the path of meditation – Catholics, Buddhists, Jainas – that they become cold because to control comes easily. Awareness is arduous. Control is very easy because control needs only a cultivation of habits. You cultivate habits, then those habits possess you, and you need not worry. Then you go on with your habits, they become mechanical, and you live a robot life. You may look like a Buddha, but you will not be. You will be just a dead stone statue.

If compassion has not arisen in you, then apathy will arise. Apathy means absence of passion; compassion means transformation of passion. Go and watch Catholic monks, Jaina monks, Buddhist monks, and you will see very apathetic figures – dull, stupid, nonradiant, closed, afraid, continuously anxious.

Just the other day I was reading an article on Oscar, the founder of Arica. The man who was interviewing him was a little surprised to see that he was continuously smoking, so he asked, "Why are you smoking so much, and why do you smoke?"

At least Oscar was true. He said, "Whenever I feel nervous, I smoke, it helps."

If a person like Oscar, who has become a master to many people in America, is still nervous and needs smoking to help his nervousness, then what is going to happen to his followers? He must have controlled himself.

Controlled persons are always nervous because deep down turmoil is still hidden. If you are uncontrolled, flowing, alive, then you are not nervous. There is no question of being nervous: whatsoever happens, happens. You have no expectations for the future, you are not performing. Then why should you be nervous?

If you go to Catholic, Jaina, Buddhist monks, you will find them very nervous; maybe not so nervous in their monasteries, but if you bring them out to the world, you will find them very, very nervous because on each step there is temptation.

A man of meditation comes to a point where there is no temptation left. Try to understand it. Temptation never comes from without, it is the repressed desire, repressed energy, repressed anger, repressed sex, repressed greed, that creates temptation. Temptation comes from within you, it has nothing to do with the without. It is not that a devil comes and tempts you, it is your own repressed mind that becomes devilish and wants to take revenge. To control that mind, one has to remain so cold and frozen that no life energy is allowed to move into your limbs, into your body. If energy is allowed to move, those repressions will surface. That's why people have learned how to be cold, how to touch others and yet not touch them, how to see people and yet not see them.

People live with clichés: "Hello. How are you?" Nobody means anything. These are just to avoid the real encounter of two persons. People don't look into each other's eyes, they don't hold hands, they don't try to feel each other's energy, they don't allow each other to pour. Very afraid. Somehow just managing. Cold and dead. In a straitjacket.

A man of meditation has learned how to be full of energy, at the maximum, optimum. He lives at the peak, he makes his abode at the peak. Certainly he has a warmth, but it is not feverish, it only shows life. He is not hot, he is cool because he is not carried away by desires. He is so happy that he is no longer seeking any happiness. He is so at ease, he is so at home, he is not going anywhere, he is not running and chasing; he is very cool.

In Latin there is a dictum: *agere sequitur esse* – to do follows to be; action follows being. It is tremendously beautiful.

Don't try to change your action: try to find out your being, and action will follow because action is secondary; being is primary. Action is something that you do; being is something that you are. Action comes out of you, action is just a fragment. Even if all of your actions are collected together, they will not be equal to your being because all actions collected together will be your past. What about your future? Your being contains your past, your future, your present; your being contains eternity. Your actions, even if all collected, will just be of the past. Past is limited. Future is unlimited. That which has happened is limited, it can be defined, it has already happened. That which has not happened is unlimited, indefinable. Your being contains eternity, your actions contain only your past.

So it is possible that a man who has been a sinner up to this moment can become a saint the next. Never judge a man by his actions; judge a man by his being because sinners have become saints and saints have fallen and become sinners. Each saint has a past, and each sinner has a future. Never judge a man by his actions. But there is no other way because you have not known even your own being, how can you see the being of others? Once you know your own being, you will learn the language, you will know the clue of how to look into another's being. You can see into others only to the extent that you can see into yourself. If you have seen yourself through and through, you become capable of seeing into others through and through.

So a few things before I enter into this beautiful story.

If by your meditations you are becoming cold, beware. If your meditation is making you more warm, more loving, more flowing; this is good, you are on the right path. If you are becoming less loving, if your compassion is disappearing and an apathy is settling inside you, then the sooner you change your direction, the better. Otherwise you will become a wall.

I have heard...

When Ford was Vice-President, he went to Israel and asked Golda

Meir to see the Wailing Wall. Prime Minister Meir took him to the wall, whereupon the Vice-President began to pray, "Help Mr. Nixon guide our country."

He turned to Mrs. Meir and asked, "Is that nice?"

"That's nice," she answered.

"Thank you for making me the Vice-President," he directed to the wall, and then to the Prime Minister, "Is that nice?"

"That's nice," she replied.

"Let Israel give back the land they took from the Arabs, so there will be peace in the Middle-East. Is that nice?"

And Golda Meir said, "You are talking to a wall."

Don't become a wall. Remain alive, throbbing, streaming, flowing, melting.

Of course there are problems. Why have people become walls? Because walls can be defined. They give you a boundary, a definite shape and form, what Hindus call *nam roop*, name and form. If you are melting and flowing, you don't have boundaries; you don't know where you are and where you end and the other begins. You go on being together with people so much that all the boundaries by and by become dreamlike. And one day they disappear.

That is how reality is. Reality is unbounded. Where do you think you stop? At your skin? Ordinarily we think, "Of course, we are inside our skins, and the skin is our wall, the boundary." But your skin could not be alive if the air was not surrounding it. If your skin is not constantly breathing the oxygen that is being supplied by the surround, your skin cannot be alive. Take away the atmosphere, and you will die immediately. Even if your skin has not been scratched, you would die. So that cannot be your boundary. There are two hundred miles of atmosphere all around the earth; is that your boundary? That too cannot be your boundary. This oxygen and this atmosphere and the warmth and the life cannot exist without the sun. If the sun ceases to exist or drops dead... One day it is going to happen. Scientists say that in four thousand years the sun will cool down and drop dead. Then suddenly this atmosphere will not be alive. Immediately. you will be dead. So is the sun your boundary?

But now physicists say this sun is connected to some central source of energy which we have not yet been able to find but is suspected because nothing is unrelated.

So where do we decide where our boundary is? An apple on the tree is not you. Then you eat it, it becomes you. So it is just waiting to become you. It is you potentially. It is your future you. Then you have defecated, and you have dropped much rubbish out of the body. Just a moment before, it was you. So where do you decide?

I am breathing. The breath inside me is me, but just a moment before it may have been your breath. It must have been because we are breathing in a common atmosphere. We are all breathing into each other; we are members of each other. You are breathing in me, I am breathing in you.

And it is not only so with breathing, it is exactly so with life. Have you watched? With certain people you feel very alive, they come just bubbling with energy. And something happens in you, a response, and you are also bubbling. And then there are people; just their face and one feels one will flop down. Just their presence is enough poison. They must be pouring something into you which is poisonous. And when you come around a person and you become radiant and happy and suddenly something starts throbbing in your heart, and your heart beats faster, this man must have poured something into you which was alive.

We are pouring into each other. That's why in the East *satsang* has become very, very important. To be with a person who has known, just to be in his presence, is enough because he is constantly pouring his being into you. You may know, or you may not know. You may recognize it today, or you may not recognize it today, but someday or other the seeds will come to flower.

We are pouring into each other. We are not separate islands. A cold person becomes like an island, and it is a misfortune, it is a great misfortune because you could have become a vast continent and you decided to become an island. You decided to remain poor when you could have become as rich as you wanted to be.

Don't be a wall, and never try to repress, otherwise you will become a wall. Repressed people are just like you; they have masks, faces. They are pretending to be somebody else.

I have heard...

A wealthy farmer went to the church one Sunday. After the service he said, "Father, that was a damned good sermon you gave, damned good."

"I am happy you liked it," said the priest, "but I wish you would not use those terms in expressing yourself."

"I can't help it," said the rich farmer. "I still think it was a damned good sermon. In fact, I liked it so much I put a hundred dollar bill in the collection basket."

"The hell you did." replied the priest.

A repressed person is carrying the same world as you. Just an opportunity is needed, a provocation, and immediately the real will come out. That's why monks disappear from the world because there are too many provocations in the world, too many temptations. It is difficult for them to remain contained, to hold on. So they go to the Himalayas or to the caves, they retire from the world so that even if ideas, temptations, desires arise, there is no way to fulfill them. But this is not a way of transformation.

The people who become cold are the people who were very hot. The people who take vows of remaining celibate are the people who were extremely sexual. The mind turns from one extreme to another very easily. It is my observation that people who are too obsessed with food one day or other become obsessed with fasting. It has to happen because you cannot remain in one extreme for long. You are doing too much of it, soon you will get fed up with it, tired of it. Then there is no other way, you have to move to the other extreme.

The people who have become monks are very worldly people. The market was too much, they had moved too much in the market, then the pendulum moved to the other extreme. Greedy people renounce the world. This renunciation is not of understanding; it is just greed upside-down. First they were holding, holding; now suddenly they see the pointlessness of it, the futility of it, and they start throwing it away. First they were afraid to lose a single *pai*, now they are afraid to keep a single *pai*, but the fear continues. First they were too greedy about this world, now they are too greedy about the other world, but the greed is there.

There are people who go on joining any and everything. I have known one person who was a member of five political parties, all against each other. When he told me, I said, "What are you doing?" He enjoyed membership.

Silverstein, the inveterate joiner, came rushing home, proudly holding a membership card to his newest organization. "Look," said Silverstein to his son, "I just joined the Prostitute Club."

"What?" said the boy. "Let me see that card." After reading it he announced, "Pa, that is the Parachute Club."

"All I know is," said Silverstein, "they guaranteed me three hundred and sixty-five jumps a year."

These people one day or other are bound to join a monastery, then they become great celibates, great renouncers. But it does not change their nature. Except awareness, nothing changes a man, nothing at all, so don't try to pretend. That which has not happened, has not happened. Understand it, and don't try to pretend, and don't try to make others believe that it has happened because nobody is going to lose in this deception except you.

People who try to control themselves have chosen a very foolish way. Control will not happen, but they will become cold. That is the only way a man can control himself: to become frozen so that energy does not arise.

People who take the vows of celibacy will not eat much; in fact, they will starve their bodies because if more energy is created in the body from food, then there will be more sex energy, and then they don't know what to do with it. So Buddhist monks eat only once a day, and then too, not enough. They eat only enough so that bodily needs are fulfilled, very minimum needs, so no energy is left. This type of celibacy is not celibacy. When you are flowing with energy and the energy starts transforming itself into love, then a celibacy, a *brahmacharya* happens which is beautiful.

The sweet old lady came into the store and bought a packet of mothballs. The next day she was back for another five packets. Another day passed, and she came in for a dozen more.

"You must have a lot of moths," said the salesman.

"Yes," replied the old dear, "and I have been throwing these things at them for three days now, and I have only managed to hit one!"

Through control you will not even be able to hit one. That is not the way. You are fighting with leaves, branches, cutting them here and there. That is not the way to destroy the tree of desire; the way is to cut the roots. And roots can be cut only when you have reached to the roots of desire. On the surface there are only branches: anger, jealousy, envy, hatred, lust. They are just on the surface. The deeper you move, the more you will understand: they are all coming out of one root, and that root is unawareness.

Meditation means awareness. It cuts the very root. Then the whole tree disappears on its own accord. Then passion becomes compassion.

I have heard about a very great Zen master, who had become very old and almost blind at the age of ninety-six and no longer able to teach or work about the monastery. Yamamoto was his name.

The old man then decided it was time to die because he was of no use to anybody, he could not be of any help. So he stopped eating. When asked by his monks why he refused his food, he replied that he had outlived his usefulness and was only a bother to everybody.

They told him, "If you die now" – it was January – "when it is so cold, everybody will be uncomfortable at your funeral, and you will be an even greater nuisance. So please eat."

This can happen only in a Zen monastery because disciples love the master so deeply, their respect is so deep that there is no need for any formality. Just see what they were saying. They were saying, "If you die now, and it is January, see, it is so cold, everybody will be uncomfortable at the funeral, and you will be an even greater nuisance. So please eat."

He thereupon resumed eating, but when it became warm again, he stopped, and not long after he quietly toppled over and died.

Such compassion. One lives then for compassion; one dies then for compassion. One is even ready to choose a right time too, so that nobody is bothered, and one need not be a nuisance.

I have heard about another Zen master who was going to die.

He said, "Where are my shoes? Bring them."

Somebody asked, "Where are you going? The doctors say you are going to die."

He said, "I am going to the cemetery."

"But why?"

He said, "I don't want to trouble anybody. Otherwise you will have to carry me on your shoulders." He walked to the cemetery and died there.

Tremendous compassion. What manner of man is this, not to give even that much trouble to anybody? And these people helped thousands. Thousands were grateful to them, thousands became full of light and love because of them. Yet they would not like to bother anybody. If they are useful, they would like to live and help. If they are not useful, then it is time to leave and go.

Now, the story.

There was an old woman in China who had supported a monk for over twenty years. She had built a hut for him, and she fed him while he was meditating.

It is a miracle that has happened in the East. The West is still unable to understand it. For centuries in the East if somebody was meditating, the society would feed him. It was enough that he was meditating. Nobody would think that he was a burden on the society, "Why should we work for him?" Just because he was meditating was enough because the East came to know that if even one man becomes enlightened, his energy is shared by all. If one man comes to flower in meditation, his fragrance becomes part of the whole society. And the gain is so tremendous that the East has never said, "Don't sit there and meditate. Who is going to feed you? Who is going to clothe you? And who is going to give you shelter?" Thousands and thousands, Buddha had ten thousand monks, sannyasins, moving with him, but people were happy to feed them, to shelter them, to clothe them, to look after them because they were meditating.

Now it is very, very impossible in the West to think that way. Even in the East it is becoming difficult. In China now monasteries are being closed, meditation halls are being converted into hospitals or school rooms. Great masters are disappearing. They are forced to work in the fields or in the factories. Nobody is allowed to meditate because a great understanding is lost. The whole mind is full of materialism, as if matter is all that exists.

If a man in a town becomes enlightened, the whole town is benefited. It is not a wastage to support him. For nothing you are going to get such tremendous treasure. People were happy to help. For twenty years this woman helped a monk who was meditating and meditating and meditating and doing nothing. He was sitting in zazen. She built a hut for him, she looked after him, she took every care. One day when she had become very old and was going to die, she wanted to know whether meditation had flowered or not, or whether this man had been simply sitting and sitting and sitting. Twenty years is a long enough time, the woman was getting old and was going to die, and she wanted to know whether she had been serving a man of real meditation or just a hocus-pocus.

One day she decided to find out...

The woman must have been of great understanding herself because the examination, the test that she tried, was full of understanding.

One day she decided to find out just what progress he had made in all this time.

If meditation is progressing, then the only criterion of its progress is love, the only criterion of its progress is compassion.

She obtained the help of a girl rich in desire, and said to her: "Go and embrace him, and then ask him suddenly, 'What now?'"

There are three possibilities. One: if for twenty years he had not touched a beautiful woman, the first possibility was that he would be tempted, would be a victim, would forget all about meditation and would make love with this girl. The other possibility was that he would remain cold, controlled and would not show any compassion toward this girl. He would simply hold himself back, hard, so that he could not be tempted. And the third possibility was: if meditation had come to fruition, then he would be full of love, understanding, compassion, and he would try to understand this girl and would try to help her. She was just a test for these possibilities.

If the first possibility happened, then all his meditation was simply a wastage. If the second possibility happened, then he had fulfilled the ordinary criterion of being a monk but he had not fulfilled the real criterion of being a man of meditation. If the second possibility happened, then it simply showed that he was a behaviorist, that he had made a habit, controlled his behavior.

You must have heard the name of Pavlov, the Russian behaviorist.

He said there is no consciousness in man or in animals or anywhere; the whole thing is just a mind mechanism. You can train the mind mechanism, and then it starts working in that way; it is all a question of conditioning. Mind functions as a conditioned reflex.

If you put food before your dog, he immediately comes running, his tongue hanging forward, dripping. He starts to salivate. Pavlov tried. Whenever he gave food to the dog, he would ring a bell. By and by, the bell and the food became associated. Then one day he simply rang the bell, and the dog came running, tongue hanging out, dripping.

Now this is absurd, no dog has ever been known to react to a ringing bell in this way. The bell is not food. But now the association has conditioned the mind.

Pavlov says man can be changed in the same way. Whenever sex arises in you, punish yourself. Go for a seven-day fast, flog your body, stand in the cold the whole night, or beat yourself, and by and by the body will learn a trick. Whenever sex arises, it will repress it automatically because of the fear of the punishment. Reward and punishment – this is the way to condition the mind if you follow Pavlov.

This monk must have been doing that, many are doing that. Almost ninety-nine percent of people in the monasteries are doing that – just reconditioning their minds and bodies.

But consciousness has nothing to do with it. Consciousness is not a new habit; consciousness is to live a life with awareness, not confined to any habit, not possessed by any mechanism, above the mechanism.

And she said to her: *"Go and embrace him, and then ask him suddenly, 'What now?'"*

"Suddenly" is the clue to the whole thing. If you give a little time, then the mind can start working in the conditioned way for which it has been prepared.

"So don't give any time. Go in the middle of the night when he will be alone meditating. Just go inside the hut" – he must have been living outside the town, alone – "go inside the hut and simply start caressing him, embrace him, kiss him. And then immediately ask, 'What now?' Watch his reaction, what happens to him, what he says, what colors pass on his face, what his eyes indicate, how he reacts and responds to you."

The girl called upon the monk and immediately started caressing

him, and asking him what he was going to do about it.
"An old tree grows on a cold rock in winter," replied the monk somewhat poetically, "nowhere is there any warmth."

He has conditioned his dog; he has conditioned his body–mind. Twenty years is a long enough time to condition. Even this sudden attack could not break his habitual pattern. He remained controlled. He must have been a man of tremendous control. He remained cold with not even a flicker of energy, and he said, *"An old tree grows on a cold rock in winter..."* Not only was he controlled and cold, he was so controlled, he remained so cold that in such a dangerous situation, provocative, seductive, he could use poetic words to reply. The conditioning must have gone very, very deep, to the roots. *"An old tree grows on a cold rock in winter, nowhere is there any warmth."*

He said, "I am like ...*a cold rock in winter, nowhere is there any warmth."* That's all he said.

The girl returned and related what he had said.
"To think I fed that fellow for twenty years!" exclaimed the old woman in anger.

His meditation had not flowered. He had become cold and dead, corpse-like; but he had not become enlightened or a buddha.

"He showed no consideration for your need..."

A man of compassion always thinks about you, about your need. He remained coldly self-centered. He simply said something about himself, *"An old tree grows on a cold rock in winter, nowhere is there any warmth."* He did not utter a single word about the woman. He did not even ask, "Why did you come? Why? What do you need? – and why have you chosen me out of so many people? Sit down."

He should have listened to her. She must be in a deep need. Nobody comes in the middle of the night to a withered-away monk who has been sitting in meditation for twenty years. Why had she come? He did not pay any attention to her.

Love always thinks of the other; ego only thinks of oneself. Love is always considerate; ego is absolutely inconsiderate. Ego has only one language, and that is of self. Ego always uses the other. Love is ready to be used, love is ready to serve.

"He showed no consideration for your need, no disposition to explain your condition."

When you go to a man of compassion, he looks at you, he looks deeply into your heart. He tries to find out what your problem is, why you are in such a situation, why you are doing the thing that you are doing. He forgets himself. He simply becomes focused on the person who has come to him; his need, his problem, his anxiety, is his consideration. He tries to help. Whatsoever he can do he will do.

"...no disposition to explain your condition. He need not have responded to passion..."

That's true. A man of compassion cannot respond in a passionate way. He is not cold, but he is cool. He can give you his warmth, nourishing warmth, but he cannot give you any fever. He has none. Remember the difference between a feverish body and a warm body. A feverish body is not healthy, a warm body is simply healthy. In passion people become feverish. Have you watched yourself deep in passion? You are almost a raving maniac, mad, wild, doing something that you don't know why, and in a great fever, with the whole body trembling, in a cyclone with no center.

A man of warmth is simply healthy. Just as when a mother takes her child to her breast, and the child feels the warmth, surrounded by the warmth, nourished by it, welcomed by it, so when you enter into the aura of a compassionate man, you enter a motherlike warmth, you enter into a very nourishing energy-field. In fact, if you come to a man of compassion, your passion will simply disappear. His compassion will be so powerful, his warmth will be so great, his love will be showering on you so much that you will become cool, you will become centered.

"He need not have responded to passion, but at least he should have experienced some compassion."
She at once went to the hut of the monk and burned it down.

It was just a symbolic gesture that those twenty years that he was meditating there, during which they had been hoping that he had been progressing, had been a wastage.

It is not enough just to be a monk superficially, just to be a monk repressed and cold because coldness is an indication of repression, a very deep repression.

That's what I have been telling you: if you move into meditation, compassion and love will come automatically, on its own accord. It follows meditation like a shadow. So you need not be worried about any synthesis. The synthesis will come. It comes by itself, you don't have to bring it. You choose one path. Either you follow the path of love: devotion, singing, dancing, *kirtan*, *bhajan*, dissolve yourself completely into your love toward the divine... On that path of dissolving, no awareness is needed. You are needed to be drunk, completely drunk with godliness, you will need to become a drunkard. Or choose the path of meditation. There you are not needed to be dissolved into anything. You are needed to become very crystallized, you are needed to become very integrated, alert, aware.

Follow the path of love, and one day suddenly you will see that meditation has flowered within you – thousands of white lotuses. And you have not done anything for them, you were doing something else, and they flowered. When love or devotion comes to its climax, meditation flowers.

And the same happens on the path of meditation. Just forget all about love, devotion. Simply become aware, sit silently, enjoy your being; that's all. Be with yourself; that's all. Learn how to be alone; that's all. And remember, a person who knows how to be alone is never lonely. People who don't know how to be alone, they are lonely.

On the path of meditation, aloneness is sought, desired, hoped for, prayed for. Be alone so much so that not even in your consciousness does any shadow of the other move. On the path of love, get so dissolved that only the other becomes real, and you become a shadow, and by and by you completely disappear. On the path of love, godliness remains, you disappear; on the path of meditation, godliness disappears, you appear. But the total and the ultimate result is the same. A great synthesis happens.

Never try to synthesize these two paths in the beginning. They meet in the end, they meet at the peak, they meet in the temple.

One of Rabbi Moshe's Hasidim was very poor. He complained to the zaddik that his wretched circumstances were an obstacle to learning and praying.

"In this day and age," said Rabbi Moshe, "the greatest devotion, greater than learning and praying, consists in accepting the world exactly as it happens to be."

The person who is moving into meditation or who is moving on the path of love will be helped if he accepts the world as it is. Worldly people never accept the world as it is, they are always trying to change it. They are always trying to make something else, they are always trying to fix things into a different order, they are always trying to do something outside. The religious person accepts whatsoever is on the outside as it is. He is not disturbed, he is not distracted by the outside. His whole work consists of moving inside. One moves by love, another moves by meditation, but both move inside. The religious world is the world of the within, and the within is the beyond.

In Latin *sin* has two meanings: one is "missing the target," and another that is even more beautiful, and that is "without." *Sin* means to be without, to be outside yourself. *Virtue* means to be within; to be inside yourself.

Soon after the death of Rabbi Moshe, Rabbi Mendel of Kotyk asked one of his disciples: "What was most important to your teacher?"

The disciple thought and then replied: "Whatever he happened to be doing at the moment."

The moment is the most important thing. So whatsoever you are doing at the moment, if you are on the path of love, do it with deep love, as if you are doing it for God. Make it a sacrifice. The word *sacrifice* comes from the same root as "the sacred." Sacrifice means making a thing sacred. If you are on the path of love, make everything that you are doing a sacrifice, a holy thing, as if you are preparing for God. He is to come, the guest is to come, and you are doing everything for him.

And, in fact, it is so. The whole of life is a preparation for the guest, and the whole of life is a preparation to become the host, so that when he comes you are ready. When he knocks at the door, everything is ready to receive him.

If you are on the path of meditation, then too this moment is the most important moment because on the path of meditation the past has to be dropped, the future has to be dropped, and you have to be just herenow.

So remember on both paths many things are similar; many things are basic requirements on both paths, but many things are very, very polar opposite.

So please, don't you try to make a synthesis. Simply follow one path. Whatsoever is essential is similar; that is, to be in the moment accepting the world as it is, remaining in a mood of celebration. The *bhakta*, the devotee, goes on celebrating life because godliness is; and on the path of meditation the *sadhak*, the yogi, the Zen follower, goes on celebrating because, "I am here, I am." That very amness, that very amness, is his celebration.

So don't be worried. Many questions have come to me full of worries, anxieties, as if, if you follow one path, you will be missing something. Nothing. You will be missing nothing. By following one, you will be following both; by following both, you will not be following either.

Enough for today.

CHAPTER 6

joy is the criterion

The first question:

Osho,
How can I know if detachment or indifference is growing within?

It is not difficult to know. How do you know when you have a headache, and how do you know when you don't have a headache? It is simply clear. When you are growing in detachment, you will become healthier, happier; your life will become a life of joy. That is the criterion of all that is good. Joy is the criterion. If you are growing in joy, you are growing, and you are going toward home.

With indifference there is no possibility that joy can grow. In fact, if you have any joy, that will disappear.

Happiness is health, and, to me, religion is basically hedonistic. Hedonism is the very essence of religion. To be happy is all.

So remember, if things are going right, and you are moving in the right direction, each moment will bring more joy, as if you are going toward a beautiful garden. The closer you come, the air will be fresher, cooler, more fragrant. That will be the indication that you are moving in the right direction. If the air becomes less fresh, less cool, less fragrant, then you are moving in the opposite direction.

Existence is made out of joy. That is its very stuff. Joy is the stuff existence is made of. So whenever you are moving toward becoming more existential, you will be becoming more and more full of joy, delight, for no reason at all. If you are moving into detachment, love will grow, joy will grow. Only attachments will drop because attachments bring misery, because attachments bring bondage, because attachments destroy your freedom. But if you are becoming indifferent... Indifference is a pseudo-coin, it looks like detachment, but it only looks like detachment. Nothing will be growing in it. You will simply shrink and die.

So go and see: there are so many monks in the world – Catholic, Hindu, Jaina, Buddhist – watch them. They don't give a radiant feeling, they don't have the aura of fragrance, they don't look more alive than you are; in fact, they look less alive, crippled, paralyzed. Controlled of course, but not in a deeper, inner discipline; controlled but not conscious; following a certain conscience that society has given to them but not yet aware, not yet free, not yet individuals. They live as if they are already in their grave, just waiting to die. Their life becomes morose, monotonous, sad; it is a sort of despair.

Beware. Whenever something goes wrong, there are indicators in your being. Sadness is an indicator, depression is an indicator; joy, celebration is also an indicator. More songs will happen to you if you are moving toward detachment. You will be dancing more, and you will become more loving. Remember, love is not attachment; love knows no attachment, and that which knows attachment is not love. That is possessiveness, domination, clinging, fear, greed; it may be a thousand and one things, but it is not love. In the name of love other things are parading, in the name of love other things are hiding behind, but on the container the label "love" is stuck. Inside you will find many sorts of things, but not love at all.

Watch. If you are attached to a person, are you in love? Or are you afraid of your aloneness, so you cling? Because you cannot be alone, you use this person so as not to be alone. Then you are afraid. If the person dies or moves somewhere else or falls in love with someone else, then you will kill this person, and you will say, "I was so much attached." Or you may kill yourself, and you will say, "I was so much attached that I cannot live without her or without him." It is sheer foolishness. It is not love, it is something else. You are afraid of your aloneness, you are not capable of being with yourself, you need somebody to distract you, and you want to possess the other person. You want to use the other person as a means for your own ends. To use another person as a means is violence.

Immanuel Kant has made it one of his fundamentals of moral life, and it is. He used to say that to treat a person as a means is the greatest immoral act there is. It is. Because when you treat another person as a means – for your gratification, for your sexual desire, for your fear, or for something else – when you use another person as a means, you are reducing the other person to be a thing. You are destroying his or her freedom, you are killing his or her soul.

The soul can grow only in freedom. Love gives freedom. And when you give freedom, you are free, that's what detachment is. If you enforce bondage on the other, you will be in imprisonment on your own accord. If you bind the other, the other will bind you; if you define the other, the other will define you; if you are trying to possess the other, the other will possess you. That's how couples go on fighting for domination for their whole life: the man in his own way, the woman in her own way. Both go on struggling. It is a continuous nagging and fighting. And the man thinks that in some ways he controls the woman, and the woman thinks that in some ways she controls the man. Control is not love.

Never treat any person as a means. Treat everybody as an end in himself, in herself. Then you are a religious person. Then you don't cling, then you are not attached. You love, but your love gives freedom, and when you give freedom to the other, you are free. Only in freedom does your soul grow. You will feel very, very happy.

The world has become a very unhappy thing. Not because the world is an unhappy thing, but because we have done something wrong to it. The same world can become a celebration.

You ask, "How can I know if detachment or indifference is growing within?" If you are feeling happy, if you are feeling happy with whatsoever is growing, more centered, more grounded, more alive than before, then go headlong into it. Then there is no fear. Let happiness be the touchstone, the criterion; nothing else can be the criterion. Whatsoever the scriptures say is not a criterion unless your heart is throbbing with happiness; whatsoever I say cannot be the criterion for you unless your heart is throbbing with happiness.

The moment you were born, a subtle indicator was placed within you. It is part of life that you can always know what is happening, you can always feel whether you are happy or unhappy. Nobody asks how to know whether he is happy or unhappy. Nobody has ever asked. When you are unhappy, you know; when you are happy, you know. Then it is an intrinsic value. You know it, you are born knowing it, so let that intrinsic indicator be used, and it will never falsify your life.

But if you look in the scriptures, then there is danger because for the person who wrote a certain book, it may have been a growth for him, but it may not be a growth for you. He felt happy. Mahavira felt very happy with fasting; Buddha never felt so happy with fasting. So what to do? To whom to listen? Both are perfect beings. If you listen to Buddha, there is a possibility that you will start distorting your own feelings; if you listen to Mahavira, there is the same possibility. Krishna lived in the world, loved many women, enjoyed himself. He was a totally different man, perfectly happy. He was always singing and dancing. He had his own feeling. Maybe his feeling suits you or not.

So never try any outer criterion; never try the outside criterion for your inside, otherwise there is a danger you may falsify your inner mechanism, the intrinsic mechanism. Listen to your heart.

I am here not to give you any criterion but just to make you aware of your own criterion, just to make you aware of your own intrinsic awareness. Feel, and it is so clear that nothing else is needed to help it.

The second question:

Osho,
When my mind is the cause of my unhappiness, either I don't know how to come out of mind, or I must still enjoy being in my mind, dreams, fantasies.

If the house is on fire and you see the flames of fire, you will escape, and you will know how to escape, you will find a way. When the house is on fire, who worries whether you are getting out of the right door, or you are getting out of the back door, or you are getting out of the window? Who bothers? Once you feel that the house is on fire, you will not even think about how to get out. You will get out first, and then you will think. And then you will wonder how it happened.

Buddha used to say that you ask about techniques because you are not yet aware that the house is on fire.

When you come across a snake on the path, do you ask how to get out of the way? And you may not have ever come across a snake in your whole life. This may be for the first time. And you may never ever have heard anybody talking about how to get out of the way of a snake, but still you will get out of the way; you will jump. You will not sit there and think about what to do, how to do it, whom to consult, where to find a guru. You will not think, you will simply jump.

The questioner says, "When mind is the cause of my unhappiness, either I don't know how to come out of mind, or I must still enjoy being in my mind, dreams, fantasies. When mind is the cause of my unhappiness..." Still it is not clear to you. You may have heard me saying again and again that mind is the cause of all unhappiness. You have listened to me, you have become like a parrot; now the question arises. But you have not yet felt it. If you have felt that mind is the cause, then you will jump out of it, you will know the way. The way is there, the way has always been there.

It is not your realization. And you must still be enjoying your dreams, your fantasies because the mind stops immediately the moment you stop enjoying it. There is no other way to stop it. It is just like a bicycle: you go on pedaling it, it goes on moving. If you stop pedaling it, it may go a little further because of the past momentum, but then it will stop.

Mind needs constant cooperation, constant infusion of energy from your side, constant identification. The mind needs your help, it is a mechanism, it cannot run on its own accord. Deep down you are helping it. When the body lies there and the soul has disappeared, the mind stops instantly. It cannot work without you.

You must be enjoying it. In fact, religion is also one of your fantasies; existence is your biggest dream. Listening to religious people, seeing their ecstasy, watching their grace, a greed has arisen in you. Your mind fantasizes. It would be beautiful to be in nirvana, it would be beautiful to be enlightened. Your mind starts dreaming about it. Then you come to hear that the mind has to be dropped.

Three persons were talking. One said, "If in a dream you get one million rupees, what are you going to do? As far as I am concerned, I am going for a world tour. That has been my dream from my very childhood. What are you going to do?"

The other said, "If I get one million rupees, I am not going anywhere. I am just going to rest in my house. Why bother? I am going to stop going and just rest and relax and enjoy. Who bothers to go from here to there?"

And they asked the third man, "If you get one million rupees in a dream, what are you going to do?"

He said, "I will immediately close my eyes and sleep again, to dream more to get many more millions. If you can get one million rupees in one dream, I will dream the same dream again to get one million more."

Your mind is your dream, your fantasy. You are still in it. Even when you are thinking about how to get out of the mind, that too is a mind fantasy. And you must be enjoying it.

I have heard...

Mulla Nasruddin stormed out of his office and yelled, "Something has got to be done about those six phones on my desk. For the past five minutes I have been talking to myself."

Mind is nothing but talking to yourself. What else is it? The inner talk, the inner chattering, the rehearsing for the future, the chewing again and again the past experiences; you are talking to yourself. It is a monologue. There is nobody else to talk to, so you talk to yourself.

If windows were possible into your mind and people could look inside, or there was a system... Someday there may be. Science will find a way to magnify your mind. Your mind can be attached, wired, to an instrument and the instrument will start broadcasting what is going on inside your mind. Then you will be simply amazed to see that you are mad. You will not allow anybody to connect your mind to an instrument. Sometimes write down what goes on in your mind on a blank paper. Close the doors and windows so nobody comes in and just write it down. Don't deceive, because nobody will ever see, you can burn it immediately. Just write down whatsoever goes on. Don't improve upon it, don't add something, don't delete anything. Photographically simply write down the way the mind goes on. Within ten minutes you will see how mad you are. What is going on? But we never look. We look outside, we never look into the mind. Looking into the mind is what meditation is all about.

Bodhidharma, the real founder of Zen, used to say, "Looking

face-to-face with the mind is all. Looking directly into your mind is all." Once you start looking directly, you will be surprised. You will come to know that you are carrying a madman; not one really, a madhouse; many madmen inside, running hither and thither, all against each other, fighting, struggling, warring.

If you look deep inside into the mind directly, first you will be amazed, mystified as to why you go on carrying this mind, and the second thing you will realize is that you are not the mind, you are the looker, the watcher, the witness, who is seeing into the mind. And that will give you a freedom that you have not known yet.

You are confined in the body, then you are confined in the mind. Once you come to know that you are neither the body nor the mind, suddenly you become unconfined; you are as big, as vast as the sky. Then there is no boundary line around you; then you are one with this ocean of life; then you are one with existence. "That art thou" – *tattvamasi*. Then you come to know "I am that," the witness.

So the only thing you can do is just to look deeply inside the mind. It will have two aspects. First you will feel very, very crazy, going mad. Don't try to escape from that madness because if you escape, again you will escape outside. Stick to it, let it be mad, but go on looking into it. Sometimes it takes months, sometimes it takes years, but it is worth it even if it takes lives. If you go on looking, unwaveringly, not getting distracted here and there, then one day the second aspect arises in you: that you are a witness. Your mind looks very, very far away, very distant, on some other planet, only sounds are heard, a few flickering waves come to you. The more you become a witness, the more your energy gathers together in becoming a witness, the more and more energy is taken away from the mind. The mind starts withering. One day you are there all alone without any mind. Then you are in a state of "nowhereness."

I have heard about two hobos who were caught by the police and were brought to the court. The policeman suspected they had not committed anything wrong, but just their way of life, their style was suspicious.

The magistrate asked the first hobo, "Where do you live?"

He said, "Nowhere."

He asked the second, "Where do you live?"

He said, "I am this guy's neighbor."

The first guy lives nowhere, and the other is his neighbor; the answer is pure Zen.

When you come to know yourself, you come to know that you are no-where, and no-when because there is no time, no space. Suddenly you are the whole, spread all over reality. This is what we in the East call *moksha*, absolute freedom.

But you must be enjoying your mind. That's why you are asking how to get out of it, what is the way to get out of it. These are the questions of people who are trying to deceive themselves. You don't want to get out of it, so you ask "How?" because with the "How?" postponement is possible. The "How?" cannot be done right now, you will have to practice it. It can happen only tomorrow, it cannot happen right now. The "How?" gives you time, tomorrow. And then you say, "Okay, so we will do it tomorrow. It cannot happen right now."

People ask me, "Can enlightenment happen right now?" If I say "Yes," they say, "But then why is it not happening?" Then they think it is not going to happen to them because if it was going to happen, it would have happened already. It happens right now! If I say to them, "You will have to work for it, you will have to do hard, arduous work, you will have to move in deep discipline," then they say, "Then it is okay. So somewhere in the future it will happen." Then they are relieved. So it is not going to happen right now – someday – so what is the hurry?

Whether it is tomorrow or the day after tomorrow, it makes no difference; it is tomorrow. Both ways they find a way to postpone.

Now let me give you a paradox to meditate on: it always happens right now, but one has to work for it. It never happens in the tomorrow, it always happens today because there is no tomorrow. But one has to work hard; one has to gather together all one's energies and to put them at stake. If all your energies are together right now, if you desire intensely, passionately, if your desire has become almost a flame and you are aflame with one desire, only with one desire – to attain to enlightenment – it can happen right now. If you are so thirsty that you disappear and only thirst remains, then godliness starts pouring into you. Then you have earned, you have earned the capacity. You have become receptive.

"When mind is the cause of my unhappiness..." Never ask such questions. You still think it is not so. This is a hypothetical question; when, if, etc., are hypothetical questions.

"When mind is the cause of my unhappiness..." No, either it is or it is not, there is no question of "when." Either you know that it is the cause of unhappiness, or you know that it is not the cause of unhappiness. Decide. If it is not the cause of unhappiness, then things are clear: then there is nothing to be done with the mind. In fact, if it is not the cause of unhappiness, then the cause must lie somewhere outside you. That's what communists say – Marx and Mao. That's what they say: that the cause of unhappiness is somewhere outside you, not inside you: in the structure of the society, the economic system of society, in the political world – somewhere outside you.

If your misery comes from outside, then there is no way to get out of it. Because the cause is outside you, how can you destroy it?

Because of this fact, Freud by and by became very despondent in his later life and finally before he died he wrote in a letter: man can never be happy; it is impossible. Man's desire to be happy is an impossible desire. Man can never be happy because it is not in his hands to be happy.

But Freud is wrong. I am here, and I say to you that I am happy. So it is not a question of my belief. It is not a belief that I am happy. Buddha is happy, Krishna is happy, Jesus is happy. But why does Freud think that man cannot be happy? And he is not a man to make meaningless statements. He is a very sincere man. Forty, fifty years of deep observation has brought him to make the statement that man cannot be happy. The reason is that he was also looking for the cause somewhere beyond man.

Marx looks for it in the social structure, Freud looks for it in the unconscious, but the very definition of unconscious is that which is not available to you, that of which you are not conscious. It is outside you, you are in your consciousness. It is outside you, it is somewhere you don't know where. From where does your misery come? How can you change it?

Religion takes a radically and diametrically opposite standpoint: you are the cause. "I am the cause of my misery" makes one sad in the beginning, but one should be really happy. If I am the cause, then there is a possibility, then there is hope, because I can stop it. I can try not to be the cause of my unhappiness.

With religion man becomes responsible; with communism, man becomes irresponsible. With religion man becomes a free agent in this world; with communism, man becomes a mechanical thing, a robotlike thing. With religion you attain to being a soul, you become a soul; with communism, the soul disappears, you are no longer there.

If the cause of happiness is outside, if the cause of misery is outside, then your soul is outside; it is not within you. Then you are to be manipulated by the state, then you are nothing but a hollow puppet, and the strings are somewhere in the Kremlin; somebody is manipulating from there. Then life is almost meaningless; not only meaningless, but horrible. Man is not a hollow puppet; man has a substantial being in him.

So when you say, "When mind is the cause of my unhappiness..." you have taken my statement as true without realizing it, without becoming a witness to it. Never do that, otherwise questions arise unnecessarily. It is better not to answer hypothetical questions because they will create more hypothetical questions. Recognize the fact that you are unhappy because of your mind.

Somebody insults you. Do you think you are unhappy because somebody insulted you, or do you think you are unhappy because you have a very subtle ego which felt hurt by this insult? Now there are only two possibilities. Either you are unhappy because he insulted you... If that is the possibility, the only possibility, then you can never be happy because the world is vast, and how can you manage that nobody will insult you ever? It is beyond you. If it is your ego which feels hurt, then the possibility exists that you can drop the ego. Then let the whole world insult you, you can go on laughing, it makes no difference.

Mulla Nasruddin and one of his friends had been drinking all evening in a bar. The friend finally passed out and fell to the floor. The Mulla called a doctor who rushed him to a hospital. When he came to, the doctor asked him, "Do you see any pink elephants or little green men?"

"No," groaned the patient.

"No snakes or alligators?" the doctor asked.

"No," the drunk said.

"Then just sleep it off. You will be all right in the morning," said the doctor.

But Mulla Nasruddin was worried. "Look, doctor," he said, "that boy is in bad shape. He said he could not see any of them animals, and you and I know the room is full of them."

What I say will not make much difference if you know that the room is full of them. Finally you are going to be the deciding factor. So watch your mind. Is your mind the cause of misery? If it is not, then you cannot be a religious man. Then one day or other you are going to be a communist. These are the two alternatives: religion and communism. Everybody has to decide. And I would suggest to you that if you feel that your mind is not the cause of misery, then become a communist; nothing wrong in it, be sincere. Sooner or later you will be frustrated, and a frustrated communist becomes religious very easily. Many people need that frustration because then that alternative is finished. Then there is only one alternative. Never hang between the two, never be in limbo.

Many people are in limbo. They go to the church, but their heart is communistic. When I say communistic, I don't mean they belong to the communist party, I mean that they believe that the cause of their misery is outside.

A stubborn old Dubliner stepped into the dentist's office with a terrific toothache. He could not, however, muster up enough courage to have the tooth pulled. So the dentist gave him a glass of whisky to bolster him. Then the dentist said, "Right, ready now?"

"Not quite," said the man smacking his lips.

Two more drinks of whisky, and finally he finished up the entire bottle.

"Now step into the chair," the dentist begged.

The Irishman came out swinging into the middle of the room.

"I would like to see the swine who would dare to touch my tooth now!"

You are almost drunk with your mind. And I am not going to touch your teeth, remember. You have to become a little sober, you have to become a little more aware. Once you have a little awareness, you will start seeing that it is your mind, nothing else but your mind, that goes on spinning new webs of misery. It is just like a spider that goes on creating a web and goes on being caught in it himself.

The first thing to be decided is whether you realize the fact that your mind is the cause of your misery, of your unhappiness. Once this is decided, everything becomes clear. Then there is no need, really, to ask how to get out of it. And if you are not yet decided and

I help you in some way to get out of it, I will be in trouble.

Let me tell you one anecdote that will make the thing clear.

The woman bather had got into a hole, and she could not swim. Nor could the young man on the end of the pier. But when she came up the first time and he caught sight of her face, he could yell, and he did. Just then a big fisherman walked by. "What is up?" he asked.

"There!" hoarsely cried the young man. "My wife, drowning. I can't swim. A hundred dollars if you save her!"

In a moment the fisherman was in the water; in another he was out of it with the rescued woman.

He approached the young man. "Well, what about the hundred dollars?"

If the young man's face had been ashen-gray before, now it was dead white as he gazed upon the features of the rescued woman.

"Yes I know," he gasped, "but when I made the offer, I thought it was my wife who was drowning, and now, now it turns out it was my wife's mother."

"Just my luck," said the fisherman sadly, thrusting his hand into his trouser pocket. "How much do I owe you?"

So first you decide whether your mind is your wife or your mother-in-law. Then only can something be done about it. Otherwise you will be angry with me. If I pull you out of your mind and you were still fantasizing and dreaming, you will be tremendously angry and annoyed and irritated. And if you were dreaming sweet dreams, then more so, because you were hoping that something was just going to be fulfilled.

One day Mulla Nasruddin's wife woke him up in the morning, and he became very, very angry, and he said, "You foolish woman. Is this the right time?"

She said, "But the sun is up."

He said, "It has nothing to do with the sun. I was dreaming about a man who was offering me a hundred rupees, and just at the moment I was going to take it, and here you come. You have destroyed the whole thing."

He tried again to create sleep, tried to close his eyes, turned this way and that, but you cannot catch hold of a dream. Once it is gone, it is gone. And he started saying, "Okay, I will accept even ninety, eighty, seventy, whatsoever you give, I will accept, but give it."

But there was nobody to give.

If you are dreaming, then dream a little more. Nobody is ever fulfilled by dreaming, but one has to figure it out oneself: "Enough is enough. I have dreamt enough, fantasized enough, and nothing comes except misery, except frustration." Each desire brings more frustration, each expectation turns finally into frustration.

Once you understand it, there will be no need to take you out of it; once you understand it, the very understanding becomes the coming out of it. The very understanding means freedom from mind.

The third question:

Osho,
You talk about a living religion, yet in some centers people kneel over the cast of your feet. I am reminded of the Catholic religion where I lost the meaning of the teachings and instead venerated the symbols. Please tell me why do we need your symbols. They are not you, nor your teaching.

It is a very subtle question. You will have to be very alert to understand it.

Yes, religion has nothing to do with symbols. Religion in its essence is absolutely pure, just an experiencing, a knowing. It has nothing to do with outside symbols. But that is not the question. That pure religion is not possible for you as you are; the way you are, you will need symbols.

Once it happened, Joshu was sitting in front of his temple. A great Zen master. A seeker came, and he asked Joshu, "Master, where is Buddha? Who is Buddha? What is this buddhahood?"

Joshu looked into the eyes of the man and said, "You ask who is Buddha? Go inside the temple. He is there."

The man laughed and said, "There is only a stone statue. And I know and you know that a stone statue is not Buddha."

Joshu said, "Perfectly right. A stone statue is not Buddha."

Then the man said again, "Then tell me, who is Buddha?"

Joshu looked again into his eyes and said, "Go into the temple, you will find the Buddha there."

Now this is very puzzling. The questioner is not yet able to understand the non-symbolic. Though intellectually he understands that the statue is just a stone statue and is not Buddha, it is only intellectual understanding.

If your lover gives you a small handkerchief, has it any more meaning than any other handkerchief of the same make, of the same value? If it is lost, tears may come to your eyes. Your mind is still symbolic, still lives in symbols. That handkerchief, a small, valueless handkerchief given by your lover or beloved, carries a certain meaning which nobody else can see. It is an ordinary handkerchief, but to you it is very symbolic. It has a message, a love message. That handkerchief is worth a kingdom. It is personal and somebody has given it to you as a deep gesture of his love. It is no longer a commodity in the marketplace, it is no longer a part of the world of things; that handkerchief has a personality, almost a soul. Have you not watched this inside you?

If this is so, then symbols are still meaningful for you, and you cannot just drop them unless the whole mind is dropped. It depends on you. If those symbols have a certain response in your heart, they are alive.

When a Buddhist goes to the Buddhist temple and bows down before the stone statue of Buddha, if it is really a heartfelt prayerful, if he is really bowing down in deep humbleness, then don't bother about the statue. The real thing is the humbleness, the desire, the love, the heartfelt urge. That stone statue is just instrumental.

If you go and you are not a Buddhist and you have no heart for Buddha, then, of course, it is a stone statue. A Buddhist has a love affair with Buddha. If you call that stone statue just a stone, he will be hurt because he sees something more in it. That something more is in his eyes, certainly so, absolutely so; it is not there in the statue. But in front of the statue something responds in him, something starts singing in his heart. His heart beats faster, he feels transfigured. That transfiguration is meaningful. It does not matter whether the statue is really Buddha or not, it does not matter at all. But it helped.

For example: you come across a rope. It is getting dark, the sun has set, the night is descending, and on a lonely path in a forest you come across a rope, and you think it is a snake. You start running, perspiring. There is no snake, but is your perspiration real or not? If there were a real snake, would the perspiration be more real? Is your running real or not? Would it have been more real if there had been a real snake? To you it is real.

Buddha has a definition of truth, a very strange definition. He says, "That which affects is true." That which affects is true. If a rope is taken as a snake and it affects you, it is true. To you it is true. It is almost a snake.

A symbol is real if it affects you; if it does not affect you, of course, it is not a symbol at all. The very word *symbol* means that a thing has some greater value than is available to the naked eyes, a thing has some greater value than a scientist can give to it. That greater value makes it symbolic.

I have heard about a Hasid rabbi, Rabbi Sadagora. He used to say to his disciples, "You can learn something from everything. Everything can teach us something, and not only everything God has made or created, but what man has made also has something to teach us."

"What can we learn from a train?" one Hasid asked dubiously.

"That because of one second one can miss everything."

"And from the telegraph?"

"That every word is counted and charged."

"And the telephone?"

"That what we say here is heard there."

Then everything becomes symbolic, and life takes on a different dimension.

If your heart feels something for the cross, then it is not just a cross, you become connected through it with Jesus. That's not a scientific thing, but religion is not a scientific thing. It is more poetic; it is more like love and less like reason; it is more like feeling and less like analysis. It is not logic, it is a very deep romance with reality.

If you drop all symbols – as many people have, thinking that symbols are just empty symbols, there is nothing in them – why do you shake hands with your friend? It is simply foolish taking somebody's hand and simply shaking it. Can't you see the foolishness of it? Why do you kiss your woman? Can't you see the lack of hygiene in it? The sheer unmedicalness of it? Two persons transferring their diseases because in each kiss millions of minute cells are transferred. What are you doing? When you say to your woman, "I love you," what are these words, "I love you"? Just words? Nothing more? Words are symbols. The word *love* is not love, so drop it. If you go on dropping in that way. what will be left?

Let me tell you one anecdote...

The battered old man got up one night during a revival meeting and said, "Brothers and sisters, you know and I know I ain't been what I ought to have been. I have stole hard and told lies and got drunk and always been getting in fights and shooting craps and playing poker and I have cursed and swore, but I thank the Lord there is one thing I ain't never done. I ain't never lost my religion."

Then what type of religion is left? If you drop all symbols, you drop language; if you drop all symbols, you drop poetry; if you drop all symbols, you drop even mathematics. Then what is left?

Man is a symbolic creature, man lives in a world of symbols. Even science cannot do without symbols. Science, which is expected to be absolutely factual, cannot work without symbols. In fact, there is no possibility of growing without symbols. That's why animals are not growing; they cannot grow unless they move into the dimension of symbols. So everything is a symbol.

Once it happened that Ramakrishna was talking to his disciples. He was talking about *anahat nad*, the soundless sound, and he said that by the constant chanting of om you will come to a point where soundless sound is heard.

An intellectual, a logician, was present there, and he was getting very irritated by this uneducated man. Ramakrishna was uneducated, he went only to the second grade, he never studied anything, never knew anything about scriptures. So the man was getting annoyed. And people were listening so intently to this uneducated fellow that he was boiling inside, and he tried to find a chance to show his knowledge.

Then he said, "Stop. This is all nonsense. Just by repeating a sound, om, om, om, nothing is going to happen. Because om is just a symbol, nothing else. It is just a word – not even a word, a meaningless sound. So what is going to happen out of it? You can go on repeating and nothing will happen."

And he started quoting scriptures. He was a learned man. Ramakrishna listened to him for half an hour, very intently, then suddenly he looked at him and said, "Stupid! Now stop! Don't utter a single word."

That man was very much disturbed. This illiterate fellow called him stupid! But he became afraid also because this man was thought to be very religious, a great mystic, and he said, "Don't utter a single word, otherwise you will repent." So he became very afraid because when this mystic's devotees were there, if he said something, they might jump on him. And who knows? This man might know something. So he kept quiet, but he was almost fire.

For two or three minutes Ramakrishna again started talking about om and *anahat nad*, the soundless sound. Then after two minutes he looked at the man. He was perspiring, yet it was a winter evening. Ramakrishna said, "Look, sir. Just a small word *stupid*, and look what it has done. You are perspiring, and you are getting so aflame that if these people were not here, you would have killed me. Just look at it. Just a small symbol 'stupid' and look what it has done."

The whole human consciousness has grown out of symbology. All our languages – the language of science, the language of religion, the language of poetry – are all symbols. Our whole life of love, relationship, is nothing but symbology.

Unless you have come to a point where the whole mind disappears, symbols are meaningful. The questioner asks: "You talk about a living religion, yet in some centers people kneel over the cast of your feet." Those feet are irrelevant, their kneeling is relevant. Those feet are just symbolic, but their kneeling is real. That is not symbolic. They are affected by it.

So when I say "a living religion," I mean a religion which is still moving the hearts. If somebody is moved by a cross, he is still encountering Christ; the religion is living to him. And if you simply bow down because it is a formality to be fulfilled, then the religion is dead. Because the symbol is dead and there is nothing inside you, the religion is dead. The symbol is always dead, but if it affects you and starts a movement in your energy, then it is alive.

A religion is alive in the heart, it has nothing to do with temples and churches. If you are moved, if a rhythm arises in you, if you start dancing seeing Krishna or his statue, suddenly the flute on his lips is no longer just a symbol to you, it has become a real dance. You can listen to his tune, you can hear his tune.

"I am reminded of the Catholic religion where I lost the meaning of the teachings and instead venerated the symbols." That was your fault. It had nothing to do with the church. If you missed the meaning and started venerating the symbols, it was your fault. Now that you have become so afraid of symbols, it simply means you have reacted to your upbringing; you have not yet become a revolutionary, you have just reacted against it.

Because a few symbols were given to you in your childhood and they never became alive, now you are afraid of all symbols. You will be very poor for that. Don't be afraid. If one set of symbols has not worked, another set of symbols can work. And now you are not a child. Those symbols did not work because they were forced on you by your parents, but if you choose your own religion… Now remember this, this is my continuous emphasis: if you want to be religious, you have to choose your religion; then it is alive. Only through choice, voluntary choice, is it alive. If it has been enforced on you, then it is dead, then it is somebody else's religion, it is somebody else's trip – your parents' trip. And you are simply carrying it like a load.

You have chosen to walk with me, it is your choice, it is your voluntary choice. It is your will to be with me. Then whatsoever transpires between me and you is going to be alive. That may not be so with your children when I am gone. You would like your children also to be in orange. Then something may not happen because then it will be your trip, and you will be enforcing your trip on your children. Never enforce your trip on anybody else.

If you choose hell, even hell is heaven; if you are forced and coerced into heaven, then heaven will become a hell. Freedom is the most fundamental value; nothing is more valuable than freedom. If you choose Christ or Krishna or Buddha – if you choose, remember – then they become contemporaries, then there is no gap of twenty centuries between you and Christ, no. Then he walks with you, then he talks with you, then he is a constant companion. Then his cross is your cross, and your cross is his cross. Then he is with you in your misery, and he is with you in your happiness, and he shares himself with you. But it has to be your choice.

"Please tell me why do we need your symbols. They are not you nor your teachings." Yes, they are neither me nor my teachings, but you cannot see me yet, and whatsoever you see is just a symbol; my body is a symbol, it is not me; my photograph is a symbol, it is not me; whatsoever I am saying is symbolic, it is not me. And even what I am saying is not my teaching because my teaching cannot be said. Nobody's – Buddha's nor Christ's – nobody's can be said. Whatsoever is being said is not the real thing. The real is elusive. Truth cannot be uttered.

But I have to talk to you to persuade you to become silent. This is a very absurd effort, but this is how it is. I have to seduce you toward silence through words. Words are just symbols; silence. Remember when I say silence, the word *silence* is not silence.

Yes, Joshu was right. The Buddha is in the temple. The man said, "But there is no Buddha, there is only a stone statue. How can an enlightened man like you say that a stone statue is a Buddha?"

And Joshu said, "You are right. It is just a stone statue."

Then the man said, "Now tell me, where is Buddha?"

Joshu said, "Go into the temple, he is there."

If you have the eyes to see, then you can see even in a stone. If you don't have the eyes to see, you may come across Jesus, and you may not recognize him. Many of you were there when Jesus was there, many of you were there when Buddha was there, and you never recognized him. Many of you are here just in front of me, and you may never recognize me. So the deepest question is of your recognition. If you can recognize something in a stone, if you can recognize something in a cast of my feet, yes, Buddha is there.

The whole thing is yours – your Buddha, your Christ, your me. Everything is yours, you are the only one. This is the beauty, the drama of life: you are the actor, you are the director, you are the audience, you are the story-writer, you are the play-back singer, you are all, alone.

Let me tell you one anecdote...

The wholesale company sold a bill of goods to a merchant at a small crossroad village. When the goods arrived, he refused them. The wholesale firm prepared to start suit for collection and wrote to the railroad agent of the village for information about the arrival of the merchandise. They also wrote the president of the bank for information concerning the financial standing of the customer, to the mayor of the town asking him to recommend a good lawyer to handle the case, and to the merchant threatening suit if he did not make payment at once.

The company received this reply: "I received a letter telling me I had better pay up. I am the railroad agent here and also received the letter you wrote to the agent. I am president and sole owner of the local bank and can assure you as to my financial standing. As mayor of the town I hesitate to refer to you a lawyer since I am the only member of the bar in this vicinity. If I were not also the pastor of the town's one church, I would tell you to go to hell."

Now this is the case – you are all in all. If a symbol is alive to you, it is alive – you bring life to it, you pour life into it.

When somebody is bowing down before the cast of my feet, for him they become alive; he pours his life into them. You may be standing there looking at the foolishness: "What is he doing?" Yes, it is foolish for you because those feet are not alive for you, that symbol is not throbbing for you, you have not poured your life into it.

So don't be bothered about others; let them do their thing. They must be finding something in it. If you are not finding something there, then find it somewhere else. You may find something in my words; words are as symbolic as the cast feet and, of course, less substantial. Words are less substantial: uttered, and they disappear. They are very dreamlike. Or you may be pouring your energy into the symbol of this body herenow; that too will disappear, that too is not the ultimate thing. The ultimate is that which always remains. You can see that ultimate anywhere; just make your eyes a little more perceptive.

And don't still be dominated by your Catholic upbringing because that will be a great loss to you. If you go on dropping all symbols, you will become very, very poor. Nobody will be at a loss, only you.

Symbols make life rich, poetic.

I have heard...

Two businessmen were relaxing in the clubhouse after a round of golf.

"I don't know why you don't sack your secretary," said one. "Her typing is atrocious, and she spends more time on your private phone than you do. Take away her gorgeous hair, her beautiful eyes, her sensuous lips, her lovely figure, and what have you got?"

The other businessman grunted and said, "My wife."

Beware. Don't go on dropping symbols, otherwise nothing will be left.

Yes, that is the highest peak; get ready for it. Symbols will help you to reach that highest peak, but if you drop them right now, you will never reach to that height. One has to move up a staircase. When one has reached the top, one has to leave the staircase. But if you leave it at the very beginning, you will remain on the bottom floor. Symbols are to be left only when you have come to see the non-symbolic, not before that. Otherwise you will remain very low – somewhere crawling on the earth.

Once you have a symbology, it gives a vision to your life, a style. Then you are not haphazard, then you become an order, you are not a chaos. Then things start crystallizing within you, and everything starts gaining a significance; your life has a direction, and you have a sense of direction.

"In the synagogue I heard men praying," said the puzzled young boy. "It must be awfully hard for God."

"Why?" asked the rabbi gently.

"The woodcutter was praying for cold weather."

"Naturally," the rabbi said. "He makes his living cutting wood for our stoves. The colder it is, the more wood he sells."

"But the fruit seller prayed for mild weather."

"Well," said the rabbi, "he stores autumn fruit to sell in winter, and severe cold would freeze his stored fruit."

"The farmer prayed for rain, and the brickmaker for dry weather. They are all godly men: how does God know how to answer all their prayers?"

"How is the weather now?" asked the rabbi.

"Dry and mild."

"And last week?"

"Let me see. On Monday and Tuesday it rained and on Thursday it was cold."

"See?" said the rabbi.

Once you have a symbol, you can see. Then God is fulfilling everybody's needs: one day it is raining, one day it is dry, one day it is hot, one day it is cold, and God is fulfilling everybody's desires.

But if you have the symbol of God, then the whole thing is no longer disorderly. If you don't have that symbol, then you are simply surprised: five persons are praying in the synagogue, and each one is asking for different weather, and it looks almost foolish. And they all are good people, religious people. How is God going to fulfill them? In fact, if you don't have the symbol of God, those five prayers are chaotic, you cannot make any sense out of them. Once you have the symbol, that symbol crystallizes everything.

"See?" said the rabbi.

The last question:

Osho,
It is an unimportant point in a very interesting inspiring discourse, but why do you say that the sun will be finished in four thousand years? My atlases of the earth and the universe give a figure for the next major change in the sun's present output – to a red giant stage – to be about five billion years or so which would annihilate life on earth. Are you trying to start a stampede? Or is this an "intentional imperfection" inserted into your discourse as in a Persian rug?

The questioner says: "It is an unimportant point in a very inspiring discourse..." – but nothing else has inspired the questioner to ask. So this must have been the most important thing.

There are people who are interested in nonessential things, and they make much fuss about them. And they forget that because of that fuss much is being missed.

If it makes you happy, you can make it five billion years, or why five billion? Why not five hundred billion? If it makes you happy, you can make as big a figure as you can.

I have heard one anecdote...

A scientist was speaking about the same truth, and he said, "In five billion years the sun will cool down."

A woman sitting in the front of the audience started trembling, perspiring, was almost going to faint. So the scientist had to stop his talking. He came down and said, "What is going on? Why are you becoming so afraid? You need not be afraid, it is five billion years."

The woman said, "Thank God! I thought you said five million."

What difference does it make? You will be dead within fifty years. Whether the earth continues, or the sun continues for five billion or five million years makes no difference. These are irrelevant things.

My point was that if the sun becomes cold someday, we will not be able to live. I was trying to explain to you that you don't end at your skin. I am not a scientist, and I am very happy that I am not. I was simply saying that your skin is not your boundary. It is difficult to say where your boundary is, and it is, in fact, nowhere.

The sun is there; without the sun you will not be able to live. Your skin will simply wither away, and you will die. That was the whole point.

And I am not trying to create a stampede. If a stampede is to be created, four thousand years won't help. Tomorrow, and that too is doubtful. Even if I said that tomorrow the sun is going to cool down completely, then too it is difficult to see that a stampede will be created. You are so lazy you will say, "Tomorrow? Tomorrow never comes." And you may start living even more madly because, "Tomorrow? Maybe this man is right." So whatsoever you have not done up to now, do it. You were thinking about murdering a man – murder. Or you were thinking about kidnapping a woman – kidnap; because, "Tomorrow? Who knows? This man may be right."

No, I am not creating, or trying to create, any stampede. To me it is an irrelevant thing: four thousand years, four million years, four billion years, four trillion years – whatsoever.

But you missed my point. And you showed your mind by raising a very unimportant question. If such questions are meaningful to you, you will go on missing me. Then you are simply watching for something absolutely meaningless.

I have heard...

Junior was in the habit of coming to the table with a dirty face, and, of course, had to be sent away to wash every day.

One time his mother, losing her patience, said to him, "Junior, why do you persist in coming to the table without washing? You know I always send you away."

"Well," replied Junior, "once you forgot."

Just once, and, who knows, you may forget again.

There are minds who go on watching for such things. Be alert about this tendency.

I am not a scientist, neither was Jesus or Buddha. Now there are many people who deny Jesus because he was not a scientist – because he said the world was created four thousand years before. Now look. This four thousand seems to be very meaningful. I said, "After four thousand years it is going to drop," and Jesus said, "Just four thousand years ago the world was created."

Now scientists find fault. It is faulty. The world was not created four thousand years ago. Then why was this man saying it? This man was not a scientist; this man was saying something not as a fact but as a parable. He was not talking about a scientific theory for the creation, he was not interested in any scientific theory, he was simply talking in parables. He was emphasizing one fact: that the world is not going to be forever, and it has not been there forever. It is dreamlike. It has been created, and it will disappear. So don't be too involved in it, it is not the real thing; seek the creator, find out who is the creator. Don't waste too much time with the creation.

But now there are scientists who will prove that he is wrong, and there are Christians who will try to prove that he is right. And both do the same foolishness: you mistake a parable for a fact, you can't understand a beautiful story, you can't understand poetry. Now I have come across scientists who have written great treatises proving that Jesus is wrong. I have come across treatises which have tried to refute him.

For example, scientists say that now there is proof – and there is proof – that the world has existed for millions of years. We have found bones in the earth, skulls in the earth which are at least fifty thousand years old. So not only the world, but man, has existed for at least fifty thousand years. And Jesus says that the world was created only four thousand years ago. Now, how to answer it?

I was reading a Christian theologian. He says, "God is Almighty. When he created the world, he created skulls fifty thousand years old just to test the faith of people."

Now what to do with these people? He has put fifty thousand-year-old skulls inside the earth. He created the earth four thousand years ago, just to see who are the doubters and who are the real believers!

Don't waste your time in such things.

Enough for today.

CHAPTER 7

not knowing is the beginning of zazen

Long ago in Japan a blind man, visiting a friend one night, was offered a paper-and-bamboo lantern to carry home with him.

"I do not need a lantern," he said. "Darkness or light is all the same to me."

"I know you do not need a lantern to find your way," his friend replied, "but you must take it because if you don't have one, someone else may run into you."

The blind man started off with the lantern, and before he had walked very far, someone ran squarely into him. "Look out where you are going!" he exclaimed to the stranger. "Can't you see this lantern?"

"Your candle has burnt out, Brother," replied the stranger.

Knowledge is not enough, and to rely on it is dangerous. Knowledge is borrowed, it is not knowing. Knowing grows within you, knowing is a growth, an inner evolution; knowledge is implanted within you from the outside, knowledge is borrowed, it is counterfeit. It looks like knowing, it is not. It deceives, it gives you a feeling that you know, and yet you don't.

On the path of Zen the first thing to beware of is knowledge: the tradition, the scripture, that which has been handed over to you by others. Those eyes are not yours, that light is not yours, and it is better to remain ignorant than to become knowledgeable because at least ignorance is yours. At least it is authentic, at least it is true, at least it belongs to you.

Out of the truth of ignorance knowing can grow, but out of the falsity of knowledge you will be lost, nothing can grow out of it. Knowledge is an accumulation of dead facts and information. It has no life in it. It is like stones piled up, one upon another. It can rise to a very great height, but it has no growth because it has no sap of life in it.

A tree is totally different. It also goes higher and higher, but it has an organic growth, a sap of life, running through it. It is growing on its own accord. It is rooted in life. It is an alive process. You can make a plastic tree. It will look just like any other tree: it can be even more green, it can be even more deceptive, more beautiful, but still it will be dead. It will not have any roots anywhere, it will not be grounded in existence, it will not be at ease and at home, it will not be an insider. It will be a foreigner, it will be alien.

This is the first thing to understand, only then can you understand the radical attitude of Zen. It is very easy to borrow knowledge. That's what the schools, the colleges, the universities are doing. They go on transferring information from one generation to another. They are the via media, and people who collect knowledge from them start feeling that they know. But how can you know if you have not known it?

I can talk about love to you, you can listen to me, you can even agree with me, but your agreement is not the point. I may be logical and clever enough to persuade you to agree with me, but that will not give you any taste of love. To know love, you will have to fall in love. To know love, you will have to travel the path of love. To know love, you will have to take the dangerous journey.

Knowledge is more of a certainty; knowing is more uncertain. That's why people choose knowledge. Knowledge is more guaranteed, it has authority, centuries are standing behind it. That's why every religion tries to prove that it is the oldest religion in the world. Why? Because the older a religion is, the greater the authority it has. Hindus say that the Vedas are the oldest scriptures in the world; Bibles and Korans and Guru Granthas are just very late arrivals. The Vedas are very, very old. Why so much insistence? Because the older a scripture is, the longer it has stood the test of time, the greater the authority it has gathered around it. Millions of seers are witnesses to it.

Zen says truth has nothing to do with authority, truth has nothing to do with tradition, truth has nothing to do with the past; truth is a radical, personal realization. *You* have to come to it.

Knowledge is certain; the search for personal knowing is very, very hazardous. Nobody can guarantee it. If you ask me, can I guarantee you anything, I would say I cannot guarantee you anything. I can only guarantee danger, that much is certain. I can only guarantee you a long adventure with every possibility of going astray and never reaching the goal. But one thing is certain: the very search will help you to grow. I can guarantee only growth. Danger will be there, sacrifice will be there; you will be moving every day into the unknown, into the uncharted, and there will be no map to follow, no guide to follow. Yes, there are millions of dangers, and you can go astray, and you can get lost, but that is the only way one grows. Insecurity is the only way to grow, to face danger is the only way to grow, to accept the challenge of the unknown is the only way to grow. So I can guarantee only growth.

Knowledge guarantees everything. There will be no danger if you follow the Veda, if you follow the Bible; then you need not worry. Now it is Christ who has to worry about it, and he knows. You have simply to imitate him. And the seers of the Vedas know, and Mohammed knows, so there is no need for you to make your own private effort. It has already been known, you simply believe. All that is required from you by ordinary religions is belief.

Zen says belief is counterfeit, borrowed.

You have to grow, and you have to take the risk. I can guarantee you risk. In the open sky of the truth one searches with trial and error, many times going astray, and again and again coming back to the right path. That's the only way.

Truth is not cheap; belief is very cheap. Truth is very costly; you will have to pay with your life. Truth requires total sacrifice, nothing less will do.

Zen says that if you believe scriptures, tradition, others, it is irrelevant whether they are wrong or right; that is not the point. Remember, Zen doesn't say the Bible is wrong, Zen doesn't say the Veda is wrong. Zen says they are irrelevant. It has nothing to do with right and wrong. They may be right, they may be wrong, but that is not the point to be considered at all. Through them growth is not possible. Those who have written them were grown-up, mature people. They have asserted something that they have known, but that was knowing for them. For you it will be knowledge.

Knowing means that you have seen it with your own eyes; knowledge means you have heard it from others. It is very poor, and one who remains with knowledge remains poor. A pundit, a so-called learned man, is the poorest man in the world. He has only counterfeit money, and he goes on counting it.

We are the hollow men
We are the stuffed men
Leaning together
Headpiece filled with straw. Alas!
Our dried voices, when
We whisper together
Are quiet and meaningless
As wind in dry grass
Or rats' feet over broken glass
In our dry cellar....

These beautiful lines from T. S. Eliot describe exactly the situation of the man, of the mind, who has remained with knowledge: "stuffed with straw" and "our voices" are like "rat's feet over broken glass."

Look at your head. It is almost rubbish: a collection, accumulation, but not knowing at all. And unless you are free from this rubbish, your eyes will not have clarity, you will remain blind. I can give you my lamp in your hand, it will not help. Sooner or later the flame will be gone. In fact, the flame goes immediately the moment I give my lamp to you. In the very transfer the flame goes out because the flame cannot be transferred. You will have to become a flame on your own accord.

You can learn how to kindle your flame, but you cannot borrow it. It is not a thing that can be transferred. At the most I can give you a thirst to seek it, I can give you almost a madness to search for it. I can drive you crazy enough to go after it, but I cannot give it to you. Nobody has ever given it to anybody else, it is untransferable.

Wittgenstein says: "Philosophy leaves everything as it is." You can become a great philosopher, you can know much, but philosophy leaves everything as it is. Nothing changes through it, it has no revolution in it.

Belief is communal, knowledge is also communal; knowing is

personal, trust is personal. You have to relate to existence or to truth directly, immediately. You have to come to truth, and it is going to be arduous because each step will require tremendous changes in you. You cannot go to truth as you are, you will have to drop many things, and the first thing, Zen says, is to drop borrowed knowledge.

If you ask Christians what is to be dropped first, they will say sin. But they have forgotten what was the original sin. The original sin was that Adam and Eve ate from the tree of knowledge. That story comes closer to Zen. They ate the fruit of the tree of knowledge. That became the fall. That is the real sin, the original sin. Sin has nothing to do with your acts – moral, immoral. Sin has something to do with knowledge. The parable is so clear, but still Christian theologians have misinterpreted it for centuries.

So the original sin is to become knowledgeable, to eat from the tree of knowledge.

Then what will be surrender? Then what will be virtue? Virtue will be surrendering the knowledge, vomiting the knowledge, cleaning your head completely, throwing all knowledge out. The apple that Adam swallowed is sticking in everyone's throat.

And, of course, for Adam knowledge was just a beginning. We have accumulated more than Adam because for centuries and centuries we have been eating from the same tree. We have completely lost the space, the inner purity, the inner innocence that comes when one throws, renounces, one's knowledge. Renounce your knowledge.

In the Bible there is another beautiful parable: the parable of the three wise men. Jesus is born in a stable in the poorest of poor situations. Then three wise men from the East go searching and seeking him because, according to their astrological analysis, they have come to feel that something of the beyond is entering into time. They are very wise men, learned, so learned that kings of many countries consult them and touch their feet. But still they go in search of this small child to touch his feet. Their learning is nothing compared to the innocence of this small child, just born.

This child has not yet eaten the fruit of knowledge, and this child is such that he is not going to eat the fruit of knowledge. He is going to insist on remaining pure of knowledge, he is not going to pollute his being, contaminate his being. Something from the beyond, something of the divine has entered into the world of time.

Those three wise men travel. It is arduous, the journey is long, and the three wise men are very, very old, very experienced, learned in many arts. They know all that can be known, but they don't know how to be in a state of knowing. And they are going to search for this boy, this small boy, to look into his pure eyes, to look into his virgin eyes, to find out how one can be simply there without any knowledge.

They are very old, and nobody knows where Jesus is born; but the story is beautiful. The story says: look into the sky to find a path on the earth. This is strange. To find a path on the earth, you have to look on the earth, but they look in the sky, and a star guides them.

If you want to find a way on earth, you have to look at the sky. If you want your feet to move rightly, you will have to look at the uttermost height of life. You will have to look at the stars. If your eyes are moving toward the height, your feet will follow the right track. That is the only way. If you are crawling on the earth and looking on the earth, you will miss all paths.

A star guides them. They reach the town, they reach the stable, and the star stops there. When you reach home everything stops because the home means simply that now there is nowhere to go. You have come to a point from where one has nowhere to go. The ultimate has come.

These wise three men bow down into the feet of this small babe. This is knowledge bowing down before knowing, experience bowing down before innocence, Adam bowing down before Jesus, respectability bowing down before revolution.

And they offer many presents to Jesus: gold they offer, incense they offer, myrrh they offer. Those are symbolic offerings. In the East gold is offered to kings, and this poorest of the poor is the king of the kings. So they offer gold. Incense is offered to the priests, and this boy is not a priest, yet he is going to be the highest priest possible. They offer incense. And in the East, myrrh is offered to somebody who is on their deathbed. Why do they offer myrrh to this boy who is just born? They know, they feel, that this boy is going to die on the cross – is destined. Because unless somebody dies totally, there is no resurrection.

They offer whatsoever they have, and they go back. The story says that they go back to their home. Their home was in Iran. So they go back home, and they bring the message that they have looked and found in the eyes of Jesus something of the unknown.

They bring the message, but Iran never became a Christian country, never. That too is very symbolic. The three wise men were the first to encounter Jesus, but still they could not bring the message back home. The experience was so deep and profound that it could not be expressed. They may have become dumb, they may have remained silent for the rest of their lives, they may not have talked to anybody, they may not have said anything to anybody. Nobody knows what happened to those three wise men. Because they had come to the very source, they may have become silent.

This is a Zen parable. The first thing to be dropped is knowledge. Once you drop knowledge, you attain to clarity. Look at small children. Let that be your ideal, and become a child again. Only children have eyes to see. Our eyes are too full of ideas.

We go on collecting knowledge, opinions, but deep down we remain the same, nothing changes. We just go on painting our personalities on the surface.

I have heard...

Cohen and Goldberg were partners in the dress business, and business was terrible.

A discouraged Cohen announced to his partner that he was going to change his name for good luck.

"From now on," he said, "I am O'Brian."

That night Goldberg decided he would change his name too.

Both men instructed the switchboard operator to answer the phones, "O'Brian and O'Brian."

Everything went well until a caller demanded to speak to Mr. O'Brian. "Which O'Brian do you want?" asked the operator. "Cohen or Goldberg?"

Everything that we go on doing on the surface will be just like changing a name. Inside you will remain the same. Your persona can never become more than skin deep; your knowledge, your identity in the world is nothing but a persona, a dressing.

Zen says you are wasting your life. Go deep, go beyond your knowledge, go beyond your name and your form, go beyond that identity that the society has given to you. Zen masters give koans to their disciples to look into their original face – the face that you had before you were born. Now you have a false face; it has been given to you by the society, it is just a formality, and if you think it is you, you are in a very bad shape.

Somebody is a Christian, somebody is a Hindu, somebody is a Mohammedan, somebody is a Buddhist, and these are just superficial things, accidents of birth. You are not a Christian because Christ has not touched your heart yet. You are a Christian because you were born in a Christian home. You are a Buddhist because it was just an accident of birth, coincidence. It happened that your father and mother were Buddhist, hence you are a Buddhist, but Buddha has not yet happened to you.

Remember, this is very cheap. Drop Christianity, drop Islam, drop Buddhism, drop that which has been given to you by the society, by birth, by association, by culture, by country. Drop all that, so that you can find out who you really are.

These things will be taken away by death; death will burn your persona, and then you will come face-to-face with your being, and you will not even be able to recognize it because you never knew that this was your face. We live very superficial lives.

I have heard...

A beggar clutched at the sleeve of a benevolent-looking passerby.

"Five cents, Sir, for a cup of coffee," he whined.

The other turned and surveyed him. "Why," he asked, "should I give you money? What brought you to this sad plight?"

"A terrible catastrophe, Sir," the beggar replied. "Two years ago I was a prosperous business man like you. I worked industriously. On my desk was the motto, 'Think Constructively, Act Decisively.' Money poured in and then, and then," the beggar's frame shook convulsively, "the cleaning woman burned my motto!"

Just the burning of the motto. "The cleaning woman burned my motto!" That has made him a beggar.

Have you anything more than just a motto? What do you call your name? What do you call your identity? It can be burned; death will take it away. Death is nothing but a cleaning woman. It will clean it away, and then you will cry convulsively. Then you will say, "Death has killed me."

Death has never killed anybody. Death has no power to kill; death is the most impotent thing in the world. You make it potent by clinging to the superficial. The power of death is not intrinsic to death, the power of death is given by you. Death is empowered by you because you go on clinging to the superficial. Death can only take the superficial, it cannot enter into the depths of your being.

But if you think your clothes are you, your body is you, your mind is you, then you have given power to the hands of death. Death will destroy this, and then you will convulsively weep, "I have been killed," and for your whole life you will be afraid of death.

Zen says that if you drop knowledge – and within knowledge everything is included, your name, your identity, everything because this has been given to you by others – if you drop all that has been given to you by others, you will have a totally different quality to your being: innocence. This will be a crucifixion of the persona, of the personality, and there will be a resurrection of your innocence. You will become a child again, reborn.

Hindus call this state *dwij*, twice born. This is a second birth. A man becomes really a brahmin when he has gone through the cross – the personality burned and destroyed by death. Or he has renounced it himself voluntarily, and then innocence arises, and he is reborn. Then he is a brahmin because only then does he come to know what truth is. But we have decided to follow the short-cut, the way of the belief. We are hoping against hope that somebody else's eyes will do the work for us.

It happened...

In Buddha's time there was a blind man in a certain village. He was a great logician, a great thinker, and nobody was able to convince him that light existed because he would argue against it.

He would say, "If light exists, I would like to touch it because anything that exists can be touched. If light exists, I would like to taste it, or at least I would like to smell it, or you can throw it on the floor; at least I can hear the sound of it."

He said, "These are the four senses, so any sense that is available to me can become a proof for it."

But there is no way to touch light, no way to smell it; it has no smell, and there is no way to throw it on the floor to create sound. There is no way to taste it. It is difficult, very difficult to prove.

And then that blind man would laugh, and he would say, "You are trying to befool me. You simply want to prove that light is, so that you can prove that I am blind, but I am not blind. Everybody is blind, and there exists nothing like light. You don't try to befool me."

One day the blind man was invited to a friend's house. A preparation of milk was made, and he liked it very much, and he asked of what was it made. They said, "Of milk."

He said, "Tell me something more about milk. How does it look?"

They said, "It looks white."

He said, "White? You will have to prove because I don't believe that colors exist. It is just an imagination of man. What is white?"

They said, "White, just like a white cow."

He said, "Now you are creating more problems. What is a cow? What does it look like?"

Finding no other way, one man innovated a method. He came near the old man, he put his hand before him, made a gesture as if this is the head of the cow, and he said, "Touch my hand. The head of the cow feels like this, and these two fingers are the two horns. Feel."

He tried to feel, and he laughed and said, "Now I know that milk looks like a bent hand."

Absolutely logical because his basic question was about milk.

Finding it difficult they brought him to Buddha – Buddha was in the vicinity – and they said to Buddha, "We have tried hard, but we cannot convince this man that light exists or that colors exist. He is blind, but he is very argumentative."

Buddha said, "He is not wrong, you are wrong. Rather than bringing him to me, take him to a physician who can cure his eyes. He does not need any other conviction because no other conviction is possible. It cannot be proved to a blind man that light exists, and if any blind man agrees, he may be agreeing only to be polite. How can a blind man agree that light exists? If he cannot feel its existence, then there is no way to feel it. Take him to a physician."

And Buddha said, "I know a great physician" – Buddha's own physician, Jeevika was his name – "Go to Jeevika. He may be able to find some way."

And it happened that the man was not really blind, he had a certain disease in the eyes from his birth. After six months of treatment, he started seeing. He danced the whole way to Buddha's place, he fell at his feet, and he said, "Excuse me, light is, but there was no way for me to recognize it before I had my own eyes opened."

The same is true about God, the same is true about truth. No argument can prove that God exists, no proof exists which can help unless your eyes are opened.

So Zen doesn't bother about philosophizing, about concepts. It says the only effort worth doing, the only thing worth putting your whole energy into, is how to attain eyes.

Lopos Pachio, a great poet, has a few beautiful lines:

Remove from my eyes this mist of the centuries.
I want to see things like a child.

That is what the whole effort of Zen is – removing the mist of centuries, removing the mist of the past. It is a great cleansing of the eyes, and once your perception is clear and once you have attained clarity to see, truth is, and nothing else is. Truth is not lost; you have lost your eyes.

People come to me, and they ask, "Where is God?" I say, "Drop that subject completely. That is irrelevant. Have you got eyes? That is the relevant question to ask. If you don't have eyes, even if I manage to produce God before you, you will not be able to see."

You can see only that which you can see. You will need a greater clarity to move into the subtle mysteries of life. Godliness is the subtlest mystery. For it, very refined eyes are needed.

So Zen says that there is no need to talk about God; all talk about God is useless. They don't talk about God; all talk about heaven and hell is useless. They don't talk about that, they don't talk about truth, they don't talk about reality; they have no metaphysics.

Buddha was very reluctant to talk about any metaphysical problem. He would either keep quiet, he would not answer, or he would say something which was totally different from what the questioner had in his mind. He was almost silent about all the great questions humanity has been discussing, arguing about, thinking about, contemplating, philosophizing about. If Plato, Aristotle, Hegel, Kant, and people like that had gone to him, they would have thought him mad. He would not answer a single question from Hegel or Kant or Plato or Aristotle. At the most he would laugh at their foolish questions. He will insist on only one thing, "*Appo dipo bhav* – be a light unto yourself." Kindle your inner light, so you can see. We can see only that which we can see.

A small girl came once to me, and I asked her, "Do you want to say something to me?"

She said, "I would like to sing a small song."

She was a very small girl, and she sang a small song, and I loved it.

The song was:

Pussycat, pussycat, where have you been?
I have been to London to look at the queen.
Pussycat, pussycat, what saw you there?
I saw a mouse under the chair.

Of course, a cat cannot see the Queen, it is impossible. A cat can only see the rat. The Queen was there sitting on the chair, but the cat could not see; she saw a mouse under the chair, and it is absolutely logical. A cat has eyes for the mouse and for the rat, she has no eyes for the Queen. We see only that which we can see.

If you don't see godliness in existence, then you have to remember one thing: you don't yet have eyes for *godliness*. So work hard to have eyes, and don't borrow eyes; eyes are not like glasses. You can borrow somebody else's glasses, and sometimes they may even fit, but eyes are not like glasses.

And when I'm talking, or Zen people are talking about eyes, they are not like your ordinary eyes. It is an inner vision. Even these eyes can be transferred; you can have my eye, my physical eye. I can have your physical eye, they can be transplanted; but the inner vision, the inner eye, the third eye, is impossible to transfer.

So remember that ignorance is better than borrowed knowledge. It is at least true. Recognize the fact "I don't know"; recognize it so deeply that your whole ego disappears because the ego exists through knowledge; knowledge is the most vital food for the ego. That's why we go on pretending about things which we don't know; we go on pretending that we know.

It happened in church...

The old priest of the church was getting ready for his morning sermon. It was Sunday, early morning, and he was preparing his notes.

A young priest came running, and he said, "Look! What are you doing? Jesus has come, and he is worshipping at the altar."

The old priest said, "Jesus?" It was almost a shock. Jesus had never come, and nobody had ever thought that he was to come.

Even priests who go on saying that he is going to come next time, that he will come again, even they don't believe. Who believes? Priests are the most unbelieving people because they know the very secrets of the trade. They say things for others.

He could not believe it, but he started trembling. He became afraid. Both came to the door and looked inside. Yes, there was a figure exactly like Jesus Christ, and he was worshipping at the altar.

The young priest said, “Now what do we do?”

He said, “Look busy. What else can we do?”

Look busy! That’s how we go on pretending. It is the most difficult statement in the world to say “I don’t know.”

If somebody asks, “Is there God?” either you say, “Yes, there is” or you say, “No, there is no God in the world.” Both answers are stupid. If you have been brought up in a religious home, you say, “Yes, there is.” If you have been brought up in Soviet Russia or China, you say, “No, there is no God.” But these are your conditionings speaking, not you.

Wait a minute, think twice. Do you know? Yes and no both show your knowledge. The man who says no is pretending absolute knowledge. He is saying that he has searched the whole of existence and has not found him. The man who says yes says, “Yes, I have looked into the Bible and the Koran and the Vedas, and they all say he is, and I believe that he is.” But the truth is that they both are asserting something which has no personal experience behind it.

A real and true person will say, “I don’t know.” The moment you say “I don’t know,” you are available, your doors are not closed. Then you can seek and search, then the whole journey opens for you. Once you say yes or no, doors are closed. You become smug in your knowledge.

Knowledge makes you blind. It closes your eyes. It fills your eyes with dust. Knowledge is a sort of blindness; you will have to come out of it, you will have to jump out of it. If you can show that much courage, only then can you walk the path of truth, can you meditate, can you sit in zazen.

“I don’t know” is the beginning of zazen. “I don’t know” – this recognition is the first step toward knowledge.

Now the story...

Long ago in Japan a blind man, visiting a friend one night, was offered a paper-and-bamboo lantern to carry home with him.

Now it is absurd to offer a lantern to a blind man because he cannot see. Both darkness and light are the same to him. It is foolish.

What is he going to do with the lamp? It will be just a burden. A lamp is beautiful and helpful and a light on your path if you have eyes; otherwise the lamp is a burden.

Knowledge, if it is yours, is a light on the path. Knowledge, if it is just learned from others, is a burden. Then your head becomes heavy, then you are carrying stones in your head. Then you cannot fly because for flying you need to be weightless. Knowledge becomes a weight on you.

It was foolish to offer a lantern to a blind man, but the man who offered it must have been very logical. He had some logic behind it. Whenever we do something foolish, we always rationalize it because it is very difficult for the ego to do a simple, foolish thing. We rationalize it, we find some argument for it. Whatsoever we do we always find some argument to give it support, to at least give it a face, so that it doesn't look foolish.

"I do not need a lantern," he said. "Darkness or light is all the same to me."

The blind man is simple, and he knows what a light can do for him. He cannot see; day and night are the same to him.

"I know you do not need a lantern to find your way," his friend replied, "but you must take it because if you don't have one, someone else may run into you."

Now he has found a beautiful argument for it, and even to the blind man it appealed. It looks right. You may not be able to see, but with a lantern in your hands at least others will be able to see you, and they will not run into you. It was difficult to deny this, the logic is clear.

That's how we have accepted many things: for some reasons, for some logic behind them. You don't know if God is, then somebody says, "Can you think of a watch being made without a maker?" Of course you cannot. It looks almost impossible that just by coincidence, by chance, a watch will come into existence. Inconceivable. It looks logical that if a small watch, a small mechanism, cannot come into existence by itself, then how can this whole universe, this cosmos, so infinite and so complex and yet running in such deep order and discipline? How can this whole existence come into being without there being a maker? It appeals, it looks logical, it is difficult to deny it. So the blind man agrees; so you say, "Yes, there must be a God."

Look! You are accepting something which you cannot see, which you have never felt. But the argument seems to be weighty, and it seems to be difficult to deny it. You have accepted God, you have accepted the soul, you have accepted a thousand and one things just because they are supported by weighty arguments. But they don't help.

Life is not an argument. You have to live it to know it. And the danger is that because of the argument, once you accept God – "Yes, God is because the maker is needed, the creator is needed for the creation," – you may forget by and by that you don't know this creator. This acceptance may become a dangerous thing, a fatal thing. Then you will not search, you will think you already know. Your knowledge can deceive you, and you can start feeling that you already know. Millions of people in the world go on thinking that they know God exists. That's what happened to this poor blind man.

The blind man started off with the lantern, and before he had walked very far, someone ran squarely into him. "Look out where you are going!" he exclaimed to the stranger. "Can't you see this lantern?"
"Your candle has burnt out, Brother," replied the stranger.

Now the danger is that the blind man, if he had no lantern in his hand, would have walked more cautiously. He has always been walking. He is a blind man; he knows he is blind, so he takes all precautions. Today he must have left all precautions behind; he had a lantern in his hand. He believed in the lantern, so there was no need to be cautious. He must have walked at leisure, thinking that the lantern was there, and nobody can run into him.

For his whole life he had been walking on the same road, and nobody had run into him because he was cautious. Today there was no need to be cautious. That is the danger of borrowed knowledge.

If you are ignorant, you are more cautious, you walk with more alertness, awareness, you behave more consciously. If you think you know, then you start moving like a robot. There is no need to be cautious, there is no need to be alert, you can fall asleep, you can become unconscious. That's what happened to the blind man. He must have walked, thinking other thoughts. There was no need to think about the road, about other people, about himself. He trusted, he believed in the lantern.

That's how millions of people are walking in life – trusting in the Bible, in the Vedas, in the Koran, trusting in others. Their very belief is dangerous. It is better to be aware and alert and to move cautiously.

The blind man started off with the lantern, and before he had walked very far, someone ran squarely into him. "Look out where you are going!"... He must have been angry, annoyed. Somebody was going against the logic, somebody was behaving very irrationally. He had a lantern, and the friend had said very convincingly, that nobody will run into him now. People will be able to see him, and here comes this man. "Are you blind?" he must have said to him. "Can't you see this lantern in my hand? What are you doing? Are you mad? Don't you understand simple logic?"

But life does not believe in logic; life is very illogical, it is very irrational, it is almost absurd. And here comes the absurdity; life always has surprises for you. The blind man was thinking that the lamp was there, and so there was no problem.

"Can't you see this lantern?" "Your candle has burnt out, Brother." Now this is a surprise, and how can the blind man see that the candle is burnt out, that he is carrying a dead lamp which has no light, that he is carrying just a dead weight?

All your beliefs are like that lamp which has no light in it. Your Koran is dead, it has no light. It may have been full of life and full of light in the hands of Mohammed. Your Gita is dead, the candle is burnt out. It may have been full of light in the hands of Krishna because that man had eyes. He could have replaced the burned-out candle any moment.

For centuries you have been carrying scriptures – burned-out candles. And everybody was running into everybody else. Can't you see that? The whole conflict of humanity – Hindus fighting with Christians, Christians fighting with Mohammedans, Mohammedans fighting with Buddhists, everybody running into each other – can't you see this agony, this conflict? The whole of humanity is struggling, is at war. Sometimes it is hot, sometimes it is cold, but all the time it is war. Sometimes you are fighting, sometimes you are preparing for a fight, but all the time it is fight.

And it is not only that religions are fighting – nations are fighting, persons... Everybody is fighting: the husband with the wife, the wife with the husband, the friend with the friend, the brother with the brother, the children with the parents, the parents with the children. Everybody, everywhere, is running into each other, as if we are all blind, and everybody thinks that he is carrying a lamp in his hand, and the candle is burned out.

In fact, as far as the candle of truth is concerned, the moment it is transferred from one hand to another, it dies. The Gita died when Krishna was transferring it to Arjuna. It is not that Arjuna will carry the light at least a few steps, it is impossible. When I am saying something to you, I can see it dying continuously between you and me. The moment it reaches you, it is already dead. There is no way to transfer it.

Then why do I go on talking? Sometimes people come and ask me, "Why do you go on talking if there is no way to transfer it?" There is no way to transfer it, there has never been a way to transfer it, but still I have to talk just to show you the impossibility. You cannot understand what I am saying, and it will be impossible for you to understand if I am silent. If you cannot understand my words, you will not be able to understand my silence. If you misunderstand my words, you will misunderstand my silence. But still I have to talk to you because that is the only way possible to communicate that there is something within me which cannot be communicated, that I am carrying something, that I am pregnant with something which is incommunicable.

Being with me, listening to me again and again, again and again, watching me, some day you may understand the point. I cannot make you understand it, but if you persist long enough, you may be able to understand it. That understanding will arise within you, it will not be a transfer from me. I can push you and pull you here and there, but I will have to wait. And if you can also wait with me, then someday your own inner flame will arise. It needs patience, it needs contact with a master, but it cannot be transferred.

The master can function only as a catalytic agent. My presence will make you more and more thirsty; my presence will make you more and more mad; a great, an intense, an impossible desire will arise in you. You will become a passionate search. In that passion your own candle will start burning. You will become your own fuel.

So all that I can do is not a transfer of truth but only a support, a help, so that you don't become impatient, so that you don't lose your interest in truth, so that you continue in your desire, and you go on putting more and more at stake. A moment will come, just as it comes when you heat water. You go on heating it. At a hundred degrees it jumps and becomes vapor, evaporates. All that I am doing is trying to heat you as much as I can. The jump will be yours, the evaporation will be yours.

If you allow and if you are able to suffer patiently the pain of waiting and the pain that the heat will bring and the pain that your intense desire will create, if you are ready to suffer happily, patiently, then one day it is your flame that will arise within you. It will be absolutely yours.

And I talk also for the reason: because whenever a truth happens, it has to be shared. Unshared, it starts dying; shared, it lives. It is not that I can give you truth, but sharing with you, making an effort to share with you, truth can remain alive. I am talking for the same reasons as birds sing or flowers bloom or stars shine. I dig it. If you also start digging it with me, if you cooperate with me, then when it will happen to you, you will know that it has not been a transfer, but that something authentically yours has arisen. It is individual. Truth is revealed individually.

I would like to tell you a few anecdotes…

The old fellow was a crossing-tender at a spot where an express train made quick work of an auto and its occupants. Naturally, he was the chief witness, and the entire case hinged upon the energy with which he had displayed his warning signal. A grueling cross-examination left him unshaken in this story. The night was dark, and he had waved his lantern frantically, but the driver of the auto paid no attention to it.

Later the division superintendent called the flagman to his office to compliment him on the steadfastness with which he had stuck to his story. "You did wonderfully," he said. "I was afraid at first that you might waver in your testimony."

"No, sir," said the fellow, "but I was afraid every minute that that damn lawyer was going to ask me if the lantern was lit."

Ask yourself again and again, "Is the lantern that you are carrying lit?" Otherwise waving it in the dark night is a sheer wastage of energy. Is your Bible lit? Is your Gita lit? If not, then drop them. Then it is better not to have these illusions.

Another anecdote…

As the rookie cop passed a store, he heard a noisy argument. He paused, listened again, then stepped inside to investigate. "What's going on?" he demanded. "What's all the noise about?"

"It's nothing," said the proprietor. "There's no argument. I'm all alone."

"Wait a minute, Mac," said the cop. "I distinctly heard an argument going on."

"You don't understand, Officer," said the store owner. "I'm alone in the store. Business is terrible. So to pass the time away, I talk to myself, and when I talk to myself, there's bound to be an argument."

"How can you argue with yourself?" asked the cop.

"It's easy," said the store owner, "because I hate a liar!"

Look, watch inside your mind, what goes on. There is a continuous inner chattering, a continuous argument with yourself.

Truth is possible only when this inner talk stops, when you are left in deep emptiness, no argument, no for–against, no pro–con, no word, no thought. When the inner talk is simply suspended, in that moment of suspended inner talk, the window opens toward the sky.

The third anecdote…

A miserly man was approached by a friend who did his best to persuade him to dress more in accordance with his station in life. "I'm surprised," said the friend, "that you've allowed yourself to become so shabby."

"But I'm not shabby," said the miser.

"Yes, you are shabby," insisted his friend. "Take your grandfather. He was always neatly dressed. His clothes were always well tailored and of the best material."

"You see," cried the other triumphantly. "These clothes I'm wearing are grandfather's."

Watch. Are the thoughts that you are carrying yours? Or somebody else's? Centuries old, long ago dead and buried, and you go on carrying those dead thoughts. Gather courage, this shabbiness of the mind is a great disrespect toward yourself. Those clothes are dirty. People are not ready to use somebody else's clothes, but they are very easily ready to use somebody else's thoughts.

I have heard...

A philosopher went to a shoemaker. He wanted his shoes to be repaired, but he had only one pair. So he said, "I will wait, you repair."

The shoemaker said, "It is difficult, it is closing time. Come tomorrow, and I will get them ready."

The philosopher said, "I have got only one pair and it will be difficult for me to walk without shoes."

The shoemaker said, "Okay, keep this pair" – he gave him a pair – "with you. Tomorrow you return it and take yours."

The philosopher was very annoyed. He said, "What! To use somebody else's used shoes? What do you think I am?"

The shoemaker laughed and he said, "If you can carry others' used thoughts in your head, then what is wrong in using somebody else's shoes? They will just be on your feet. Your head is borrowed, so what is wrong in it?"

We are at ease to borrow our soul, hence we are beggars. Stop this borrowing. If you don't have your own soul, it is better not to have any soul at all. And once you gather that courage, you will start attaining to your own soul. It is not very far away, it is just hidden behind these borrowed clothes, thoughts, philosophies, doctrines, dogmas. Be yourself.

You have heard the famous Greek dictum of Socrates: "Know thyself." But that is not a primary thing. More primary is: "Be thyself." If you are not yourself, whom are you going to know? So I would like to tell you that more basic and more fundamental is the dictum: "Be thyself." Then there is a possibility to "Know thyself." If you are not, then whom are you going to know, and who is going to know?

A religious man is not a borrowed man, a religious man is not a hollow man, he is not a stuffed man. A religious man is absolutely empty of others. And the moment you are empty of others, you fill your own inner space. That is what fulfillment is, that is what nirvana is, that is what liberation is.

Enough for today.

CHAPTER 8

you are already there

The first question:

Osho,
As a child, Sundays were something very special to me. Now, since a few days, I wake up every morning, look out, see the sun shining through the trees, hear the birds singing, and get this feeling, "Ah, another Sunday." I put on my best clothes and have Sunday for the whole day. What is happening to me?

Don't make a problem out of it.

The mind is constantly searching for something to pounce upon – even happiness. It makes a problem out of happiness also. If you are feeling happy, you ask, "Why?" That question is dangerous.

If you are suffering, it is good to ask why because the suffering has to be dissolved, transcended. Ways and means have to be found to get out of it; the "Why?" is relevant. But when you are happy, then to ask why is to disturb it. There is no need to ask any questions. When happiness surrounds you, accept it totally without any questioning. If you are ill, diagnosis is needed, analysis is needed because the disease has to be found. But if you are healthy, you don't go to the doctor to ask,

"Why am I healthy? Diagnose my health. What is happening to me?" You don't go.

It is an old habit of the mind because it has been always living in misery, unhappiness, and always the "Why?" has been relevant. So when clouds disappear for the first time and the sun shines in your life, the old question goes on persisting – "Why?" Learn to accept happiness, learn to enjoy it without any questioning, learn to trust happiness. Don't doubt it because the very doubt will be a poisoning. Happiness rarely happens. Those moments are very few and far between. When they come, welcome them, open your door, receive them with your full heart, don't withhold anything. Even a question will become a very, very strong wall between you and your happiness.

Every day is a Sunday. It should be so. Every day is a holiday. It should be so because all days belong to him. Each moment is holy. Once you understand it, you will stop asking questions like this.

Don't think that any particular day is needed for you to be happy, only a particular mind. It has nothing to do with time; everything depends on the attitude, how you look at life. There are people for whom even a Sunday is not a Sunday. There is no light, no sun rising even on a Sunday. They are clouded in their own darkness, shrouded in their own misery. They carry their hell around them. Even if you force them into heaven, they will go on carrying their hell. They will live in their hell. Nobody can force them out of their hells unless they decide to drop it. It is your decision to be happy or to be unhappy.

I have heard about a Sufi mystic who was always happy, always and always. Nobody had ever seen him unhappy. It was as if he did not know that language, as if the only way he knew to be was happiness.

He became very old, and one day a man asked him, "Will you please tell me your secret? How you remain so happy? How you remain so unperturbed? How each moment one can be so blissful? It is impossible. It is unbelievable. What is your secret?"

The old man laughed, and he said, "Long before I found one simple thing – each morning when I opened my eyes, there are two alternatives to choose for that day: either to be happy or to be unhappy. And I always choose to be happy. My secret is simple. Each day gives me only two alternatives to choose: to be happy or to be unhappy. And I always choose to be happy, that's all. There is nothing more to it."

But you will not believe in it. You will say this old man is deceiving. He must have some other secret. But I also tell you this is the secret.

All great truths are simple truths, very simple. Try tomorrow morning. Before you open your eyes, have a clear-cut vision of two alternatives: being in hell or heaven. Visualize misery on one hand, visualize blissfulness on another hand. See deep into both. Don't be in a hurry. Look into both as deeply as possible and wait, and then decide. If you want to be unhappy, then decide. Let it be your decision, and then be truly unhappy the whole day. Be committed to your decision, and then don't try to escape from it. Then whatsoever happens, you remain miserable. And if you decide to be happy, then stick to it, and soon you will realize that your life is your decision.

You are suffering because you go on deciding that way; you are suffering because you go on clinging to your suffering. You have made a habit out of it. It is just mechanical.

It is good. You should feel grateful that it is happening to you that every day is becoming a holiday. Holidays are disappearing from the world. In the legal sense people are having more holidays. Workdays are being reduced all over the world, from six to five, from five to four, and soon even that will not be so. People will need... At least in the very highly developed technological societies, one day of the week will do, and for six days people can have holidays. But "holiday" is disappearing; that quality of sacredness, that quality of holiness is disappearing.

I have heard about a very reformed temple. Of course it is in Southern California because everything in Southern California is a little far-out, even religion.

There is a reformed temple in Beverley Hills that is so reformed that on the holiest of the days, Yom Kippur, there is a sign on the door saying: "Closed for the Jewish Holidays."

That quality, that consciousness is disappearing from the world.

People have more leisure; that is another thing. But what do they do with their leisure? They create more misery for themselves or for others. Finding nothing to do, they do harm to themselves or to others. More accidents happen on the holidays, more car accidents, more murders, more suicides. And after the holiday people are so tired that they need a whole week's rest to recuperate, to recover. They do a thousand and one things on holidays just to keep busy because not to be busy is to be with oneself, and that has become almost impossible. The dimension of being with oneself and being happy with oneself is completely lost.

That's what a holiday is, or should be. One is so full of godliness, so full of being, that there is no need to do anything, there is no need to be occupied. Occupation is just an escape. It is a good way to avoid encountering yourself, encountering life. Holidays are disappearing.

It is good that every day a feeling arises in you that it is a holiday. It is. If it was not so before, then you were missing something. Now it has started happening, don't make it a question.

I used to know a man who was an atheist. Once I heard that he had become a theist. I could not believe it. So when I came across him I asked him, "How come you decided to become a theist?"

"Well," he said, "I used to be an atheist, but I gave it up."

"Why?" I inquired.

He said, "No holidays."

If you are an atheist, then there are no holidays, then there is no God, then there are no Sundays. The Christian parable says that God created the world in six days and on the seventh day, Sunday, he rested. That rest was very beautiful, it was out of great creation. He was feeling fulfilled. He had created the whole world and, on the sixth day, he looked and he said, "Good, very good." And he rested. He was happy, like a small child who has made something and looks from every side and says, "Good. I have done it." He rested on the seventh day. That rest day was a fulfillment day.

The parable has much significance. It says that you can have a rest only after creation. If you don't create anything, your life will be restless; you will not be able to have a holiday. Create something; only then can you rest. Rest is a byproduct. You cannot directly rest; first you have to be so creative, you have to feel so good about yourself, so happy with yourself, so worthy, that you can allow rest for yourself, that you can allow a day just for fun.

Ordinarily people can't allow a day of rest for themselves because they feel so condemnatory about themselves, they feel so unworthy because they have not done anything worthwhile, that they have not experienced any fulfillment. Nothing has come to fruition, they have not blossomed. Hence continuous occupation, continuous activity is needed.

Many people go on working and working and working, and one day they die because their work is not creative. When is the work creative? The work is creative when you love it, the work is creative when you feel in tune with it, the work is creative when you enjoy it, the work is creative when you choose it, when it fits with your being, and there is a great harmony between you and your work. Once that happens, whatsoever you do is creative. And when after each creative moment you can relax, that relaxation is earned. Yes, God earned relaxation for the seventh day. For six days he worked hard, he created the whole world; on the seventh day he had earned relaxation, he was worthy of it. That's the meaning of the parable.

If you are creative, only then can you have holidays, not otherwise. So if you want to have holidays, become more and more creative. I am not saying be creative in the eyes of others – that is irrelevant. Just be creative in your own eyes, whatsoever you do. If you love it, then do it; otherwise don't do it, then choose some other way. Life is vast. Says Jesus, "There are many mansions in my God's house." There are many dimensions in life. There is enough opportunity to choose.

If you are not feeling fulfilled in something that you are doing, then don't do it because this will be a sheer wastage, and you will not have earned holidays. A man who has lived according to his being, who has done his own thing, earns death. Then he dies, but the death is a Sunday; then he dies, but he dies fulfilled. He has no complaints. He lived the way he wanted to live.

If I am going to die and God asks me, "If I send you back, how would you like to live?" I will say, "The same. I loved it. I enjoyed it. I would like to live the same way."

Just think about you. If you die and God asks you, "If you are sent back to the world, what changes would you like to make in your life?" Will you be able to say that you would like to live the same way, absolutely the same way? If not, then you are doing something wrong with your life. Then you are dragging your life, then you are not living it. Then you are simply killing time, as they say. Then you are simply wasting; your energies are simply dissipated. They will not become an integral force, and there is not going to be any blossoming; your tree is going to remain without any fruits and flowers. How can you be happy, and how can you enjoy?

Time as a holy opportunity, that is the meaning of holiday – a holy day, a day which is not profane, a day which is not ordinary. And once you know how to be creative, each moment becomes holy.

Whenever you create something, you participate with the creator; you have become a small creator in your own right. If you write a small poem, maybe nobody likes it, or you sing a song, nobody applauds it, that is irrelevant, but you enjoyed it. Singing, you were happy, you participated in that moment with existence, you helped it to create a song, you became instrumental. In fact, whatsoever is created, is created by existence; you allowed it to create a small song through you. Then you feel tremendously good, good about yourself.

And that is one of the basic qualities of a religious man: he always feels good about himself. He is not in any way guilty, guilt does not exist in him because he lived life as he wanted to live it. He loved his life the way it happened; it was the only life that he wanted to live. Then there is no guilt. Remember, a guilty person is not a religious person. A guilty person is ill, a guilty person is neurotic, a guilty person needs psychiatric help.

A religious person feels tremendously good about himself; whatsoever he is doing, he is doing something intrinsically valuable. This should be insisted upon as much as possible: worth in life arises only when you do something intrinsically valuable.

There are two types of value in life. One is intrinsic value. You sing a song; it has an intrinsic value, it is the means and it is the end also. Or you sing a song in the marketplace to earn a little money. That money is not intrinsic to the song, that money is an outside value. And if you are singing your song only for the money, then the activity is no longer holy, it is profane. If you are singing your song for the happiness that it brings to you... Maybe as a byproduct it brings money also, but that is irrelevant. If it brings money, it is good. If it does not bring, that too is good, but your activity has an inner glow to it, it is intrinsically valuable in itself. If you are happy that you could sing, you are happy that you had an opportunity to sing, then every day will become meditative, holy.

If you are doing the meditations here correctly, this is going to happen to everybody. That's my whole effort here: to help you enjoy each moment as it comes.

"As a child, Sundays were something very special to me. Now, since a few days, I wake up every morning, look out, see the sun shining through the trees, hear the birds singing and get this feeling: 'Ah, another Sunday.' I put on my best clothes and have Sunday for the whole day. What is happening to me?"

Something tremendously beautiful is happening to you. Allow it to happen.

Don't help your mind to create any trouble. The mind will try because the mind feels happy only when there is some misery. The mind's happiness is not your happiness, and your happiness is never the mind's happiness. Your goals are different; in fact, diametrically opposite. The mind feels happy only when you are miserable; then there is something to do. Then the mind becomes dominating, then he can dictate: do this, do that. Because one has to fight with the misery, one has to take the advice of the mind. When you are happy, mind is not needed. You can discard it, there is no need for it.

It is just like when the country is at war, then the army is needed. Then suddenly you see the army becomes predominant; everywhere you see soldiers, the military, moving from here to there, all the trains full of them. When the war disappears, they also by and by disappear, then you don't see them so much, then they are discarded. Not completely because our peace is not complete. Our so-called peace is nothing but the gap between two wars. So they recede into their cantonment areas, into their camps, but they go on parading there, preparing there for some war that can happen any moment, but they are no longer dominant. And if a country really attains to peace, then the military will have to be disbanded, it will not be needed.

Or think... You are ill, then suddenly the physician, the doctor, becomes important in your mind. When you are healthy, you forget completely that doctors exist. When you are ill, then suddenly passing on the street you read doctors' nameplates. They become predominant, they become the figure, and the rest of life becomes just a background. When you are not ill and you are healthy, they are no longer figures. They recede. The gestalt changes.

The same is happening with the mind. If you are miserable, mind is needed to get rid of the misery. If you are happy, mind is not needed; you can simply throw it, you can put it aside.

Mind feels neglected when you are happy, so it starts creating problems about happiness. The mind can say, "Look, don't be foolish. It is not possible. Every day cannot be Sunday. Look at the calendar:

this is Monday or Friday, and every day cannot be Sunday. This is just illusion. And every moment cannot be a moment of happiness. Who has ever heard that a person can live always in happiness? This is not possible. You must be getting some wrong notions, some delusions, or you have hypnotized yourself. Or something has gone wrong. Beware! This is not humanly possible."

Mind thinks that only misery is possible; it has a great investment in misery.

Remember it. Working here with me, by and by this moment will come to everybody. It has to come. That's what we are working for. When it comes, don't listen to the mind.

People come to me. They come here feeling so happy. How come? They have never felt so happy. And if I look at their faces, it seems that something has gone wrong. They are feeling happy, it appears to them that something has gone wrong.

I have heard about a great priest who was teaching his disciples about how to give religious sermons.

The priest was instructing his newly minted ministers on the importance of facial expression harmonizing with the speech.

"When you speak of heaven," he said, "let your face light up, let it be irradiated with a heavenly gleam, let your eyes shine with reflected glory. But when you speak of hell, well, then your ordinary faces will do."

Misery has settled; it has almost become your character. To be miserable has become your ordinary existence. When happiness comes, you cannot believe in it, you cannot trust in it.

This is a very ill state of affairs, but it is how it is. You will have to learn how to trust happiness, you will have to learn how to trust joy, you will have to learn how to be non-doubting when happiness comes, to be vulnerable, open. If you cannot learn that, happiness may knock at your door, and you may not open it.

Watch your patterns, and don't be so identified with them. People go on repeating the old tapes again and again and again. It is not that happiness has not knocked at your door, it has knocked many times. And it is not that God has not stretched his hand toward you; he has been groping for you for millennia. But you have become so clever and cunning in dodging him.

If the Devil comes and gets hold of you, you immediately surrender because you say, "What can I do?" If God comes to you, you cannot surrender because in the first place you cannot believe that God exists. This is really something. There are people who say there is no God, but still they believe in the Devil. It is difficult to believe in God, it is not so difficult to believe in the Devil. It is easier; in fact, without the Devil how will you be miserable? Without the Devil on whom will you throw your responsibilities? Whom will you find as an excuse? The Devil is your excuse. You can remain miserable, and you can say the Devil is making you miserable.

And this Devil goes on changing his form. It has taken many forms throughout history: sometimes it was fate; sometimes it was the Devil. Now according to Freudians it is your unconscious; and according to Marxists it is the social structure. But there is somebody who goes on creating misery for you. Nobody is creating misery for you. You are clinging to it. But this is very hard to accept because then your whole image becomes neurotic, and you carry a very golden image of yourself.

I have heard a very beautiful anecdote. It is a rare beauty...

Senior citizens, Israel and Emma, met at a singles' dance on Miami Beach, and within two weeks they were married. They felt it was a perfect match for they were both ninety years old.

On the first night of their honeymoon they got into bed, and the old man squeezed Emma's hand. She squeezed back, and they fell asleep.

The second night Israel squeezed her hand again. Emma squeezed back, and they went right to sleep.

On the third night Israel once more squeezed his bride's hand. "No, not tonight," said Emma, "I've got a headache."

People go on repeating old tapes to the very end.

This is an old tape that is creating the question, "What is happening to me?" as if something like a catastrophe, or something like a calamity is happening to you. Nothing is happening to you, you are coming back home. Nothing is happening to you, you are dropping nonsense, you are dropping the rotten mind, you have stopped playing the old tapes.

The second question:

Osho,
I am having a great struggle deep inside me before taking the final step, but last night when I slept in orange clothes, I felt myself a different person. What are you doing?

It is dangerous to take responsibility for you because one day things are going well, another day they are going bad. I'm not doing anything.

I have heard about a Sufi mystic who had a small school, and guests used to visit him from faraway places. One day a prince came to visit him, and the Sufi did not have the right pots, utensils, in which to prepare and offer food to this prince. So he went to the king, and he told him, "A prince has come to our poor school, and we will need a few pots, golden and silver, from you. We will return them tomorrow because by tomorrow morning he will be leaving." So he took seven pots.

The next day he came with nine pots. The king asked, "You took only seven, why have you brought nine pots? These two small pots don't belong to me."

He said, "What can I do? Last night your big pot gave birth to two twins. These are the twins."

The king could not believe it, could not think that it could happen, but greed overtook him. He said, "What is wrong in it? This man by some mistake has brought these pots, so why not accept?" He accepted. He said, "Very good. You are a very honest man. Otherwise who brings babies? If pots have babies, people keep the babies."

After a month the Sufi came again. He said, "Again the prince has come, and we need more pots because he has brought a few friends also." So he took almost twenty pots. But then he never came for two, three days.

The king called him, "What happened? You have not returned."

He said, "I am sorry. Ten of them died."

Now the king was very mad. He said, "Have you gone mad? How can pots die?"

He said, "Just think of that other time. If pots can give birth to babies, why can't they die?"

So today it was good, but I am not going to accept responsibility because tomorrow it will be bad, and then you will come to me and say, "Osho, what are you doing to me?"

It is you and only you. Don't throw your responsibilities anywhere.

This night you were a little good to yourself, you allowed something to happen. "I am having a great struggle deep inside me before taking the final step, but last night when I slept in orange clothes, I felt myself a different person. What are you doing?"

I am not doing anything at all; it was just the gesture of wearing orange. The person is not a sannyasin yet; that is his struggle. He is thinking continuously whether to take sannyas or not to take sannyas.

You allowed something. It was just like a rehearsal: you slept in orange clothes just to see what happens. The very idea that something was going to happen helped it happen. You relaxed in orange clothes, the mind was more at ease. At least you have done something, a very small gesture, but yet you have done something. At least you decided to sleep in orange.

For a person who has been continuously in conflict, even a slight decision gives such a relaxation that others cannot imagine. It will be difficult for others to see because they sleep in orange every night; they cannot believe that something could happen just because of orange.

But you don't know the person who has asked the question is in deep conflict, struggle, divided. Even this small gesture helped him to relax. Even this much courage, although it was not much because he must have put the light off so nobody could see. It was not much, but still something! He took courage in the darkness of the night to become a sannyasin. He must have felt good, relaxed.

Whenever you come to any decision, you feel good. And if the conflict is very great, the greater the conflict, the greater the happiness that will come out of this decision. But don't bring me in because it is very dangerous. I don't play that game at all.

Let me tell you one anecdote...

"Rabbi Jacobs, I need fifty dollars to get out of debt," sobbed Gottlieb. "I keep praying to God for help, but he doesn't send it!"

"Don't lose faith," said the rabbi. "Keep praying."

After Gottlieb left his house, the rabbi felt sorry for him. "I don't make much money," he thought, "but that poor man needs it. I'll give him twenty-five dollars out of my own pocket."

A week later the rabbi stopped Gottlieb and said, "Here, God sent this to you."

Back in his home, Gottlieb bowed his head. "Thank you, Lord," he said. "but next time you send money, don't send it through Rabbi Jacobs. That crook kept half of it."

So please be direct. Don't bring me in. Otherwise some day or other you are going to be angry with me.

So from the very beginning it is better to be clear. Now this man is going to take sannyas some day – he will have to – so I have to make it completely clear to him that it is his decision to take sannyas. It is not my persuasion. It is his decision to jump into the fire. I will keep myself completely clear, out of it. Only then does your decision help you to crystallize. When you take it on your own, absolutely on your own, you become centered.

Sannyas will make you more free, not less. Sannyas is not a sort of slavery, it is freedom – freedom from the formalities of the society, freedom from the oppressive burdens of the others, freedom to be yourself. Sannyas is an effort to become an individual. My help is available here, but it is only your decision which will change you. Even if you take my help, it is you who takes it. I am like a river flowing; it is your decision to drink out of me or not. It is absolutely yours, and let it be so. It needs much courage to take all the responsibility on one's shoulders, but that courage is a device.

It happened...

Feingold was on his deathbed. He was surrounded by his children. "Don't worry, Papa, we'll have a big funeral," declared his eldest son. "There'll be a hundred limousines, ten cars with flowers."

"We don't need all that!" interrupted Feingold's second son. "Fifty limos and five cars with flowers is more than enough."

"Whatta ya makin' such a big deal?" said the dying man's youngest son. "We don't need any flowers. We'll just have the immediate family. Two cars is enough."

At that moment Feingold raised himself up and said, "Listen, boys. Just hand me my pants, and I'll walk to the cemetery."

You have to walk! Don't wait for one hundred limousines and ten cars full of flowers. Nothing doing. Get into your pants and walk, but be on your own. Only that way one grows. There is no other way to grow.

The mind always wants to throw responsibility onto somebody else; the mind always wants to become a slave. The mind is a slave. It is afraid of freedom, it is afraid of responsibility; hence so many churches and so many organizations exist in the world because so many people are ready to fall in their traps. In fact, churches are not responsible. It is the people's need. Because they need certain types of imprisonments, somebody is going to provide them.

The economists say that in life there is a subtle law working of supply and demand, demand and supply. You demand and somebody is bound to come along to supply it. People demand slaveries for themselves; hence the existence of Hinduism, Christianity, Islam, and thousands of others who are ready to make a sheep out of you. They say, "Come here. Here is the shepherd." and you become just part of the crowd.

I am not here to make you a sheep. You have been a sheep for too long already. I am here to make a man out of you. It is going to be arduous, and you have to start becoming responsible for your own life. Once you start feeling responsible for your own life, you start growing because then there is no point in wasting time in postponing, in waiting. Nobody is coming to help you. All waiting is futile, all waiting is sheer wastage.

So if there is a conflict, go deep into it. Decide something. Only through decisions do you become more and more conscious, only through decisions do you become more and more crystallized, only through decisions do you become sharp. Otherwise one becomes dull.

People go on from one guru to another, from one master to another, from one temple to another, not because they are great seekers but because they are incapable of decision. So they go from one to another. This is their way to avoid commitment.

The same happens in other human relationships: a man goes from one woman to another, goes on changing. People think he is a great lover – he is not a lover at all. He is avoiding, he is trying to avoid any deep involvement because with deep involvement problems have to be faced, much pain has to be gone through. So one simply plays safe; so one makes it a point never to go too deep into somebody – because if you go too deep, you may not be able to come back easily. And if you go deep into somebody, somebody else will go deep into you also, it is always proportionate. If I go very deep in you, the only way is to allow you also to go that deep in me. It is a give and take, it is a sharing, and one may get entangled too much, and it will be difficult to escape, and the pain may be much. So people learn how to play safe: just let surfaces meet – hit-and-run love affairs, and before you are caught, you run.

This is what is happening in the modern world. People have become so juvenile, so childish. They are losing all maturity because maturity comes only when you are ready to face the pain of your being; maturity comes only when you are ready to take the challenge. And there is no greater challenge than love. To live happily with another person is the greatest challenge in the world. It is very easy to live peacefully alone, it is very difficult to live peacefully with somebody else because two worlds collide, two worlds meet – totally different worlds. That's how they are attracted to each other because they are totally different, almost opposite, polar opposites.

It is very difficult to be peaceful in a relationship, but that is the challenge. If you escape from that, you escape from maturity. If you go into it with all the pain, and still continue going into it, then by and by the pain becomes a blessing, the curse becomes a blessing. By and by, through the conflict, the friction, crystallization arises. Through the struggle you become more alert, more aware.

The other becomes like a mirror to you. You can see your ugliness in the other. The other provokes your unconscious, brings it to the surface. You will have to know all hidden parts of your being, and the easiest way is to be mirrored, reflected, in a relationship. Easier, I call it, because there is no other way, but it is hard. It is hard, arduous, because you will have to change through it.

And when you come to a master, an even greater challenge exists before you: you have to decide, and the decision is for the unknown, and the decision has to be total and absolute, irreversible. It is not a child's game; it is a point of no return. So much conflict arises, but don't go on continuously changing because this is the way to avoid yourself. And you will remain soft, you will remain babyish. Maturity will not happen to you.

I have heard...

After taking off her clothes for an examination, Mrs. Greenberg sat on the table.

"Lady," said the doctor, "I have to tell you that you are by far the dirtiest, filthiest, most unclean woman I have ever examined in my life."

"How d'ya like that!" said Mrs. Greenberg. "The doctor I went to yesterday said the same thing."

"Then why did you come here?"

"I wanted to get another opinion." answered Mrs. Greenberg.

People go on collecting opinions. Be finished. Take courage. You already have enough opinions with you. Decide.

One thing is certain: the past which you have lived has not been an enrichment for you, so there is nothing there for you in choosing it. Choosing the known has nothing for you, only the unknown. Only the unknown should have a call for you because that you have not lived yet; you have not moved in that territory. Move! – because something new may happen there. Always choose the unknown, whatsoever the risk, and you will grow continuously. If you go on choosing the known, then you will move in a circle with the past again and again. You will go on repeating it: you will become a gramophone record.

And decide, the sooner you can do so, the better. Postponement is simply stupid because tomorrow you will also have to decide, so why not today? And do you think that tomorrow you will be wiser than today? Do you think that tomorrow you will be livelier than today? Do you think that tomorrow you will be younger than today, fresher than today?

Tomorrow you will be older, your courage will be less; tomorrow you will be more experienced, your cunningness will be more; tomorrow death will come closer, you will start wavering and being more afraid. Never postpone for tomorrow. And who knows? Tomorrow may come or may not come. If you have to decide, you have to decide right now.

Dr. Vogel, the dentist, finished his examination on a pretty young patient. "Miss Baseman," he said, "I'm afraid I'm going to have to pull out your wisdom teeth."

"Oh my!" exclaimed the girl. "I'd rather have a baby!"

"Well," said Dr. Vogel, "could you make up your mind, so that I can adjust the chair?"

Make up your mind. Don't go on postponing indefinitely.

The third question:

Osho,
Sometimes it seems that wherever I go, I am facing the wall.

The wall is not outside, the wall is inside you. So wherever you go, you carry your wall. When you are alert, you feel it; when you are not alert, you don't feel it, but the wall is inside you. The wall is of your own ego; ego surrounds you like a wall. It persuades you that by surrounding you in this way, it will protect you. That's the seduction of the ego. It goes on telling you again and again, "If I am not there, you will be unprotected, you will become too vulnerable, and there will be too much risk. So let me guard you, let me surround you."

Yes, there is a certain protection in the ego, but the wall becomes your imprisonment also. There is a certain protection, otherwise nobody would suffer the miseries that ego brings. There is a certain protection, it protects you against the enemies, but then it starts protecting you against the friends also.

It is just as if you close your door and hide behind it because you are afraid of the enemy. Then a friend comes, but the door is closed, and he cannot enter. If you are too afraid of the enemy, then the friend also cannot enter into you. And if you open the door for the friend, there is every risk that the enemy may also enter.

One has to think about it deeply; it is one of the greatest problems in life. And only a very few courageous people tackle it rightly. Others become cowards and hide, and then their whole life is lost.

Life is risky; death has no risk. Die, and then there is no problem for you, and nobody is going to kill you because how can anybody kill you when you are already dead? Enter a grave and be finished. Then there is no illness, then there is no anxiety, then there is no problem; you are out of all problems.

But if you are alive, then there are millions of problems. The more alive a person, the more problems there are. But there is nothing wrong in it because struggling with problems, fighting with the challenge, is how you grow.

The ego is a subtle wall around you. It does not allow anybody to enter into you. You feel protected, secure, but this security is deathlike. It is the security of the plant inside the seed. The plant is afraid to sprout because – who knows? – the world is so hazardous, and the plant would be so soft, so fragile. Behind the wall of the seed, hiding inside the cell, everything is protected.

Or think of a small child in the mother's womb. Everything is there. Whatsoever is the need of the child is fulfilled immediately. There is no anxiety, no fight, no future. The child simply lives blissfully, and every need is fulfilled by the mother. But would you like to remain always in your mother's womb? It is very protective.

If it was given to you to choose, would you choose always to be in the mother's womb? It is very comfortable, what more comfort is possible? Scientists say that we have not yet been able to make a situation more comfortable than the womb. The womb seems to be the last, the ultimate in comfort. In fact, Freud and his followers say that the desire of *moksha* is nothing but the desire for the same lost womb of the mother. So comfortable – no anxiety, no problem, no need to work. Sheer existence. And everything is supplied immediately, automatically; the need arises and immediately it is supplied. There is not even the trouble of breathing: the mother breathes for the child. There is no bother about food: the mother eats for the child. But would you like to remain in the mother's womb? It is comfortable, very protective, but it is not life. Life is always in the wild. Life is there outside.

The English word *ecstasy* is very, very significant. It means: to stand out. Ecstasy means to get out, out of all shells and all protections and all egos and all comforts, and all deathlike walls. To be ecstatic means to get out, to be free, to be moving, to be a process, to be vulnerable, to be open, so that winds can come and pass through you.

We have an expression, sometimes we say, "That experience was outstanding." That exactly is the meaning of ecstasy: outstanding.

When a seed breaks and the life hidden behind starts manifesting, it is ecstasy. When a child is born and leaves the womb behind, and leaves the mother behind, and all the comforts and all the conveniences behind, moves into the unknown world, it is ecstasy. When a bird breaks the egg and flies into the sky, it is ecstasy.

The ego is the egg, and you will have to come out of it. Be ecstatic! Get out of all protections and shells and securities, then you will attain to the wider world, the vast, the infinite. Only then you live, and you live abundantly.

But fear cripples you. The child before he gets out of the womb must also be hesitating about whether to get out or not. To be or not to be? It must be taking one step forward and another step backward.

Maybe that's why the mother goes through so much pain. The child is hesitating, the child is not yet totally ready to be ecstatic. The past pulls it back, the future calls it forth, and the child is divided.

This is the wall of indecision, of clinging with the past, of clinging with the ego, and you carry it everywhere. Sometimes in rare moments when you are very alive and alert, you will be able to see it. Otherwise, it is a very transparent wall, and you will not be able to see it. One can live his whole life – and not one life, but many – without becoming aware that one is living inside a cell, closed from everywhere, windowless. It is what Leibnitz used to call "monad." No doors, no windows, just closed inside, but it is transparent, a glass wall.

"Sometimes it seems wherever I go, I am facing the wall." Yes, not facing it exactly, you are carrying the wall in front of your eyes. When your eyes have a clarity, then you see it; when your eyes are dull and you are unconscious, you can't see it.

This ego has to be dropped. One has to gather courage and shatter it on the floor. People go on feeding it in millions of ways, not knowing that they feed their own hell.

I have heard...

Mrs. Cochrane was standing beside the coffin of her dead husband. Their son stood at her elbow. The mourners, one by one, passed in review.

"He's feeling no pain now," said Mrs. Croy. "What did he die of?"

"Poor fella," said Mrs. Cochrane. "He died of gonorrhea!"

Another woman gazed at the corpse. "He's well out of it now," she said. "He's got a smile of serenity on his face. What did he die from?"

"He died of gonorrhea!" said the widow.

Suddenly the son pulled his mother aside. "Mom," he said, "that's a terrible thing to say about Pop. He didn't die of gonorrhea. He died of diarrhea."

"I know that," said Mrs. Cochrane. "but I'd rather have them thinking he died like a sport, instead of the shit that he was."

To the very end they go on continuously playing games.

The ego does not allow you to be true, it goes on forcing you to be false. The ego is the lie, and one has to decide that. It needs great courage because with it will shatter all that you have been nursing up to now. It will shatter your whole past. With it you will shatter completely. Somebody will be there, but you will not be that person. A discontinuous entity will arise in you, fresh, uncorrupted by the past. Then there will be no wall, then wherever you will be, you will see the infinite without any boundaries.

The old man, entering his favorite bar, found that the usual barmaid had been replaced by a stranger. He was nonplussed at first, but gallantly told her that she was "the best-looking girl I've seen in a long time."

The new barmaid, a haughty type, tossed her head and replied acidly, "I'm sorry I can't return the compliment."

"Oh well, my dear," the old man answered placidly, "Couldn't you have done as I did? Couldn't you have told a lie?"

All our formalities are nothing but helping each other's ego. They are all lies. You say something to somebody, and he returns the compliment. Neither you are true, nor he is true. We go on playing the game: etiquette, formality, the civilized faces and masks.

Then you will have to face the wall, and by and by, the wall will become so thick that you will not be able to see anything. The wall goes on getting thicker and thicker every day, so don't wait. If you have come to feel that you are carrying a wall around you, drop it. Jump out of it. It takes only a decision to jump out of it, nothing else. Then from tomorrow don't feed it. Then whenever you see that you are again nursing it, stop. Within a few days you will see it has died because it needs your constant support, it needs breastfeeding.

The last question:

Osho,
When the other bank is this very bank, then there is no need for enlightenment. If one is alive in this moment, then why should one dream of enlightenment?

These questions with "then" and "if" are very cunning questions, and you are not deceiving anybody else. You are deceiving yourself. Listen to the question again. "When the other bank is this very bank, then there is no need for enlightenment."

If you have come to know that the other bank is this very bank, then you have already become enlightened; there is no need. This is what enlightenment is all about. If you have come to know that this moment is all, and the place where you are is the whole, and that this world is the other world you have attained – you are liberated. Because if there is no other world, there cannot be desire. If this moment is all, all desiring ceases.

"When the other bank is this very bank, then there is no need for enlightenment." Absolutely true. "If one is alive in this moment, then why should one dream of enlightenment?" There is no need, but these questions won't help. It has not happened to you. This bank is not yet the other bank, and this moment is not yet the eternity.

You have listened to me, and you have become parrotlike. I say "There is no need for any enlightenment, the very search for enlightenment is nightmarish," but that is not going to help. You will have to drop all searching, then you will be able to realize the fact that you are already enlightened.

There is nowhere to go, you are already there, you have always been there from the very beginning, there has been no going astray. We have lived in godliness, we have lived as gods, there is no other way.

If you have understood this, then there is no need for enlightenment, it has already happened. If you have not understood it – you have simply listened to me, and you are playing with words – then you will be getting into more and more confusion.

Your desire will not stop by these "whens" and "ifs"; it will continue. Your ambition will not disappear. Be more practical; don't become theoretical, don't become metaphysical, don't become philosophical. Be more practical. Listen to your own state. You have desires of the other shores, you have desires for tomorrow, a better tomorrow, you have hopes for a future, you are continuously hoping that something is going to happen, something great, something extraordinary, something special. And only to you and to nobody else.

These "ifs" and "whens" will not stop that. If you can drop all hoping, all desiring – what Zen people call *trishna* – if you can drop all desire to become somebody or something, if you can drop becoming, if you understand the foolishness of hoping and desiring and it disappears and you are left without any trace of desire, that's what enlightenment is.

Then there is no need, but be practical.

I have heard...

Scientists concluded that the ice cap was going to melt, and the whole world would be flooded within six months.

When the news broke, religious leaders went into deep conference. The Protestant hierarchy released a statement: "Because of the impending disaster, Protestants will go to church and pray for two hours every day."

Then the Catholics made an announcement: "Because of the coming deluge, Catholics will make every other day, all day, a day of prayer, for the next six months."

Rabbis from all over the land convened, then they too issued a message to the world: "Because the whole world will be flooded within six months, Jews will learn how to live under water."

Be more practical, be more of a Jew. Otherwise my words can mislead you. I have no intention even to guide you, but my words can misguide you because you can take them on the surface.

You can say, "Yes, Osho says there is no need for enlightenment, so forget all about meditation and be the fool you have always been." This is not going to change you. Try to understand each word that I say to you. Each word that I utter is pregnant with tremendous meaning, but you will have to decode it.

The rabbi had stood before the synagogue's board of directors for almost an hour pleading with them to buy a chandelier for the temple.

When he'd finished, Blum, the elderly president, stood up. "What're we wasting time talkin' for?" he demanded. "First of all, a chandelier; we ain't got nobody who could even spell it."

"Second, we ain't got nobody here who could play it."

"And third, what we need in the synagogue is more light."

That's how things go. That's what the poor rabbi is saying all the time: a chandelier is needed.

What I am saying to you is that you need a deep centering in the herenow so that no desire of the world distracts you, no desire of liberation distracts you. You are so deeply herenow that you are simply herenow; your mind is moving nowhere else, your mind is not wandering anywhere.

In that pure moment, completely centered and grounded, you are enlightened. But you will have to attain to that moment, and that cannot be attained by great philosophical talk. You will have to work hard, you will have to be very practical. Right now as you are, you are completely drunk, drunk with desire.

He had been to a party and had imbibed a little too freely. Along about four in the morning he was staggering home. Crossing a bridge he met a policeman; the cop was a friend, and they leaned over the bridge rail to converse a bit.

"What's that down there in the water?" the drunk suddenly asked.

"Look again. That's the moon," said the cop.

He looked again, shook his head, and then demanded, "Okay, okay. But how the hell did I get way up here?"

Because the moon is so far down, how the hell did I get way up here?

I go on talking to you knowing well that you are drunk with a thousand and one desires. I am telling you to drop these thousand and one desires. And you are ready to drop them if I can give you a new desire for them, if I can give you a bigger substitute, if I can give you one great desire so that all desires can be sacrificed for it. You are ready to drop your desires, but you are ready to drop them only for a greater desire. That I cannot do because the greater desire will be a greater bondage to you. Hence Zen people say that enlightenment is a nightmare. Hence Zen people say, "Don't try to become a buddha, otherwise you will fall into the seventh hell. Don't try to reach to the ultimate reality because your very desire to reach it will hinder you." All desiring is a hindrance; the desire for godliness and liberation also.

You would like me to give you a big desire, a desire with capital letters, so big that you can pour your small, tiny desires into it. But that is not what I am going to do. I want you to drop all your desires and not to substitute them with anything else. Only then can you be desireless.

Desireless, you are enlightened.

Enlightenment is not somewhere waiting for you, it is already here. It surrounds you right now. It is within you and without you. It is in every beat of your heart. Enlightenment is here; you are not here. You are chasing your desires far away, somewhere in the future, on some planets. You are not to find enlightenment somewhere else, the only thing that you have to do is to come back home, enlightenment is waiting for you there. You simply don't go anywhere, that's all. The whole effort is negative – don't go anywhere. Enlightenment is not a journey, it is your deepest core of being.

It is like you sleep in Pune, and you dream in the night that you are in Philadelphia. And you are in Pune all the same, whether you dream of Philadelphia or not. You are lying down here sleeping in your room, and in your dream you are in Philadelphia. In the morning you open your eyes, and you say it was all a dream because you find yourself in Pune, not in Philadelphia.

Those who have awakened have found themselves in enlightenment. Philadelphia was a dream. This world is a dream; when you awake, this world disappears, and you find yourself in the other world. This bank is a dream. When you awake, suddenly you find you have been always on the other bank, and you were dreaming about this bank. Desire is a dream, desire is a dreaming process. It leads you away, but it leads you away only in the mind, not in reality. In reality you are gods; in minds it depends. You can make anything out of your mind.

That's what Hindus say: that it is mind which makes you a tree, it is mind which makes you a tiger, it is mind which makes you a cuckoo, it is mind which makes you a man. When there is no mind, you are a god. Godliness is your reality, and everything else that you see is just dream.

If you understand, there is no need for any enlightenment. If you don't understand, then be alert: listening to me can be dangerous. You can stop all meditations, you can stop all work, and you can say there is no need, but then you will remain in Philadelphia.

Enough for today.

CHAPTER 9

the nondual has come

Ho-shan used to give the following sermon: "To discipline ourselves in learning is called hearing; to reach a point where any more learning no more avails is called approaching. When one goes beyond these two stages, he is said to have truly transcended."
Once a monk asked, "What then is true transcending?"
Without uttering a word Ho-shan motioned as if beating a drum, saying, "Dang, dang, doko dang, doko dang."
To all such questions Ho-shan's answer was always the same: "Dang, dang, doko dang, doko dang."

What is truth?

This is the question every man has to answer on his own, and unless a man answers this question he is not truly a man.

This question has haunted humanity down the centuries. It is as old as man himself because man became man only when he asked this question: "What is truth?" Unless we know what truth is, our whole effort to live, our whole effort to make a meaning out of life is futile.

It is ultimate, but urgent also, to know from where life has arisen, and to want to know the source and the goal, to know the inner running current that holds everything, to know the thread which is the ultimate law of existence. When we ask the question, "What is truth?" we are entering into the world of man for the first time. If you have not asked the question yet, then you live below human being. Ask the question, and you become part of humanity. And when the question is dissolved, you go beyond humanity, you become a god.

Below the questioning you remain part of the animal kingdom. With the question you enter on the path; and again being without the question, you have come to realize that you have come home. The question is very difficult because just by asking, it cannot be solved. One has to put one's whole life at the stake.

This is the question that Pontius Pilate asked Jesus. At the last moment when Jesus was going to be crucified, Pontius Pilate asked him, "What is truth?" And Jesus did not answer him. Christian mystics have pondered over it. Why did Jesus not answer it? Why did he remain silent?

There are three possibilities. One, that the question was not sincere. And a man like Jesus answers only when the question is sincere. When is a question sincere? A question is sincere when a questioner is ready to do something about it. If it is just curiosity, then it is not worth answering. If it has an intense passion, a deep desire, so deep that the questioner is ready to put his whole life at the stake – because nothing less will do – only then is the question sincere. A man like Jesus will answer only when the question has been asked from the very core of one's being. So the first possibility is that Pilate's question was not sincere. Seeing the insincerity, Jesus remained silent.

Pilate was a well-educated man, a man who had succeeded at least in the eyes of the world. He was the viceroy, a Roman Governor-General. He was at the peak of his career – power, prestige, wealth, everything was his. Whatsoever he had been doing in his life had paid him well. Standing facing him was Jesus, almost a hobo, a failure, who had not achieved anything at least in the eyes of the world. He had no power, no prestige, not even respectability. He was just at the other end of life, a tremendous failure, mocked, jeered, insulted. Whatsoever he had been doing had all failed. It had not paid him in any way. His life was futile, at least for others.

The successful man asked the failure, "What is truth?"

There are two types of successes in the world. One, the worldly which is not really a success but just trying to deceive yourself, just trying to keep up faces, appearances. The eyes are full of tears, but you go on smiling; the heart is miserable, but you go on showing something else, just the opposite, to the world. They say "Nothing succeeds like success," but I would like to tell you nothing fails like success. As far as the inner journey is concerned, as far as the transcendental is concerned, nothing fails like success, and nothing succeeds like failure.

The first possibility is that the question was not sincere, it was asked just by the way. The man was well educated, well trained in philosophical concepts. He could have asked the question as a philosophical question. Then Jesus remained silent because the question was not really asked, and there was no need to answer it.

The second possibility is that the question was sincere, that the question was not just a childish curiosity, there was passion behind it, it was authentic. Then why did Jesus remain silent? He remained silent because if this ultimate question is asked authentically, then silence is the answer because there is no way to answer it except silence. The question is so profound that words will not be capable of answering it. The question is so deep that words will not be able to reach it, to touch it – only silence will.

If the second is the case, then Jesus did answer it, but he answered it by silence.

There is also a third possibility: that the question was sincere, and yet not so sincere – that it was ambiguous, split, which was probably the case because where can you find a man who is total? A part of him was authentically asking, another part was pretending, "Even if you don't answer, I am not in a hurry. Even if you don't answer, I don't mind because, in fact, I don't need it. In fact, I know the answer already, I am asking just to test you."

The question was ambiguous, Janus-faced. That seems to be more probable because that is how man is and has always been – split. A part of Pilate feels the truth of this man who is standing before him – a complete, utter failure, but yet his eyes are luminous, yet he has a glow. Pilate can feel it, can almost touch it. Yet another part, the egoistic part, is not ready to surrender, so he pretends that he is asking only casually, "Even if you don't answer, don't be worried. It is not my need. In fact, I already know the answer."

If this ambiguity was the case, then Jesus would also remain silent because when a question is ambiguous and the person is divided, no answer is possible. Because the answer can be understood only in your undivided consciousness, the question can be answered only when you are no longer split, when you are one, when you are in a unison, unity. Only then can you understand it.

Jesus' silence before Pontius Pilate is very significant, pregnant with many meanings. But Jesus has answered the question somewhere else. It is recorded in the New Testament. Somewhere else he says, "I am the Truth."

I would like you to go a little bit into history then it will be very easy to understand today's parable.

Homer asked the same question in 850 B.C. and he answered that "The whole is supported by fate, and fate is the truth."

This is not really an answer; in fact, it is avoiding. When you say, "It is fate," you don't say much; in fact, you are not saying anything, you are simply playing with a word. You have simply shifted the question. It doesn't answer. If somebody is miserable and you say, "It is fate," how have you answered it? Your answering has not added anything to the already-known situation. You have simply labeled it. "One is suffering because it is fate." But why is it so? Why is fate so? No, it is not a real answer. In fact, it is a lie, but one can believe in such things. Many people still do the same as Homer did. They have not risen above that level of consciousness.

Then came Thales, 575 B.C. He said that the whole consists of nothing but water. Water is the basic element of truth, of life, and of existence.

Better than fate, something more tangible, but very fragmentary. Water does not go very deep, does not explain much. It is reducing the higher to the lowest. Thales must have had a scientific mind; that's what science goes on doing. You ask about mind, and they say it is nothing but matter. The higher is reduced to the lower; the sky is explained by the earth. Mind is a great evolution. To explain the mind by matter is a scientific fallacy.

Thales was the first scientist of the world. He tried to explain the unknowable by something known: he called it water, the liquid element, the liquidity, the flow. But the answer is very fragmentary. It has something of truth in it but not all of it. And a fragmentary truth is even more dangerous than a lie because it has a certain appearance of truth, and it can deceive more. That fragment of truth can become very deceptive; it can cover the whole lie, and make it appear as if it were the truth.

Then came Pythagoras, 530 B.C. He says that the whole consists only of numbers, mathematical symbols. He has even more of a scientific attitude than Thales – mathematics. Meaningful, but mathematics is not life. In fact, all that is very alive is non-mathematical. Love is non-mathematical, you cannot reduce it to numbers. Poetry is non-mathematical. Just think of life consisting only of numbers – one, two, three, four – all poetry disappears, all love disappears, all dreaming disappears. Life would not be worth living.

That's how it is happening today. Scientists have reduced everything to mathematical equations. Life is not equal to equations howsoever accurate the equations; life is more than mathematics can ever explain. The mathematics cannot explain the mathematician, the mathematician who deals in numbers is higher and bigger than numbers. It has to be so; those numbers are just toys in his hands. But who is this player? Whenever life is reduced to mathematics, it loses charm, it loses charisma, it loses mystery, and suddenly everything seems to be worthless. Mystery is needed; it is subtle nourishment for growth.

I have heard two mathematicians talking. One said to another, "Is there any meaning in life? Is there any worth? Is there any purpose?"

The other said, "But what else can you do with it?"

The first asked, "Is there any meaning to live for in life?" and the other says, "What else can you do with it?" If life has to be lived just as if you were a victim, as if somebody were playing a trick upon you, as if you were being thrown into this torture chamber, into this concentration camp called the earth, then even if you live, you don't live enough. You slowly commit suicide. You by and by, by and by, go on disappearing. Suicide becomes a constant thought in the mind if life has no mystery.

Then came Anaxagoras, 450 B.C. and his answer is mind. Certainly he took a great leap from water, number, fate; he took a great jump. Anaxagoras is a great milestone in the history of humanity. "Mind," he says. "The whole existence is made of the stuff called mind."

Better, but Jesus would not agree, Buddha would not agree. Yes, certainly better than what others were saying, but Zen would not agree. Matter, mind... Zen says no-mind. One has to go higher still because mind still carries the duality with matter.

Good, great in a way, a radical step; from object Anaxagoras turns to the subject, from the outer he turns to the inner. He opens the door. He is the first psychologist in the world because he emphasizes mind more than matter. He says matter is also made of mind; he explains the lower with the higher.

You can explain it in two ways. Go and see beautiful white lotus flowers in a pond; they come out of dirty mud. Then there are two possibilities: either you explain the lotus by the dirty mud or you explain the dirty mud by the lotus. And each will lead you in totally different dimensions. If you say that this lotus is nothing but dirty mud because it comes out of it, your life will lose all significance, meaning, beauty. Then you will live in the dirty mud.

That's what Freud has been doing; that's what Marx has done. They have great skill in reducing everything to the dirty mud. If Buddha attains to enlightenment, ask Freud; he will say it is nothing but sex energy. There is a truth in it because it arises out of sex, but the sex functions like dirty mud, and out of it arises the lotus.

Ask Buddha; he will say sex is nothing but the beginning of enlightenment, the very first steps of nirvana. That's how Tantra was born.

These are two ways, and you have to remember that your life will depend more or less on the way you interpret, on the way you choose. If you try to reduce the lotus to dirty mud, it can be done, and it is very scientific. It can be done very scientifically because all that this lotus has was in the mud. It can be dissected, and everything can be found, and then the mud can be dissected, and whatsoever the lotus has, everything will be found in the mud; there is nothing special, nothing extra, nothing from the outside has entered into the lotus, so it is nothing but the mud. But then you are choosing your life with this attitude, your life will be just nothing but mud.

And the person who says that the mud is nothing but potential white lotuses, that the mud is nothing but a waiting to manifest its beauty in lotuses, has a higher standpoint, the standpoint of a religious man. Then the whole life becomes full of splendor, significance, glory. Then wherever you look, you can find godliness, you can find the white lotus. Then everything is moving toward the peak. Then there is evolution. Then there is future, possibility. Then even the impossible becomes possible.

With the first attitude – the dirty-mud attitude I call it – even the possible seems to be impossible. But with the second attitude – the lotus attitude I call it – you can see deeply into mud, and you can see hidden lotuses there. And the dirty mud is no longer dirty mud, it is just potentiality. Then sex becomes potentiality for *samadhi*, the body becomes potentiality for the soul, and the world becomes the abode of godliness.

Anaxagoras was one of the greatest revolutionaries, a radical thinker. This word *radical* is beautiful. It means pertaining to the roots. He changed the outlook. He said, "Mind." He took a necessary step, but that too was not enough.

Then came Protagoras, 445 B.C. and he said, "Man." Now his standpoint is more total. Mind is a fragment of man. Man is many things more, mind plus. If Anaxagoras is thought to be absolutely true, then you will remain in the head; that is what has happened to many people. They have not moved beyond Anaxagoras. They go on living in the head because mind is all. Then mind becomes dictatorial, it goes on a great ego trip. It starts dominating everything and crippling everything. It becomes a destructive force.

No, you are not only mind. You are mind, certainly, but plus. Many more things are there.

A lotus cannot exist alone, the flower cannot exist alone, it will need many more things to exist, the pond, the water, the air, the sun, its connection with the mud, and leaves, and a thousand and one things. So if you think only in terms of the lotus and you forget all connections with the universe, your lotus will be a plastic lotus. It will not be a real lotus, it will not be interconnected, it will not be rooted in existence.

Protagoras has a more holy attitude, holistic attitude. Man and the totality of man – the body, the mind, the soul – becomes truth.

Then came Socrates, 435 B.C. and he said, "Wisdom, knowing, knowledge." When man attains to maturity, he becomes wise; when man comes to fulfillment, then wisdom arises. Wisdom is the essence of man, the fragrance of the lotus flower. A still higher attitude.

And then came Jesus who says, "I am the truth." This one statement is one of the greatest statements ever made in the world. Either it is the greatest truth ever uttered, or it is the most egoistic and arrogant statement ever made. "I am the truth." It depends how you decode it. Ordinarily when you hear that Jesus says, "I am the truth," you think this man is a megalomaniac, has gone mad. He is uttering nonsense. This man is truth? Jesus is truth? Then what about us all?

Jesus is not saying that, you have misunderstood him. When he says, "I am the truth," he is not saying, "Jesus, son of Mary and Joseph, is the truth." What he is saying is totally different. He is saying "I amness, I am is the truth," so wherever there is this "I amness" there is truth. When you say "I am," you are uttering truth. Your "I am" and my "I am" are not two things, we both participate there. Your name is different, your form is different, my name is different, my form is different, but when I say "I, I am" and you say "I am" we refer to some common experience, we refer to some common root. Your "I amness" and my "I amness" are not different, are not separate, they belong to one "I amness" of existence. When Jesus says "I am the truth," he means wherever this integration is felt of being totally "I am," there is truth.

Ordinarily you are many i's – you don't have any capital I; you have many i's, lowercase. Gurdjieff used to say that we should not use the word *I*, only God can use it because you don't have any single I, you have many I's like a crowd. For one moment one I comes on the top and becomes the ruler; in another moment it is gone, and another I comes over and rules.

You can watch it. It is so simple. One moment you say, "I am happy. I am tremendously happy, at the top of the world" and the next moment you are unhappy, at the lowest bottom of the world, in the seventh hell. Are both these I's the same? One moment you were flowing, and you were compassionate and loving, and another moment you were closed and frozen and dead. Are these two I's the same? One moment you could have forgiven anything, and another moment just any small tiny thing, and you cannot forgive. Are these two I's the same? One moment you are sitting in silence, in zazen, meditating, and you look so buddhalike, and another moment for a small thing you are nagging, fighting. You will yourself feel ridiculous later on. For what were you getting so hot? For what were you creating so much fuss? It was not worth it. But another I was ruling over you.

You are like a wheel of many I's; those I's are like spokes. The wheel goes on moving, one spoke comes on top; hardly before it has come it starts declining. It goes on changing. Again it will come up, and again you will feel a different being existing there within you. Watch. Have you got an I? Any substantial I? Any essential I? Can you say that you have some permanent I in you? A crystallized I in you?

You promise, and next moment you have forgotten your promise. Gurdjieff used to say that unless you have a permanent I, never promise. You will not be able to fulfill it. Who will fulfill it? You say to a woman, "I love you, and I will love you forever and ever." Wait! What are you uttering? What nonsense. Forever and ever? How can you promise? You don't know what is going to happen tomorrow, you don't know who is going to rule you tomorrow. Your promises will create trouble for you. You cannot promise because you are not there. Only a man like Gurdjieff or Jesus can promise. Yes, he can promise because he knows that he will remain the same; whatsoever changes in the world will not affect him. He will remain the same, he has come to a crystallized soul. Now he knows that his wheel has stopped. He is in total possession of his being. He can promise.

But ordinarily people go on promising, and you never see the fact that no promise has ever been fulfilled by you. You completely forget about it. You don't even remember it because that remembrance will be like a wound, and you find out ways and means to rationalize it: you cannot fulfill it because the other person has changed, you cannot fulfill it because the circumstances have changed, you cannot fulfill it because you were foolish at the time you made it. And again you will make promises.

Man is an animal who goes on promising, never fulfilling any promise because he cannot fulfill it; man as he exists has too many I's.

When Jesus says "I am the truth," he is saying that whosoever attains to "I amness" is truth. And this truth is not something philosophical, this truth is something existential. You cannot come to it by logic, argumentation. You cannot come to it by finding a right premise and then moving toward a right syllogism and then reaching to a right conclusion. No, that is not the way. You will have to come to it through an inner discipline. That's what Zen is all about.

Now this story.

This story says everything that is needed for a seeker to come to truth, the truth of "I amness." It is "I am" that holds the whole existence together. Moses asked God on Mount Sinai, "I will go back to my people, and I will say that I have seen God, but they will not believe me. So please tell me how I am to convince them. And they will ask "Who is this God?" So please tell me what is your name, who you are, so that I can convince them. Otherwise they will not be ready to believe me." And God said to Moses, "Go and tell them

I am, I am." No name, simply "I am, I am." This is what Jesus is saying – "I am the truth."

It has nothing to do with Jesus, it has nothing to do with any person, it is your innermost core, which is absolutely impersonal. It is never born and never dies. It is your innermost current of life. It is from where you are connected with godliness. It is from where you are one with existence.

This has to be found, not by thinking but by a great, deep discipline.

Now this story.

Ho-shan used to give the following sermon: "To discipline ourselves in learning is called hearing..."

This is the first step. *"To discipline ourselves in learning is called hearing..."* First one has to discipline oneself. What is discipline?

Ordinarily the word has very wrong connotations. Somebody else disciplines you – your parents, the society. Always it is the other who disciplines you, so the very word has wrong associations. It has been wrongly used, misused. A beautiful word has been very much corrupted. Discipline is not from the outside. Nobody else can discipline you. Discipline is from the inside; discipline is an understanding, and that is the word's meaning also. It comes from the same root as *disciple.* Can somebody make you a disciple? Think of it. Can discipelhood be thrown over you? Can you be forced to become a disciple? No, you can either take it or reject it, but the ultimate decision is yours. To become a disciple means to voluntarily surrender. If the surrender is not voluntary, it is not a surrender. If you are being forced to surrender, then deep down you will resist, and you will wait for the right moment when you can throw off this slavery.

The first Christians, those who had the great opportunity to live with Jesus, to imbibe his spirit, used to call themselves slaves of Jesus. The first Christians used the word *slave* for themselves, but their slavery was not a slavery forced on them. Even if a freedom is forced on you, it is a slavery, and if you accept a slavery on your own, it is freedom. They were freed by Jesus, liberated by Jesus, and they loved the man so much they called themselves slaves.

A disciple is one who surrenders according to his own heart. Nobody is forcing him to surrender. If any force is used, then exactly there something goes wrong. If you are a Christian because your parents forced you to become a Christian, or if you are a Hindu because your parents forced you to become a Hindu... And that's how people are Hindus and Mohammedans and Christians. They have been forced. The parents have somehow conditioned their minds to be Hindus, Christians or Mohammedans, it is not their own choice. Then out of it discipline cannot arise; in fact, out of it rebellion arises, out of it a great resistance arises, out of it your innermost life energy becomes angry, annoyed, irritated, and for your whole life you can never forgive those people who forced you.

And religion is a very delicate matter – more delicate than love. Just think: if you are forced to love a woman or a man, the very effort that you are being coerced into loving will destroy love. Even if there was love, it will disappear, it will evaporate.

I have heard a very beautiful story about an Egyptian king. He was in love, deeply in love with a woman, but the woman was not in love with him. He could have forced it on her, but his wise advisors prevented him.

They said, "Don't do that. You can force it, she is your subject. You can simply bring her to your palace, but it will be almost a rape, not a love. You may even get children out of her, but you will never get her heart. That is not the way."

Then the king said, "What to do? I cannot live without her, and she is not in love with me, that's a fact, so the only way is to force. What do you suggest?"

They asked him, "Is she in love with somebody else?"

The king said, "Yes, she is in love with one of my servants, and this is foolish, stupid. She is blind!"

That's what so-called clever people have always been saying. They think of other things: economics, finance, respect and other things, but not of love.

The king said, "She is foolish. She cannot see the point. It is so simple. She is blind, mad. I can give her a thousand and one slaves, and she is in love with one of my poor servants. And I am the king. So what to do?"

Those wise people suggested a very novel experiment. It had never been done before, and I don't know that it has ever been done again. They said, "Catch them both. Bring them both to the palace, and just in front of the palace, bind them both together naked, in deep embrace. And bind them to the pillar and leave them there."

The king said, "What will that do?"

They said, "Just wait."

So they both were caught and undressed. They were ordered to embrace each other, forced to be loving to each other, and they were bound to a marble pillar. And for twenty-four hours they were left there to be looked at by the whole town.

By and by they started getting angry at each other because the lover thought, "It is because of her I am suffering this calamity." And the woman started thinking, "Because of him." And because they were forced to be together, they started resisting. They wanted to separate, but there was no way. They were bound in chains. Twenty-four hours – just think – with your beloved, bound on a pillar.

By and by, more and more anger arose. Then they started smelling each other's perspiration, it was hot. And then they couldn't sleep. And they pissed on each other. And they vomited. And it became a very ugly affair, horrible, a nightmare.

And the story says that after twenty-four hours, when they were released, they escaped in different directions and never saw each other ever again.

If you are forced to love, forced to be together with someone, that very enforcement will kill something subtle within you. That's why husbands cannot forgive their wives, and wives cannot forgive their husbands. It is impossible to forgive those with whom you are forced to live by the law, by society, by responsibility, or by your own conscience – but forced.

Disciplehood is an even higher thing than love. Nobody can force you to become a disciple. And *discipline* comes from the same root; it means "with full awareness you accept something on your own." It is your heart's desire.

"To discipline ourselves in learning is called hearing..." And Buddhists call the first step of learning, of knowing, hearing; right-hearing – *samyak shravan.* If somebody has attained the truth, if somebody has attained, then listen to him. Nothing else is needed. Listen to his vibes, listen to his being, listen to the murmur of his inner sound. Just listen. If you can find a person who has come home, then just listen to his calmness, his tranquillity, his bliss.

By "right-listening" is meant "to be rightly receptive." Learning is not active, it is passive. You are not to do anything about it, you cannot be aggressive about truth, you can simply allow it, that's all. You can simply be there in front of it, in close vicinity, passive, allowing, not resisting, not creating any barrier. Remove all barriers and be in the presence of a man who has attained, and this is right-listening. If he says something, listen to his word; if he does not say something, listen to his silence.

When he is not saying something, then too go on listening, and in his nonsaying you will find tremendous expression. And when he is saying something, go on listening deeply because when he is saying something, he is at the same time transferring his silence to you. When he is speaking, he is silent also, and when he is silent, he is speaking also. A tremendous quality of listening is needed.

If you cannot find any person, don't be worried, then listen to nature, then listen to the winds passing through the pines, then listen to the waterfall, go and listen to the wild ocean. Go and listen to the birds; anything will do. This is something very important to remember: if right-listening is there, then even listening to a waterfall will do. And if right-listening is not there, then even listening to Jesus or Buddha won't do.

The truth happens when you are in the mood of right-listening. It has nothing to do with the object of listening; it has everything to do with the quality of listening. But we have forgotten how to listen. Even when we are silent, we are not listening. Even when we pretend to show that yes, we are listening, we are not listening; we are doing a thousand and one things in the mind. Many thoughts are crowding in. Politely we show that yes, we are listening, politely sometimes we nod also; we are listening, but deep inside is the madhouse. How can you listen?

To listen you will have to drop your thinking. With thoughts, listening is not possible. If you are speaking inside and I am speaking here, how can you listen to me? Because you are closer to yourself than me, your thoughts will be closer to you, they will make a ring around you, and they will not allow my thoughts to enter. They will allow only those thoughts which are in tune with them, they will choose and select. They will not allow anything that is strange, unfamiliar, unknown. Then it is not worth listening because you are simply listening to your own thoughts. And it is dangerous because now you will think that you have listened to me. Right-listening means to be in a totally receptive, silent mood.

In Zen the disciple sits for many months, sometimes years, before he becomes capable of listening. Whenever anybody would come to Buddha, he would say, "For one year or two years simply sit here. Nothing else has to be done. Simply learn how to sit."

People would say, "We know already how to sit."

And Buddha would say, "I have never come across a person who naturally knows how to sit because when I say sit, I mean sit – no turmoil, no movement of thought, totally silent, utterly silent, no movement in the body, no movement in the mind. A pool of energy with no ripples."

"To discipline ourselves in learning is called hearing..." So the whole Buddhist discipline, Zen discipline, starts by right-listening.

> *"...to reach a point where any more learning no more avails is called approaching."*

Then there comes a moment when you become so silent that the listener disappears. First your thoughts disappear, then your thinker disappears because the thinker cannot remain without thoughts. The thinker is nothing but the interlink between thoughts. The thinker cannot exist without thoughts. When thoughts are no longer there, suddenly the thinker evaporates. When you are listening so totally that there is no thought arising, passing, coming and going, then the listener also disappears.

"...where any more learning no more avails..." Then this is the moment where nothing can be got from the outside – *learning no more avails* – now there is no need, now you are enough unto yourself. This is what Zen people call "approaching." Now you are coming home, approaching, closer, closer, closer.

So first you are full of thoughts. To drop those thoughts, hearing is emphasized – hear the master, or the winds, or the thundering clouds. Listening is used as a device to drop thoughts. When thoughts are dropped, one day you will realize the thinker has disappeared. Now there is no longer anything like a listener. The device has worked, the work is over. Now there is no need to listen to the outside because there is nothing to learn from the outside. This is what Zen calls "approaching." Now you are approaching home, now everything is within you, you are coming to the innermost shrine.

Thoughts do not allow you to listen, and the thinker does not allow you to enter into yourself. The thinker is the subtlest part of thoughts; thoughts are gross thinker, and thinker is subtle thoughts. Thoughts prevent you from listening to the outside, and the thinker prevents you from listening to the inside. First drop thoughts because the gross can be dropped more easily so that you can listen to the outside. Then the thinker disappears. Now you can listen to the inside. Then the master speaks from the innermost core of your heart. The outer master is just a help to create the inner master; the outer master is just a provocation for the inner master to come into its full swing, to come into its full being. The outer master is just a situation so that the inner master can awaken.

And,

When one goes beyond these two stages, he is said to have truly transcended.

Now comes the last point. First you drop thoughts, then you drop the thinker. First the outside master disappears, the outside object disappears, then you come to the inside. But the inside can exist only with the outside. As I told you, the thinker can exist only with thoughts; in exactly the same way, the inside can exist only with the outside. If the outside disappears, the inside also disappears because they are both two aspects of the same coin. So first the outside disappears, then you come in, and suddenly you find one day that the inside is also disappearing because it is nothing but the innermost core of the outer. They are both together. How can you have an inside if you don't have an outside?

Just think of a house which has only an inside, no outside. How can it have only an inside without the outside? Or how can it have only the outside without any inside? They both exist together.

When inside and outside both disappear, Ho-shan says, *...one is said to have truly transcended.* Then there is neither out nor in, neither thoughts nor thinking, neither outside master nor inside master. It is a tremendous emptiness. Nothing is, or only nothing is. This is transcendence, this is nirvana, enlightenment. Then freedom is utterly complete because there is no boundary; you are without boundary.

This is what Jesus means when he says, "I am the truth." This is what "I am" is.

Once a monk asked, "What then is truly transcending?"

Now this is a foolish question to ask, a stupid question to ask. Because when there is no outside, no inside, no thinker, no thought, then there is no possibility of any answer. If you have understood, then you will not ask what this transcendence is. It is meaningless. You have come to a point where no question can be asked.

This monk must not have understood. So he asked, *"What then is truly transcending?"* The question again brings you back to the first step. Now right-listening is needed. Do you see it? The question again brings you to the first step. The monk has not transcended the first step yet. He has not listened otherwise he would have understood. He must have been there listening ordinarily. He had ears, so he could listen. And he must have understood these words because he could use the words, *"What then is truly transcending?"* He must know language, of course, and he has ears, so he can hear. He is not deaf, that's certain, but still he missed.

Now the master has to start from the very beginning, and Ho-shan used to tell this story almost every day. That was his only sermon. Every morning he will start his sermon the same way. *To discipline ourselves in learning is called hearing; to reach a point where any more learning no more avails is called approaching. When one goes beyond these two stages, one is said to have truly transcended.*

No question can be asked if you understand. You can touch the master's feet and thank him, or you can have a good laugh, or you can roll your mat and go home, but a question is now irrelevant.

But the monk asked, "What then is truly transcending?" And what did Ho-shan do?

Without uttering a word...

It is useless to utter a word now because he will have to repeat the same.

Without uttering a word Ho-shan motioned as if beating a drum...

Many things are implied in it. With this gesture *...as if beating a drum...* he is saying, "Are you deaf or something? Do you need a drum to be beaten only then you will understand? Are you deaf or something? Your question simply shows that you have not heard what I have been saying all the time."

Ho-shan motioned as if beating a drum, saying, "Dang, dang, doko dang, doko dang."

One meaning just on the surface is that he is saying to the person that he is deaf. "You don't need me, you need a drum to be beaten. Only then will you listen, otherwise you will not listen. These things are very subtle. They are not for you." That is one thing just on the surface.

The second thing: the drum is a very, very meaningful symbol in Buddhism because a drum is empty inside, and Buddhism believes in emptiness. Emptiness is virtually the godliness of Buddhism. A drum is empty, but if you beat it, it creates much sound. Buddhism says that the innermost core of existence is empty, only just on the surface is it like a drum. You can go on beating and creating sound.

All language is like beating a drum, but all meaning is more in tune with emptiness than in tune with the beating of the drum. All is noise, the innermost core can be known only in silence. All philosophy is beating the drum. If you enjoy, good, you can enjoy, but you will never enter into the really real, the ultimately real. It is empty.

And the third meaning: answering a question in this way is very absurd. Only Zen masters are courageous enough to do that. You cannot think of any other tradition which is so courageous to use such outlandish methods of expression: *"Dang, dang, doko dang, doko dang."* He is saying, "Your question can only be answered in an absurd way. The question is absurd, the answer cannot be anything else than that. You are illogical, so I will have to be illogical with you."

One great Christian, Tertullian, has said a tremendously meaningful thing. He says, "*Credo quia* impossible" – "I believe because it is impossible." He says, "I believe in God because God is impossible." In fact, logically he should not be. In fact, if the world is rational, God should not be. Tertullian says, "I believe because it is impossible."

Rationally there is no reason to believe, but life is more than reason, deeper than reason. Life is more than logic, vaster than logic; logic is very narrow. Logic is man-made, life is not man-made; on the contrary man is life-made. Life is bigger than man, so naturally it has to be bigger than logic.

The third meaning of Ho-shan's gesture is that you are asking such an absurd question that it can only be answered through an absurd gesture: *To all such questions Ho-shan's answer was always the same: "Dang, dang, doko dang, doko dang."*

He had found even a better way than Buddha; he must have had a better sense of humor than Buddha himself. Buddha always kept silent whenever somebody asked a metaphysical question. About something which transcended language, logic, he would keep quiet, or he would change the subject, or he would talk about something else. But Ho-shan found a more alive way with a certain sense of humor. Somebody was asking a question which by its very nature was absurd because by its very definition the transcendental is that which goes beyond, beyond all dualities. We can talk about dualities, but we cannot talk about the nondual.

Let me tell you a story, a very famous story from the Upanishads...

Vidagdh Sakalya asked a great upanishadic teacher, Yagyavalkya, "How many gods are there, Yagyavalkya?"

He answered in the words of a prayer, "There are as many gods as there are in the hymn to the Vishwa-devas – three thousand, three hundred."

"Yes," he said, "but how many are there *really*, Yagyavalkya?"

"Thirty-three."

"How many?"

"Six."

"How many?"

"Three."

"No, how many really?"

"Two."

"How many?"

"One and a half."

"Now come on. How many really?"

"One."

Now if you ask beyond this, then Yagyavalkya will also have to beat a drum.

It happened...

There was a great discussion in the court of Janak, a great emperor and a very wise man. He had requested all the wise persons alive to come to the court, and they were trying to define the nature of God.

Yagyavalkya went there, he defeated all the participants, and he was just going to be declared victorious when a woman arose. Yagyavalkya must have felt a little afraid because it is very difficult to communicate with a woman. If you argue with a woman, either you are defeated, or the argument remains incomplete; there is no other way. Because the feminine mind functions in a totally different way, it has no logical coherence. It jumps from one place to another; it leaps. The male mind goes step-by-step, so they never meet. The greatest and most impossible thing is to communicate with a woman, and if you are in love, then it is even more impossible. If you are not in love, then maybe a certain way can be found.

Yagyavalkya must have felt a little shiver around his spine. The woman asked, "Who is holding up this existence? Who is supporting this existence?"

And Yagyavalkya said, "Of course, God, Brahma is the support of all." He said, "He is the support of all. He is the ultimate support."

And the woman asked, "Then who is supporting him?"

Now this was going beyond. He had said, "He is the support of all. Nothing is left." He had said that it was the ultimate, so you cannot ask logically who is supporting God because now nothing is left.

Yagyavalkya said, "This is an absurd question." What in India they call *utee prasan*, absurd question. Absurd because by the very definition of the word *ultimate*, nothing is left. It cannot be asked. If you want to be logical, if you want to be coherent, if you want to communicate rightly, then it cannot be asked. And if it can be asked, then there is going to be no end to it.

He said to Janak, "If this question is allowed, then it is better that I should stop now because then there is no end. It will become a regress ad infinitum. If I say that God is supported by something, then she will ask, "Who is supporting that something?" And if I say something else, she will say, "Who is supporting that something?" It is going to be foolish and endless if it is going to be allowed; it is better that I should drop out of it right now."

He was right because when we say, "all," then nothing is left.

Ho-shan was saying, "All duality is transcended," and language can function only in duality. A man has to be defined by a woman. A man is one who is not a woman, and a woman is one who is not a man. Matter is to be defined by mind; night is to be defined by day; God is to be defined by the Devil; language exists in duality, otherwise there is no possibility of defining it. The other is needed, and the transcendental means that now there is no other, the nondual has come. Now it is all one, you have reached to the indefinable.

But Ho-shan, of course, is a better man than Yagyavalkya. Yagyavalkya must have been very serious; he said to the king, "I had better stop now because if this woman is allowed to ask, she will create regress ad infinitum." And he was a little angry also. He said to the woman, "No more questioning, otherwise your head will fall off." He was right but a little irritated and annoyed.

Ho-shan has more sense of humor, he is not so serious. And that's how an enlightened person should be. About Yagyavalkya I have always felt that he may have been a great philosopher, a great man of learning, learned, but he was not yet enlightened. Otherwise there was no need; he could have laughed. He could have also gestured as if he was beating a drum; he could have said, *"Dang, dang, doko dang, doko dang."*

But no, this quality of Zen is special to Zen. It is tremendously beautiful. They can turn an ugly situation into laughter, and laughter brings you home as nothing else.

The one cannot be expressed. To know that one, one has to become more and more silent, silent and silent. To know that one, to experience that one, one has to lose language by and by, so that language completely disappears, and you are left without any language, without any mind.

Last night I was reading a few lines of Pablo Neruda. Beautiful...

So that you can hear me,
at times my words get fainter and fainter,
like the marks made by seagulls on the sand.

A master, the more you grow with him, starts becoming more

and more silent, and his words get fainter and fainter, "...like the marks made by seagulls on the sand."

"So that you can hear me..." The more you become capable of hearing, the more the master has nothing to say to you. When you are not capable of hearing, he has to say many things to you to make you capable of hearing. When you become capable of hearing – look at the absurdity of it all – when you become capable of hearing, his words become fainter and fainter. When you are really capable of hearing, he stops because now there is no need to say anything, now silence can meet with the silence, now silence can melt and merge into silence. Now, language dropped, mind put aside, being can communicate with being. Communication can be direct, immediate. Now something can transpire, existentially.

But at that moment don't be stupid like that monk who asked, *"What then is truly transcending?"* because his question, if accepted, brings you back to *abc*. Again he has to be taught how to hear.

Ho-shan did well. He said, "Are you deaf or something?" by making the gesture of beating a drum. And he said, "Sound and words and mind and language and concepts and philosophies and creeds and dogmas and scriptures are just on the surface. Deep inside the drum is nothing."

Have you ever tried to open a drum and see what it is inside which makes so much sound – so much beautiful sound also? Small children do it sometimes.

Somebody gave Mulla Nasruddin's child a drum, and it became a nuisance for the whole neighborhood. One day I was sitting at his home, and the child came running in with a broken drum. He had a knife in his hand with which he had broken it.

I said, "What happened?"

He said, "The neighbor gave me the knife and said, "Try to see what is inside." So I looked inside, there is nothing.

The same happens with all philosophies. A master is there to give you a knife to look inside the drum. If you push your knife deep enough into philosophies, there is nothing, only emptiness. All words are empty. They make much sound, that's right, but don't be befooled by the sound. Have a penetrating knife, a sharp knife, with you; that's what meditation is all about. It is like sharpening a knife, so you can put it through all words and reach to the innermost core of it all, which is empty.

Yes, Ho-shan did well. His assertion about all metaphysical questions, *Dang, dang, doko dang, doko dang,* was absurd but tremendously beautiful. He says, "We here in Zen are not concerned with words, logic, intellect, syllogism. We here in Zen are concerned with existence, with being. And if you ask an absurd question, you will get an absurd answer."

The story says nothing about what happened to the monk who asked it. If he had been a little alert, he may have even become more alert. This sudden absurd response of the master, *Dang, dang, doko dang, doko dang,* may have brought him a little satori, but the story says nothing. The man may not have been even that alert that he could understand this. He may have turned away thinking that the man was mad.

The Zen people are mad in a way because they are trying to pull you toward the ultimate, which is beyond you. They are trying to pull you beyond yourself; they are trying to pull you out of yourself. They are mad people, but if you allow them, they can give you a glimpse of the eternal; and once the glimpse happens, you are never the same again.

Let this story penetrate your heart as deeply as possible, and whenever you are becoming a victim again of theories, dogmas, doctrines, philosophies, say loudly, *"Dang, dang, doko dang, doko dang."* It will be helpful; it will suddenly bring you back to the earth.

Ludwig Wittgenstein used to say that he did not solve philosophical problems, he dissolved them. Everything is left as it is, but perhaps for the first time we come to see things as they are.

Zen is a way of dissolving philosophical problems, not of solving them. It is a way of getting rid of philosophy because philosophy is a sort of neurosis.

Enough for today.

CHAPTER 10

happiness is always herenow

The first question:

Osho,
I have too much sexual energy burning within my body. When I dance, sometimes I feel as if I am going to kill the whole world, and at some stage so much anger and violence bubbles within my body that I can't channel the energy into meditation techniques, and it drives me crazy. I don't feel to go into the sex act, but violent energy is still burning like volcanic fire. I can't bear it, and it makes me sometimes suicidal. Please, explain how to give a creative outlet to this energy.

The problem is created by the mind, not by the energy. Listen to the energy. It is showing you the right direction. It is not sexual energy which is creating the problem; it has never created any problems in the animals, in the trees, in the birds. The energy creates problems because your mind has a wrong attitude about it.

This question is from an Indian lady. In India the whole upbringing is against sex. Then you create the problem. And then, whenever there is energy, you will feel sexual because something is incomplete within you. Something unfulfilled will always wait, and it will assert energy, exploit energy.

In the dynamic methods of meditation much energy is created. Many hidden sources are tapped, and new sources become available. If sex has remained an unfulfilled desire, then this energy will start moving toward sex. You will become more and more sexual if you meditate.

Let me tell you one thing that happened in India. Jaina monks completely stopped meditating just because of sexual energy. They forgot all about meditation because they were repressing sex so much that whenever they meditated, energy would rise. Meditation gives you tremendous energy. It is a source of eternal energy, you cannot exhaust it. So whenever energy arose, they would start feeling sexual. They became afraid of meditations. They dropped them. The most essential thing that Mahavira had given to them they dropped, and the nonessential, fasting and rituals, they continued. This fits with an anti-sexual attitude.

I am not anti-sexual because I am not anti-life. So the problem is not where you think it is; the problem is in your head not in your sexual glands. You will have to change your attitude, otherwise whatsoever you do will be colored by your sexuality. You meditate, and it will become sexual; you look at somebody, and your eyes will become sexual; you touch somebody, and your hand will become sexual; you eat something, and eating can become sexual.

So people who deny sex start eating more. You can watch it in life. Freely flowing, sexually flowing people will not be very fat, they will not eat too much. Love is so satisfying, love is so fulfilling they will not go on stuffing their body with food. When they can't love, or when they can't allow themselves to move into love, they start eating too much. That becomes a substitute activity.

Go and see Hindu monks. They go on gathering unnecessary fat. They become ugly. That is another extreme. On one extreme are Jaina monks who cannot eat because they are afraid that once they eat, food will release energy, and the energy will immediately move to the incomplete desire waiting for it. First it goes to the incomplete experience which is hanging in the middle; that is the first requirement, so energy moves there. The body has a certain economy: wherever energy is needed first, energy moves there first.

There is a hierarchy of needs. A person who has been denying sex will have a hierarchy; sex will become first on the list. And whenever any energy is available, it will start moving to the most unfulfilled desire. So Jaina monks cannot eat well, they are afraid, and Hindu monks eat too much. The problem is the same, but they have solved it in two extreme ways.

If you eat too much, you start getting a certain sexual enjoyment by eating, by filling your belly too much. Too much food brings lethargy. And too much food is always a substitute for love because the first thing the child comes in contact with is the mother's breast. That breast is the first experience in the world, and the breast gives two things to the child: love and food. So love and food become deeply entangled with each other.

Whenever love is missing, your childish mind will think, "Get more food. Complement it." Have you watched? When you are feeling very full of love, your desire to eat disappears, you don't feel so much appetite. But whenever love is missing, you start eating too much, you don't know what to do now. Love was filling a certain space inside you. Now that space is empty, and you don't know any other way to fill it than food. You create problems by denying nature, by rejecting nature.

So I would like to tell the questioner that it is not a question of meditation. Lady, you need love. You need a lover, and you need courage to move into it.

It is difficult to move into love; there are very hidden fears in it. Love creates as much fear as nothing else because the moment you start approaching the other, you have to go outside yourself. And who knows? The other may accept you or may reject you. The fear arises, you start feeling hesitant, whether to take the move or not, whether to approach the other or not. Hence all over the world the coward ages of the past have decided for marriage instead of love, because if people were left open to love, very few people would be able to love. Many more would die without love; they would live and drag out their lives without love because love is dangerous.

The moment you start moving toward somebody else, you are coming to collide with another world. Who knows if your approach will be accepted or rejected? How can you be certain the other is going to say yes to your need and to your desire? That the other is going to be compassionate, loving? How do you know? He may reject you. He may say no. You may say, "I love you," but what is the guarantee that he will also feel love for you? He may not. There is no necessity for it, and the fear of rejection is very shattering.

So cunning and clever people decide not to move at all. Keep to yourself, then at least you are not rejected. And you can go on enhancing your ego with the idea that nobody has ever rejected you, even though that ego is absolutely impotent and is not enough to fulfill you. You need to be needed; you need somebody to accept you. You need somebody to love you because only when somebody else loves you, will you be able to love yourself, not before. When somebody accepts you, you will be able to accept yourself, not before. When somebody else feels happy with you, you will start feeling happy with yourself, not before. The other becomes a mirror.

Each relationship is a mirror. It reflects you. How can you know your face without the mirror? There is no way. Others' eyes become mirrorlike, and when somebody loves you, that mirror is very, very sympathetic toward you; very, very happy with you; delighted with you. In those delighted eyes you are reflected, and for the first time a certain acceptability arises.

Otherwise, you have been rejected from the very beginning. It is part of the ugly structure of society that each child comes to feel that he is not accepted for himself. If he does something good – of course, whatsoever the parents think is good – if he does that, he is accepted. If he does something wrong – what the parents think is wrong – then he is rejected. The child sooner or later starts feeling, "I am not accepted for myself, not as I am, not intrinsically, but for what I do. My being is not loved but my doing." And that creates a deep self-rejection, a deep self-hatred. He starts hating himself.

If you don't fall in love, if you don't find lovers and friends who can accept you, you will remain with that rejection your whole life. Love is a must. You must move through it. You can come out of it one day, you can transcend it one day – it has to be transcended – but how can you transcend it if you never enter into it?

So don't be afraid, and drop all nonsense from the head. Yes, there is fear. You may be rejected, but don't be afraid of that fear because that risk has to be taken; only then somebody will come and accept you. If you knock at a hundred doors and ninety-nine remain closed, don't be afraid; one will open. Somebody is waiting for you. Somebody will be fulfilled through you as you will be fulfilled through somebody. Somebody is waiting to become a mirror for you because somebody is waiting to make you a mirror for himself. And there is no other way to find out who that one is than to go on knocking, groping. It is risky, but life is risky.

So very clever people miss life, they never take the risk. Afraid of falling, they never walk; afraid of drowning, they never swim; afraid of rejection, they may never move in love; afraid of failure, they never make any effort to succeed in anything. Their life is not life at all. They are dead before their death. They die so many times before they really die. Their whole life is nothing but a gradual death.

Live, and live intensely, and don't take it as a personal offense if somebody cannot love you; there is no necessity. You were ready, you were available. If the other is not willing, that is for him to decide. Don't make it a wound, it is not. It simply says that you two don't fit, that's all; it doesn't say anything about you or about the other. Don't say that the other is wrong, and don't think that it is because you are wrong that you are not accepted. It is just you could not fit.

Move on, and it is good that the other did not deceive you, that the other was true and authentic. He said, "Sorry, I don't feel any love for you." At least he was sincere and authentic. Because if he had said a formal yes, then your whole life would have been a mess. Be true. When you love, say it, and when you don't, say that too. Be true and sincere.

There are so many beautiful people in the world, why remain with yourself? Walk a few steps with somebody. Feel that rhythm also. That rhythm will satisfy you, and the urge will disappear. And when the urge disappears, your meditation will be the first in the hierarchy. Meditation can be the first in the hierarchy only if you have not been denying yourself that which is natural.

A person who has been fasting cannot meditate because whenever he meditates, he thinks about food; whenever he closes his eyes, he visualizes food. A man who is denying love cannot meditate; whenever he meditates, immediately sexuality surrounds him.

Fulfill all natural needs, nothing is wrong in them. What is wrong in food, in sex? Nothing is wrong. Fulfill them. Be so natural that when you meditate, there is no other thing waiting for your attention. If you fulfill your natural needs, you will see that your dreams will disappear. In the night you will not dream because there is nothing to dream about. Fast, then you will dream about food; force celibacy on yourself, then you will dream about sex. If you are moving naturally, if you have found a tune between you and nature, that's what I call *dharma*, that's what I call the ultimate law of life. Find yourself almost always in rhythm. Sometimes even if you go out of step, come back again; remember and fall into line again. Remain with nature, and you will reach the goal; remain with nature, and you will find godliness. You can even forget about godliness, then too you will find it if you remain true to nature. Because when lower needs are fulfilled, higher needs arise; when higher needs are fulfilled, ultimate needs arise. This is the natural economy of life.

If a person is hungry, how can he understand music? It is sheer absurdity to ask him to listen to classical music when he is hungry or to tell him to meditate or sit in zazen. He cannot think anything about Buddha, cannot think anything about God or Jesus. He cannot meditate, his mind will flicker and waver; it will go again and again to his empty stomach. No, he cannot love poetry, and he cannot love music when the first needs are unfulfilled. Give him fulfillment of the first, primary needs – food, shelter, love – and then suddenly the energy is released from the lower world, and he will start reading poetry, listening to music; he will enjoy dancing. Now higher needs are arising; he would like to paint or sculpt. These are luxuries. They only come into existence when lower needs are fulfilled. And when these higher needs are also fulfilled – you have loved music, listened to music; you have loved poetry, enjoyed it; you have painted, danced – one day you will see a new realm of needs is arising which are called the ultimate needs: meditation, godliness, prayer.

If the first needs are not fulfilled, the second will not arise, and the third is out of the question. If the first needs are fulfilled, then there is the possibility for the second needs to arise, and a glimpse of the third to happen also. When the second is fulfilled, the third arises automatically on its own accord.

Just the other day in Kundalini Meditation two dogs were watching. After a while one dog looked at the other and said, "When I act like that they give me worm pills."

Of course, a dog has a dog's mind. He has his own world, terminology, understanding, concepts. He can only think that people who are doing Kundalini either have worms in their stomach or have gone crazy. And that is natural to a dog's understanding.

Your mind has been conditioned for centuries by people who have not understood your real needs. They have not bothered at all. They were looking for something else, and they have managed that very well; they were looking for the way to dominate people, and the easiest way is to create a guilty conscience. Then it is very easy to dominate people. Once the guilt exists, you will be dominated by one or the other, by this or that, but you will be dominated. A guilty person never feels at ease with himself, he cannot have any confidence; he knows that he is wrong, so he goes to find a leader, he goes to find some church, he goes to find somebody to guide him. He is not confident, hence the need arises. Politicians and priests have worked very hard to create a guilty conscience in everybody. Now that guilty conscience is creating trouble.

Now drop it. Life is yours. It belongs to nobody else. No politician, no priest has anything to do with it. Don't allow anybody to meddle with your life. It is totally yours.

And your body is giving you the right indication; the body is very wise. The mind is a very late arrival. The body has lived millions of years, it knows what is needed. It is the mind that interferes. Mind is very immature, body is very mature. Listen to the body.

When I say listen to the body, I don't mean to remain confined to the body. If you listen to the body, the body will not have anything to say to you; things will be settled. And when the body is at ease, relaxed, and there is no tension, and the body is not fighting for something, is not trying to attract your attention because you are not fulfilling any need, when the body is calm and quiet, you can float high, you can fly high, you can become a white cloud. But only when the body needs are really, truly looked after. The body is not your enemy, it is your friend. The body is your earth, the body has all your roots. You have to find a bridge between you and your body. If you don't find that bridge, you will be constantly in conflict with your body, and a person who is fighting with himself is always miserable.

The first thing is to come to a peace pact with your body and never break it. Once you have come to a peace pact with your body, the body will become very, very friendly. You look after the body, the body will look after you; it becomes a vehicle of tremendous value, it becomes the very temple. One day your body itself is revealed to you as the very shrine of godliness.

The second question:

Osho,
For the last ten days I have felt tremendously happy as I never did before. Just being myself and accepting me as I am feels great. Sometimes this incredibly good feeling is disturbed by two thoughts. First, will this stay that way? Can I keep this feeling in the future? And second, why did I have to become so old before I reached this point? I cannot forget and still I feel sorry for all those years that I did not live at all. Please explain how to get rid of these disturbances of my happiness.

This has been asked by Prem Dhyan. When he came just six months ago, he was one of the most miserable persons I have ever come across. And it has been a miracle. He has changed totally. Now I can say just the opposite, he is one of the most happy persons around here.

These two questions are natural because now he is going to leave, he will be going back home. The fear arises. Will he be able to keep this happiness that has happened to him? The future... And the second question: he feels sorry for all those years that he lived but did not really live, that he missed. He could have lived those years as happy as he is now. The past...

These are the two dangers to be alert about. Whenever you become tremendously happy, immediately mind starts spinning its web. And there are two methods of the mind because mind exists either with the past or with the future. It immediately says, "Look, you could have been so happy your whole life." Now the mind is distracting you. Say to the mind, "What does it matter? Those twenty years, or thirty years, or fifty years, are gone. Whether I lived them happily or unhappily, they are gone; it makes no difference." In the morning when you awake, what difference does it make that you dreamed a very sweet dream, or that it was a nightmare? What difference does it make? When you awake in the morning, both were dreams. And the night is over, and you are no longer asleep.

When the mind says, "Look, you could have always been this happy," the mind is creating an absurd desire. You cannot go back, you cannot do anything about the past, the past is gone and gone forever, irreversibly gone. Just think, even if you had been happy all those fifty years, what difference does it make now?

Whether happy or unhappy, it is just a memory. In fact, whether your past existed or not, what difference does it make now?

Bertrand Russell has written somewhere that sometimes he starts brooding about whether the past really existed or whether he simply imagines that it existed. Were you a child really, or did you simply dream about being a child? How can you differentiate now? Both are in the memory; whether you dreamed about it or whether you really lived it, both are part of memory, and there is no way to differentiate. The past is in the memory – both real and unreal.

And psychologists say that when people say anything about their past, don't trust them because in their past many imaginations and dreams have melted and have become mixed. Their past is not factual, and there is no way now because everything is contained only in the memory. Whether you were really living it, or you had just dreamed it, both have been mixed and melted into each other.

Past is just memory, but the mind can create great trouble, and by creating that fuss, it will deprive you of the happiness that is available right now. Just say to the mind, "I am finished with the past, and I don't care a bit whether it was happy or unhappy, it is gone and gone forever. Now is the only moment."

If you don't listen to this trap, then the mind has another trap for you. It will say, "Okay, the past is gone but the future, what about the future? At least you can manage the future, it has yet to happen, you can plan for it. And wouldn't you like this beautiful space in which you are now to be there forever and ever?" Again the desire will arise. Don't say yes to it because again it will lead you away from the present. And happiness is always herenow.

Happiness is something that belongs to the present. Now say to the mind, "I am not worried about the future at all because if I can be happy now, this moment, I can be happy forever – because the future never comes as future, it always comes as the present. And now I know the secret of being happy in the present, so why bother about the future? Tomorrow will not come as tomorrow, it will come as today. And I have the key to open the door. At least this moment I am happy, and I know how to be happy in this moment. All moments that will come will come always like this moment."

Have you watched? There is no difference between one moment and another moment. Time is completely beyond discrimination. It is always pure *now*.

So beware. These are the two traps of the mind. Mind cannot live without misery, so it is trying to create misery so that it can disturb your peace. Then the mind will be perfectly happy. Once you start feeling sorry for your past – it does not matter for what you feel sorry – you feel sorry, you start getting sad, depressed. And once you start getting too concerned about the future, you become full of desire, tense, worried whether you will be able to manage or not, whether you will be able to perform or not.

Between these two rocks the fragile moment of the present is crushed. So you have to be very alert. When one is unhappy, one can remain without alertness; he has nothing to lose. When one is happy, one has to be very careful and cautious; now he has a treasure to lose. And it can be lost within a second, within a split second. One wrong step and it can be lost. And these are the two directions in which you can lose your treasure.

A person who is poor, a beggar, need not be worried that he can be robbed, but a person who has treasures has to be very cautious. When Buddha walked so cautiously, why was he walking so cautiously? He had something, something tremendously fragile which could be dropped in any moment of unawareness and could be lost.

There is a Zen story...

A king in Japan used to visit his capital every night. He became aware that a beggar was always sitting alert under his tree; he never found him asleep. The king went at different times, but the beggar was alert the whole night, just sitting there, completely immobile, with his eyes open.

Out of curiosity he asked the beggar, "What are you being so cautious for? What are you guarding? I can't see that you have anything that could be stolen or that anybody could cheat you. Why do you go on sitting like that and watching?"

The beggar laughed, and he said, "Sir, as far as I am concerned I would like to ask you the same question. Why so many guards? Why such an army around the palace? I don't see that you have anything to be guarded. I have never seen a bigger beggar than you. You are completely empty, I can see through and through you. I don't see any treasure there. About what are you creating so much fuss? As far as I am concerned, I have a treasure, and I have to be alert about it. A single moment of unconsciousness and it can be lost."

And the beggar said, "Look into my eyes because my treasure is hidden within me."

And it is said that the king looked into the eyes of the beggar, entered into his eyes, and was completely lost. It was a tremendously luminous space. He became a disciple to this beggar.

This beggar was a Zen master, and the king had been in search for many years, and he had been to many masters, but he could never feel the vibe of the unknown. With this beggar he could feel it almost crystallized in front of his eyes, he could touch it. Something divine had happened to this man.

So when you have a little treasure to guard, guard it. Now these two will be the thieves, the past and the future. Be alert. Nothing else is needed, just alertness. Just shake yourself out of sleep. Whenever you start falling into the trap, give yourself a jerk and remember.

I would like to tell you one of the most beautiful parables that has been written down the centuries. Parables have almost disappeared from the world because those beautiful people, Jesus, Buddha, who created many parables have disappeared.

A parable is not an ordinary story, a parable is a device, a device to say something which cannot ordinarily be said, a device to hint at something which can be hinted at only very indirectly.

This parable is written in this age; a very rare man, Franz Kafka, has written it. He was really a rare man. He struggled hard not to write because he said what he wanted to write could not be written. So he struggled hard, but he could not control the temptation to write, so he wrote. And he wrote in one of his diaries, "I am writing because it is difficult not to write, and knowing well that it is difficult also to write. Seeing no way out of it, I am writing." And when he died, he left a will in the name of one of his friends to say, "Please burn everything that I have written, my diaries, my stories, my parables, my sketches, my notes. And burn them without reading them because this is the only way that I can get rid of that constant anxiety that I have been trying to say something which cannot be said. And I could not resist, so I have written. Now this is the only way. I have written it because I could not control myself. I had to write knowing well that it could not be written, so now, without reading it, destroy, burn everything utterly. Nothing should be left." But the friend could not do it, and it is good that he did not.

This is one of Kafka's parables. Listen to it, meditate over it.

I gave an order for my horse to be brought from the stable. The servant did not understand me. I myself went to the stable, saddled my horse and mounted. In the distance I heard a bugle call. I asked him what this meant. He knew nothing and had heard nothing.

At the gate he stopped me, asking, "Where are you riding to, Master?"

"I don't know," I said, "only away from here. Away from here, always away from here. Only by doing so can I reach my destination."

"And so you know your destination?" he asked.

"Yes," I answered. "Did not I say so? Away from here, that's my destination."

"You have no provisions with you," he said.

"I need none," I said. "The journey is so long that I must die of hunger if I don't get anything along the way. No provisions can save me because the journey is so long, I cannot carry enough provisions for it. No provisions can save me, for it is, fortunately, a truly immense journey."

Now this is the parable. "The destination," he says, "is away from here. Away from here is my destination." That's how the whole world is moving: away from here, away from now. You don't know where you are going; only one thing is certain – you are going away from here, away from now.

The parable says it is an immense journey. It is really endless because you can never reach away from here. How can you reach "away from here"? Wherever you will reach, it will be here. And again you will be trying to go away from here. There is no way to reach this destination. If away from here is the destination, then there is no way to reach it. And we are all escaping away from here.

Watch. Don't allow this parable to become your life. Ordinarily everybody is doing this – knowingly, unknowingly. Start moving into the here, start moving into the now. And then there is tremendous happiness, so much so that it starts overflowing. Not only *you* delight in it, it starts overflowing, it starts becoming your climate, it becomes like a cloud around you. So whoever comes close to you becomes full of it. Even others will start partaking of it, participating in it.

And the more you have, the more you will be drowning into the herenow. Then a moment comes when you don't have any space left for yourself; only happiness exists, you disappear.

But be alert of two things, the past and the future.

And now you have something to lose; you are fortunate because you have something to lose. And you have a tremendous responsibility not to lose it. The mind will go on trying its ways for a time being. When you become so alert that the mind cannot penetrate you and cannot disturb and distract you, then by and by the mind starts dropping. One day it understands well that now there is no way with you, so it leaves you. Then it stops haunting you.

That day will also come. As you could not believe before that this happiness was possible, you may not be able to believe what I am saying now. That day will also come when there will be no distraction.

Then again you will have to be even more alert because you will start crying, "Why did I waste so many years with distraction?" And then you will become again concerned with the future. Many times you will come to face this past and future in many, many different ways. It is like a person going to the peak of a hill. He moves round and round the hill, the path moves round and round, and many times he comes to the same view, to the same place. A little higher, but the same place, the same trees, the same sky. Again and again, many times before he reaches to the peak, he comes to the same point, a little higher of course, but the same point, again and again. Many times he will come again and again to this same distraction of past and future. This is just the beginning.

But one day, one reaches the peak, and when one reaches the peak, all becomes available simultaneously: the valley, the sky, the clouds, the height, the depth. Everything becomes available. That's what enlightenment is.

The third question:

Osho,
The other day I took a piece of paper and did a little doodling or free writing, and I was pained to find that I was full of self-condemnation and self-pity. I had not a nice word for myself in that long note. Is it that I am too idealistic and self-centered, and is there a way out of this darkness?

Everybody is brought up in such a way that everybody has become idealistic. Nobody is realistic. The ideal is the common disease of humanity.

Everybody is brought up in such a way that everybody goes on thinking that they have to be something, somebody, somewhere in the future. An image has been given that you have to be like it. That gives you a tension because you are not it, you are something else, yet you have to be it. So one goes on condemning the real for the unreal; the unreal is unreal. And the ideal goes on pulling you toward the future, out of the present.

The ideal becomes a constant nightmare because it goes on condemning. Whatsoever you do is imperfect because you have an ideal of perfection. Whatsoever you attain is still not fulfilling because you have a mad expectation which can never be satisfied.

You are human in a certain time, in a certain space, with certain limitations. Accept those limitations. Perfectionists are always on the brink of madness. They are obsessed people then whatsoever they do is not good enough. And there is no way to do something perfectly; perfection is not humanly possible. In fact, imperfect is the only way to be.

So what do I teach you here? I don't teach you perfection, I teach you wholeness. That is a totally different thing. Be whole. Don't bother about perfection. When I say be whole, I mean be real, be here; whatsoever you can do, do it totally. You will be imperfect, but your imperfection will be full of beauty because it will be full of your totality.

Never try to be perfect otherwise you will create such anxiety. So many troubles are there already; don't create more troubles for yourself.

I have heard...

It happened that bedraggled, worried Garfinkel sat in a train holding a three-year-old boy. Every few minutes Garfinkel spanked the child.

"If you strike that baby one more time," said a woman sitting across from him, "I'll give you so much trouble you won't forget it!"

"Trouble?" said Garfinkel. "You're gonna give me trouble? Lady, my partner stole all my money and ran off with my wife and car. My daughter is in the parlor car, six months pregnant, and she ain't got no husband. My baggage is lost, I'm on the wrong train, and this little stinker just ate the tickets and threw up all over me. And lady, *you're* gonna give me trouble?"

Now what more trouble can there be? Don't you think enough is enough?

Life itself is so complicated. Please, be a little more kind toward yourself. Don't create ideals. Life is creating enough problems, but those problems can be solved. If you are in a wrong train, you can change the train; if the tickets are lost, they can be purchased again; if your wife has run away, you can find another woman. The problems that life gives to you can be solved, but the problems that idealism gives to you can never be solved; they are impossible.

Somebody is trying to become Jesus. Now there is no way; it does not happen that way, nature does not allow it. Jesus happens once, and only once; nature does not tolerate any repetition. Somebody is trying to become a Buddha; now he is trying to do the impossible. It simply does not happen, cannot happen; it is against nature. You can be only yourself. So be total. Wherever you are, and whatsoever you are doing, do it totally. Move into it, let it become your meditation. Don't be worried whether it will be perfect or not; it is not going to be perfect. If it is total, it is enough. If it were total, you enjoyed doing it; you felt a fulfillment through it, you moved into it, you were absorbed into it, you came out of it new, fresh, young, rejuvenated.

Each act that is done totally rejuvenates, and each act that is done totally never brings any bondage. Love totally and attachment does not arise; love partially and attachment arises. Live totally and you are not afraid of death; live partially and you are afraid of death.

But forget the word *perfection*. It is one of the most criminal words. This word should be dropped from all languages of the world, it should be dropped from the human mind. Nobody has ever been perfect, and nobody can ever be. Can't you see it? Even if God is there and you come to meet him, can't you find faults with his creation? So many, that's why he is hiding. He is almost afraid of you. Faults and faults and faults. Can you count them? You will find infinite faults. In fact, if you are a fault-finder you cannot find anything right, in the right time, in the right place. Everything seems to be just a mess. Even God is not perfect; God is total. He enjoyed doing it, he is still enjoying doing it. But he is not perfect. If he were perfect, then the creation could not be imperfect. Out of perfection, perfection will come.

All the religions of the world say that God is perfect. I don't say that. I say God is whole, God is holy, God is total, but not perfect. He is still trying. How can he be perfect? If he were, the world would be dead by now. Once something is perfect, death happens because then there is no future, then there is no way. Trees are still growing, babies are still born, things continue. And he goes on improving. Can't you see the improvement? He goes on improving on everything. That's the meaning of evolution: things are being improved. Monkeys have become man; that's an improvement. Then man will become divine and gods; that is evolution.

Teilhard de Chardin says that there is an omega point where everything will become perfect. There is none. There is no omega point, there cannot be. The world is always in the process; evolution is there; we are approaching and approaching, but we never reach because once we reach – finished. God still goes on trying in different ways, improving.

One thing is certain: he is happy with his work otherwise he would have abandoned it. He is still pouring his energy into it. When God is happy with you, it is sheer nonsense to be unhappy with yourself. Be happy with yourself. Let happiness be the ultimate value. I am a hedonist. Always remember that happiness is the criterion. Whatsoever you do, be happy, that's all. Don't be bothered whether it is perfect or not.

Why this obsession with perfection? Then you will be tense, anxious, nervous, always uneasy, troubled, in conflict. The English word *agony* comes from a root which means: to be in conflict. To be constantly wrestling with oneself, that is the meaning of agony. You will be in agony if you are not at ease with yourself. Don't demand the impossible, be natural, at ease, loving yourself, loving others.

And remember, a person who cannot love himself because he goes on condemning, cannot love anybody else either. A perfectionist is not only a perfectionist about himself, he is about others also. A man who is hard on himself is bound to be hard on others. His demands are impossible.

In India just a few years before, there was Mahatma Gandhi, a perfectionist, almost a neurotic. And he was very hard with his disciples; even tea was not allowed. Tea! Because it has caffeine. If somebody was found drinking tea in his ashram, it was a great sin. Love was not allowed. If somebody fell in love with somebody, it was such a great sin that it was as if the whole world was going to be drowned because of it. He was continuously spying on his disciples, always sitting at the keyhole. But he was that way with himself. You can be with others only as you are with yourself.

But this type of person becomes a great leader by creating much guilt in others. The more guilt you can create in people, the greater the leader you can become. Because more and more people feel that, yes, you can help them to become perfect. They are imperfect, so you can help them to become perfect.

I am not here to help you to become perfect; I am not concerned with any sort of nonsense. I am just here to help you to be yourself. If you are imperfect, beautiful; if you are perfect, that too is beautiful. Don't try to become imperfect because that can become an ideal! You may be perfect already; then listening to me you can create a trouble for yourself. This man says be imperfect! There is no need. If you are perfect, accept that too.

Try to love yourself. Don't condemn. Once humanity starts a deep acceptance, all churches will disappear, and all politicians and priests will disappear.

I have heard...

A man was fishing in the north woods, and one night around the campfire his guide was telling him of the time he had guided Harry Emerson Fosdick on a fishing trip. Fosdick was a Christian missionary, a teacher, and a thinker.

"Yes," said the guide, "he was a good man except for his swearing."

"But look," said the fisherman, "surely you don't mean to say that Dr. Fosdick was profane?"

"Oh, but he was, Sir," protested the guide. "Once he caught a fine bass. Just as he was about to land him in the boat, the fish wiggled off the hook. So I say to the Doctor, 'That's a damned shame!' and the Doc comes right back and says, 'Yes, it is!' But that's the only time I ever heard him use such language."

Now this is the mind of a perfectionist. The Doctor has not said anything. He simply says, "Yes, it is." But that too is enough for a perfectionist to find fault with.

A perfectionist is neurotic. And not only is he neurotic, he creates neurotic friends around him. So don't be a perfectionist, and if somebody is a perfectionist around you, escape away from him as fast as you can before he pollutes your mind.

All perfectionism is a sort of deep ego trip. Just to think of yourself in terms of ideals and perfection is nothing but to decorate your ego to its uttermost. A humble person accepts that life is not perfect. A humble person, a really religious person, accepts that we are limited, that there are limitations.

That is my definition of humbleness. Not to try to be perfect is to be humble, and a humble person becomes more and more total because he has nothing to deny, nothing to reject. He accepts whatsoever he is, good or bad. And a humble person is very rich because he accepts his wholeness; his anger, his sex, his greed. Everything is accepted, and in that deep acceptance a great alchemical change happens. All that is ugly by and by disappears on its own accord. He becomes more and more harmonious, more and more whole.

I am not in favor of a saint, but I am in favor of a holy man. A saint is a perfectionist; a holy man is totally different. Zen masters are holy men; Catholic saints are saints. The very word *saint* is ugly. It comes from *sanctus* – one who has been given sanction by the authority that he is a saint. Now who can authorize anybody to be a saint? Is it a sort of degree? But the Christian Church goes on doing that foolish thing.

Even posthumous degrees are awarded. And a saint may have died three hundred years before, then the Church revises its own ideas, or the world has changed, and after three hundred years the Church gives a posthumous degree – a sanction: "That man was really a saint. We could not understand it at the time." And the Church may have killed the man; that's how Joan of Arc became a saint. They killed her, but later on they changed their idea. People by and by came closer and closer to Joan of Arc, and it became difficult not to accept her. First they killed her, then they worshipped her. After hundreds of years her bones were found and worshipped. She was burned by the same people, by the same Church.

No, the word *saint* is not good. A holy man is a holy man because of himself, not because some church decides to award him sainthood.

I have heard...

Jacobson, aged ninety, had lived through beatings in Polish

pogroms, concentration camps in Germany, and dozens of other anti-Semitic experiences.

"Oh, Lord!" he prayed, sitting in a synagogue. "Isn't it true that we are your chosen people?"

And from the heavens boomed a voice: "Yes, Jacobson, the Jews are my chosen people!"

"Well, then," wailed the old man, "isn't it time you chose somebody else?"

Perfectionists are the chosen people of God, remember. In fact, the day you understand that you are creating your own misery because of your ideas, you break all ideas. Then you simply live out of your reality whatsoever it is. That is a great transformation.

So don't try to be chosen people of God, just be human. For God's sake, just be human!

The fourth question:

Osho,
The other day you said that effort is dangerous, but hard work is needed in the meditations. For my German mind, effort equals hard work. Is there hard work without effort?

The point is delicate. Effort is always half-hearted, effort is always partial. You are doing it because you don't see any way without doing it that you can attain the result that you desire. If there was any way you would drop the effort and jump to the conclusion… One is never totally in his effort, cannot be because the idea is of the future, the end result. Effort is future-oriented, result-oriented. One is doing it only for the sake of some future result, some profit, some greed, some good pay-off.

That's why Zen masters say effortless effort is needed. What do they mean by effortless effort? They say hard work is needed, but it should not be future-oriented. You should enjoy it not for some other goal; even if nothing is attained through it, it is beautiful in itself. And that is the hardest thing for the human mind to do. That's why I call it hard work. The hardest thing is to do something for its own sake, to sing a song for its own sake, to meditate for its own sake, to love for its own sake. That is the hardest thing for the human mind because mind is future-oriented. It says, "For its own sake? Then why? What is going to happen out of it?"

People come to me, and they ask, "We can meditate, but what will we attain? We can become sannyasins, but what are we going to gain out of it?" This is what mind is, always greedy.

Let me tell you...

One day Mulla Nasruddin was watching the street through the window when he saw his creditor approaching the house. Knowing what the fellow was up to, Mulla called his wife and told her to handle the visitor.

Accordingly the wife opened the door and said, "Yes, sir, I know we haven't yet been able to pay you. And although Mulla himself is not home at this moment, he thinks day and night about ways to get some money and pay you back. He has even asked me to watch the street, and whenever a flock of sheep passes, to go out and pick up any pieces of wool that might have been caught on the bushes. This way, when we get enough wool, we can spin it, make a couple of shawls, sell them and with the money pay you back."

When she got to this point, the man started to laugh, whereupon Mulla came out of his hiding and said, "You rascal, now that you smell money, you start to grin."

The mind is that rascal. Once it gets any hint of any sort of future, it starts to grin. It immediately jumps on it, catches hold of it; you are no longer herenow. Meditation is for its own sake as love is for its own sake.

Ask a rose why he flowers. He simply flowers. It is so beautiful to flower. There is no motive in it. Ask the birds why they are singing. They are simply singing. They enjoy, they delight in it, there is no motive in it.

Drop the motive, and mind disappears. At least for a few hours in a day go on doing things for their own sake: dance, sing, play on the guitar, sit with friends, or just watch the sky. At least for a few hours go on devoting your time to intrinsic activities. These activities are the hard work. And I know, mind is very lazy. It likes to dream, it doesn't like to work, that's why it continuously thinks of the future. But mind is very lazy. It only thinks of the future so that the present can be avoided and the challenge of the present can be avoided.

I have heard an anecdote...

While walking along a creek bank, a man came across a young fellow lying lazily under a tree with a fishing line in the water, on which the cork was bobbling frantically.

"Hey, you've got a bite!" he said.

"Yeah." drawled the fisherman. "Would you mind pulling it out?"

The walker did so, only to have the recumbent one ask, "Would, you mind taking the fish off, rebaiting the hook, and tossing it back into the creek?"

This was done, and the man commented jokingly, "As lazy as you are, you ought to have some kids to do these things for you."

"Not a bad idea," yawned the fisherman. "Got any idea where I could find a pregnant woman?"

That's how the mind is; it does not want to do anything. It simply hopes, desires, postpones. The future is a trick to postpone the present; the future is a trick to avoid the present. Not that you are going to do anything in the future, no, because again the same mind will be there and it will say tomorrow, tomorrow. You will die, and you will not do anything, you will only think. And that thinking helps you to keep face; you don't feel lazy because you think so much of doing, doing great things always, dreaming about great things, and not doing the small things that are really to be done right now.

Hard work means to be in the present, and to do that which the present has brought you as a challenge.

"The other day you said that effort is dangerous, but hard work was needed in the meditations." Yes, hard work because you will have to go against the mind. The hardness is not in the work; the work is beautifully simple, the work is very easy. The hardness comes from the fact that because you are so much fogged by the mind, you will have to come out of it.

"For my German mind, effort equals hard work." That I understand, but all minds are German. That's why everybody is in such trouble, that's why everybody finds his own fascism, his own nazism, his own Adolf Hitler. Everybody does find. Mind is fascist, and mind looks continuously for leaders, watching for somebody to lead. It was a surprise to the whole world when Germany fell into the trap of Adolf Hitler.

Nobody could believe it, it was almost illogical. Such a beautiful race with such a great tradition of learning, of learned men, of great philosophy, of Kant, Hegel, Feuerbach, Marx... Such a great culture with very refined intellect; a culture of great scientists, of great musicians, of great novelists and poets; the country of the philosophers and professors... *Professor* has never been such a respectable word in any other country as in Germany. What happened to such an intelligent race that it fell into the hands of a stupid, almost idiotic person like Adolf Hitler?

But this has to be understood: that all learning, if it is superficial, if it is of the mind, is not going to help. The learning only remains at the surface; deep down you remain childish. Those professors, even a man like Martin Heidegger, a great philosopher – you could say the greatest that this century has produced – also became a follower of Adolf Hitler. What happened to these giants following this man who was almost mad?

It has to be understood; it can happen, it has always happened because these great minds are just great on the surface. Deep down their existence is very childish. Only their intellect, their minds have grown; they have not grown.

Martin Heidegger's mind is very grown-up, his being is childish. His being is as childish as if it is waiting for somebody to lead it. A really mature person does not throw his responsibility onto anybody else; he becomes responsible for his own being.

Now this whole country of scientists, philosophers, professors, poets, giant intellectuals fell victim to a very ordinary, mediocre man, and that man ruled over it.

This must help everybody to understand the foolishness of intellect. Intellect is superficial. One should grow in being, otherwise one is always prone, one always tends to become a victim of such people. They always happen.

Mind is conditioned from the outside; it can be ruled from the outside. You have to grow into no-mind, only then can you not be ruled from the outside. Only a man of no-mind is a free man, independent. He is neither German, nor Indian, nor English, nor American; he is simply free. American, Indian, German are the names of your prisons, they are not your freedom skies. These are not skies to fly in, these are the prisons to live in.

A free man belongs to himself and nobody else. A free man is simply free energy with no name, no form, no race, no nation. The days of nations and races are past, the days of the individual are coming. In a better world there will be no Germans, no Indians, no Hindus, no Christians; there will be pure individuals, in total freedom, living their life in their own way, not disturbing anybody's life and not allowing anybody to disturb their lives.

Otherwise mind is childish and yet cunning. It can fall victim to any Adolf Hitler, to any chauvinist, to any mad person who is bold enough. And mad people are bold, they never hesitate. That was the appeal of Adolf Hitler. He was so mad that he was absolutely bold. He would never hesitate, he was absolutely certain, and people who are uncertain in their being immediately have a deep appeal for such a person. This is a man who is so certain about truth that he must have attained to truth. They start falling in line with him. Because of your uncertainty you become a victim to somebody who is mad. But mad people are always certain, and only very, very alert and aware people hesitate. Their hesitation shows their awareness and the complexity of life.

And mind is very cunning. It can rationalize everything.

I have heard...

Berger, hiding with his wife from the Nazis in a secluded Berlin attic, decided to get a breath of fresh air. While out walking he came face-to-face with Adolf Hitler.

The German leader pulled out a gun and pointed to a pile of horse manure in the street. "All right, Jew!" he shouted. "Eat that, or I'll kill you!" Trembling, Berger did as he was ordered.

Hitler began laughing so hard he dropped the weapon. Berger picked it up and said, "Now, you eat the manure, or I'll shoot!" The Fuhrer got down on his hands and knees and began eating.

While he was occupied, Berger sneaked away, ran through an alley, climbed over a fence, and dashed up the stairs to the attic. He slammed the door shut, bolted and locked it securely. "Hilda! Hilda!" he exclaimed to his wife. "Guess who I had lunch with today."

Mind goes on rationalizing. Even if you eat horse manure, it can make it a lunch, and "Hilda, Hilda, guess who I had lunch with today!" Beware of the traps of the mind, and the more you become alert, the more you will be able to live in the moment, in the act totally. Then there is no motivation; you do it because you delight in it.

And that's why I call it the hardest work. To get out of the mind is the hardest work. But it is not effort, it is awareness; it is not effort, it is intense alertness.

The last question:

Osho,
For enlightenment does one need a human body? Can't a dog or a tree which is flowering get enlightened?

Dang, dang, doko dang, doko dang.
Enough for today.

Osho comments in this work on excerpts from:

Zen Flesh, Zen Bones, Compiled by Paul Reps ©1957/First Published: Charles E. Tuttle, Company, Inc. Published Pelican Books 1971: Penguin Books Ltd (Reprinted 1972, 1973) Harmondsworth, Middlesex, England. Penguin Books Australia, Ltd, Ringwood, Victoria, Australia

The World of Zen: An East-West Anthology Compiled, Edited, and with an Introduction by Nancy Wilson Ross ©1960/Published: Nancy Wilson Ross, Random House, New York, USA

Zen: Poems, Prayers, Sermons, Anecdotes, Interviews
Edited/Translated by Lucien Stryk and Takashi Ikemoto ©1963, 1965: Lucien Stryk and Takashi Ikemoto. Published: Doubleday Anchor Books, Doubleday & Company, Inc., Garden City, New York USA

about Osho

Osho's unique contribution to the understanding of who we are defies categorization. Mystic and scientist, a rebellious spirit whose sole interest is to alert humanity to the urgent need to discover a new way of living. To continue as before is to invite threats to our very survival on this unique and beautiful planet.

His essential point is that only by changing ourselves, one individual at a time, can the outcome of all our "selves" – our societies, our cultures, our beliefs, our world – also change. The doorway to that change is meditation.

Osho the scientist has experimented and scrutinized all the approaches of the past and examined their effects on the modern human being and responded to their shortcomings by creating a new starting point for the hyperactive 21st Century mind: OSHO Active Meditations.

Once the agitation of a modern lifetime has started to settle, "activity" can melt into "passivity," a key starting point of real meditation. To support this next step, Osho has transformed the ancient "art of listening" into a subtle contemporary methodology: the OSHO

Talks. Here words become music, the listener discovers who is listening, and the awareness moves from what is being heard to the individual doing the listening. Magically, as silence arises, what needs to be heard is understood directly, free from the distraction of a mind that can only interrupt and interfere with this delicate process.

These thousands of talks cover everything from the individual quest for meaning to the most urgent social and political issues facing society today. Osho's books are not written but are transcribed from audio and video recordings of these extemporaneous talks to international audiences. As he puts it, "So remember: whatever I am saying is not just for you...I am talking also for the future generations."

Osho has been described by *The Sunday Times* in London as one of the "1000 Makers of the 20th Century" and by American author Tom Robbins as "the most dangerous man since Jesus Christ." *Sunday Mid-Day* (India) has selected Osho as one of ten people – along with Gandhi, Nehru and Buddha – who have changed the destiny of India.

About his own work Osho has said that he is helping to create the conditions for the birth of a new kind of human being. He often characterizes this new human being as "Zorba the Buddha" – capable both of enjoying the earthy pleasures of a Zorba the Greek and the silent serenity of a Gautama the Buddha.

Running like a thread through all aspects of Osho's talks and meditations is a vision that encompasses both the timeless wisdom of all ages past and the highest potential of today's (and tomorrow's) science and technology.

Osho is known for his revolutionary contribution to the science of inner transformation, with an approach to meditation that acknowledges the accelerated pace of contemporary life. His unique OSHO Active Meditations™ are designed to first release the accumulated stresses of body and mind, so that it is then easier to take an experience of stillness and thought-free relaxation into daily life.

Two autobiographical works by the author are available:
Autobiography of a Spiritually Incorrect Mystic,
St Martins Press, New York (book and eBook)
Glimpses of a Golden Childhood,
OSHO Media International, Pune, India

OSHO international meditation resort

Each year the Meditation Resort welcomes thousands of people from more than 100 countries. The unique campus provides an opportunity for a direct personal experience of a new way of living – with more awareness, relaxation, celebration and creativity. A great variety of around-the-clock and around-the-year program options are available. Doing nothing and just relaxing is one of them!

All of the programs are based on Osho's vision of "Zorba the Buddha" – a qualitatively new kind of human being who is able *both* to participate creatively in everyday life *and* to relax into silence and meditation.

Location

Located 100 miles southeast of Mumbai in the thriving modern city of Pune, India, the OSHO International Meditation Resort is a holiday destination with a difference. The Meditation Resort is spread over 28 acres of spectacular gardens in a beautiful tree-lined residential area.

OSHO Meditations

A full daily schedule of meditations for every type of person includes both traditional and revolutionary methods, and particularly the OSHO Active Meditations™. The daily meditation program takes place in what must be the world's largest meditation hall, the OSHO Auditorium.

OSHO Multiversity

Individual sessions, courses and workshops cover everything from creative arts to holistic health, personal transformation, relationship and life transition, transforming meditation into a lifestyle for life and work, esoteric sciences, and the "Zen" approach to sports and recreation. The secret of the OSHO Multiversity's success lies in the fact that all its programs are combined with meditation, supporting the understanding that as human beings we are far more than the sum of our parts.

OSHO Basho Spa

The luxurious Basho Spa provides for leisurely open-air swimming surrounded by trees and tropical green. The uniquely styled, spacious Jacuzzi, the saunas, gym, tennis courts...all these are enhanced by their stunningly beautiful setting.

Cuisine

A variety of different eating areas serve delicious Western, Asian and Indian vegetarian food – most of it organically grown especially for the Meditation Resort. Breads and cakes are baked in the resort's own bakery.

Night life

There are many evening events to choose from – dancing being at the top of the list! Other activities include full-moon meditations beneath the stars, variety shows, music performances and meditations for daily life.

Facilities

You can buy all of your basic necessities and toiletries in the Galleria. The Multimedia Gallery sells a large range of OSHO media products. There is also a bank, a travel agency and a Cyber Café on-campus. For those who enjoy shopping, Pune provides all the options, ranging from traditional and ethnic Indian products to all of the global brand-name stores.

Accommodation

You can choose to stay in the elegant rooms of the OSHO Guesthouse, or for longer stays on campus you can select one of the OSHO Living-In programs. Additionally there is a plentiful variety of nearby hotels and serviced apartments.

www.osho.com/meditationresort
www.osho.com/guesthouse
www.osho.com/livingin

for more information

www.**OSHO**.com

a comprehensive multi-language website including a magazine, OSHO Books, OSHO Talks in audio and video formats, the OSHO Library text archive in English and Hindi and extensive information about OSHO Meditations. You will also find the program schedule of the OSHO Multiversity and information about the OSHO International Meditation Resort.

http://OSHO.com/AllAboutOSHO
http://OSHO.com/Resort
http://OSHO.com/Shop
http://www.youtube.com/OSHO
http://www.Twitter.com/OSHO
http://www.facebook.com/pages/OSHO.International

To contact OSHO International Foundation:
www.osho.com/oshointernational,
oshointernational@oshointernational.com